A GUIDE TO PROGRAMMING IN LEVEL II BASIC

BRUCE PRESLEY

LAWRENCEVILLE PRESS, INC.

DISTRIBUTED BY

VNR VAN NOSTRAND REINHOLD COMPANY

NEW YORK   CINCINNATI   TORONTO   LONDON   MELBOURNE

First published in 1982

Copyright ©1982
by

LAWRENCEVILLE PRESS, INC.

Library of Congress Catalog Card Number 82-60365
ISBN 0-442-25892-5

VNR

Educational orders may be placed by writing or calling:

Van Nostrand Reinhold Inc.
76 25 Empire Drive
Attn: Department T
Florence, Kentucky 41042
Telephone 606-525-6600

Van Nostrand Reinhold Company
135 West 50th Street, New York, NY 10020

Van Nostrand Reinhold Ltd.
1410 Birchmount Road, Scarborough, Ontario M1P 2E7

Van Nostrand Reinhold Australia Pty. Ltd.
17 Queen Street, Mitcham, Victoria 3132

Van Nostrand Reinhold Company Ltd.
Molly Millars Lane, Wokingham, Berkshire, England RG11
2PY

16 15 14 13 12 11 10 9 8 7 6 5 4 3

PREFACE

The publication of this first edition of A GUIDE TO PROGRAMMING IN LEVEL II BASIC represents the latest achievement of faculty members and students at The Lawrenceville School in developing curricular materials to assist students in learning to program computers.

Based on experience gained in our classrooms over the past fifteen years, we are convinced that a structured, concisely written computer text is invaluable in teaching and learning programming. This latest manual, written specifically to instruct students in Level II BASIC, not only retains but expands on the features which have resulted in the wide acceptance of our previous publications, A GUIDE TO PROGRAMMING IN APPLESOFT and A GUIDE TO PROGRAMMING IN BASIC PLUS.

The production of this manual has involved the cooperation and talents of many individuals. Lester Waters, Robert Lynch, Eli Hurowitz, and Donald Mikan, have all made contributions to this publication which have been invaluable. Each has authored and taken responsibility for specific areas of the manual. The clarity and accuracy of each chapter reflect their considerable effort and expertise. Majorie Vining, of the Rhode Island School of Design, has produced the imaginative cover design, and William Sunfest of Trentypo the art work, while Dr. Theodore Fraser of The College of the Holy Cross has edited the text to ensure that it is both grammatically and stylistically correct. A very special thanks is due Harold Simmons and his staff at Trentypo. Their assistance in producing this and our earlier manuals has been invaluable.

To all of these people I am deeply grateful. Thanks to their combined efforts we have produced what I believe to be one of the very finest computer texts available today.

Bruce Presley

TABLE OF CONTENTS

INTRODUCTION TO PROGRAMMING

To communicate with a computer a special language is required. The language described in this manual is LEVEL II BASIC which consists of simple English words understood by the computer. In this chapter the user will be introduced to the most fundamental statements required to write a program on the TRS-80 computer.

What Is a Program?

A program is a sequence of instructions that informs the computer of the tasks which the user wants it to perform. From the very beginning, it is important to realize that the user must determine the order in which the computer performs all tasks assigned to it. It is also essential to realize that the computer operates with a limited vocabulary and that it can understand only certain key words which serve as commands. Hence, words which make perfect sense to the user may make no sense at all to the computer if they are not part of its vocabulary. This manual will present one of the special vocabularies of the TRS-80 and will explain how it can be used in a variety of applications.

Line Numbering

To establish the sequence of instructions for any given program, line numbers must be assigned to each line within a program. This operation is essential since the computer reads instructions beginning with the lowest line number, then progresses to the next higher number, and ends with the highest numbered line.

It is permissible to type the program lines out of order because the computer puts them back into their proper order. For example, line 20 may have been typed before line 10; but, when the program is run, the computer automatically reads line 10 first. Such a system has the advantage of allowing any forgotten instructions, say between lines 10 and

20, to be entered later as lines 15, or 12, or 17, etc. For this reason it is best to number the lines of the program in units of ten (10, 20, 30, etc.) since this leaves nine possible line numbers that can later be inserted. It is also important to realize that the capital letter O cannot be used in place of zero.

An error in any instruction may be corrected at any time by depressing the return key and retyping the entire line using the same line number. If two lines are given the same line number, the computer uses only the last one typed and erases the first. By typing only a line number followed by a RETURN the line is eliminated entirely. The highest line number allowed on the computer is 65529.

PRINT

There are two basic types of information which the computer can utilize: numbers and words. What distinguishes one from the other is the fact that a number can be used in a mathematical calculation, whereas a word cannot. The PRINT statement is used to print both numbers and words.

PROGRAM 1.1

This program uses the PRINT statement at each line to print the results shown below.

```
10 PRINT 5 * 3
20 PRINT 12 + 8
30 PRINT 7 / 2
40 PRINT "SAND"
50 PRINT "5*3"
READY
>RUN
 15
 20
 3.5
SAND
5*3
READY
>
```

Line 10 instructs the computer to print the product of 5 and 3. Note than an asterisk (*) is used to indicate multiplication. Line 20 adds 12 and 8 while line 30 divides 7 by 2, with the slash (/) indicating division. At line 40 the word SAND is printed. When a word or any set of characters is printed, they must be enclosed within quotation marks. Line 50 prints "5*3" rather than 15 because quotation marks are used. Information enclosed in quotation marks is called a string. Both lines 40 and 50 contain strings. If a printer is available, the command LPRINT, rather than PRINT, will send the output to the printer rather than to the video display.

The command RUN is typed after a program has been entered to execute the program, but it is not part of the program.

Typing Errors

An error in a program can be corrected in one of three ways. First, the program line can be retyped using the same line number. For example,

```
>40 PRINT "ROCKS"
>RUN
 15
 20
 3.5
ROCKS
5*3
READY
>
```

changes only that part of the output which is produced by line 40. The second method of correcting an error involves the use of the key marked (←) which can be employed if the error is detected while the line containing the error is being typed. Each time the (←) key is pressed, it causes the computer to erase one character to the left of the cursor on the screen. The third method of error correction consists in the use of the built in line editor. To learn how to use this feature refer to Appendix A.

LIST

The LIST command is used to print the program currently in the computer's memory. Typing LIST followed by a RETURN will print the entire program, while LIST followed by a line number and a RETURN will cause only that line to be printed. To list portions of a program, type LIST followed by the first and last line numbers of the portion desired, separating the two numbers with a hyphen (-). For example:

```
>LIST
10 PRINT 5 * 3
20 PRINT 12 + 8
30 PRINT 7 / 2
40 PRINT "ROCKS"
50 PRINT "5*3"
READY
>

>LIST 50
50 PRINT "5*3"
READY
>
```

1.3

```
>LIST 20-40
20 PRINT 12 + 8
30 PRINT 7 / 2
40 PRINT "ROCKS"
READY
>
```

To send the program listing to a printer, type LLIST instead of LIST.

NEW

Before entering a program into the computer, the NEW command should be used to clear the computer's memory. The use of this command insures that program lines from a previous program do not affect the new program.

```
10 PRINT 5 * 3
20 PRINT 12 + 8
30 PRINT 7 / 2
40 PRINT "ROCKS"
50 PRINT "5*3"
READY
>NEW
READY
>LIST
READY
>
```

Observe that after the NEW command is used, a subsequent LIST shows that no program is currently in the computer's memory.

What Is a Variable?

One of the most useful properties of a computer is its ability to manipulate variables. A variable is a symbol that may assume many different values. The computer uses variables to represent numbers or strings.

Numeric variables are represented by letters or by letters and numbers. A, D, A1, and B1 are all legal names for numeric variables. The computer allows the use of longer names for variables, but for the sake of simplicity only a single letter or a single letter followed by a single digit will be used in the early chapters of this manual.

Variables can change in value as the name itself implies. For example, suppose that program line

$$20 \ X = 5$$

is typed. When the program is run and reaches line 20, X will be assigned the value 5.

Suppose a later statement such as

$$50 \ X = 7$$

is entered. Then at line 50 the value of X will change from 5 to 7.

Just as in algebra, the computer can have one numeric variable defined in terms of another. For example, when the statement Y = 4*X is executed by the computer, Y will be assigned the value 20 if X=5, or Y will be assigned 28 if X=7, and so on.

It is important to realize that the equal sign (=) is interpreted as "is assigned the value." Therefore, when assigning a value to a variable, the statement must be in the form: 'variable = value', *not* 'value = variable'. Therefore, the statement

$$50 \ 7 = X$$

is invalid.

PROGRAM 1.2

This program assigns values to the variables X and Y, where the value of Y depends upon the value of X.

```
10 X = 12
20 Y = 3 * X + 5
30 PRINT X, Y
40 X = 15
50 PRINT X, Y
60 Y = 3 * X + 5
70 PRINT X, Y
READY
>RUN
 12                    41
 15                    41
 15                    50
READY
>
```

The value of X is originally 12 at line 10 and then becomes 15 at line 40. Y changes its value at line 60 because X changed at line 40. Note than when X and Y are printed at line 50, X is now 15, but Y is still 41 because the variable Y is not changed until it is reassigned at line 60. A comma is used in the PRINT statements at lines 30, 50, and 70 to allow the values of X and Y to be printed on a single line. Up to four variables can be printed on a single line of the display by the use of commas to separate each variable name.

String variable names are used in the same way as numeric variable names, except that a string variable name must end with a dollar sign ($). For example, A$, D$, A1$, C5$ all represent string variables. To assign characters to a string variable the characters must be enclosed in quotation marks. For example, the statement

$$10 \ A\$ = \text{``HARRY''}$$

will assign "HARRY" to the string variable A$. At some later point in a program it is possible to assign different characters to the same variable. For example, the statement

$$50 \ A\$ = \text{``SHERRY''}$$

will replace "HARRY" with "SHERRY".

PROGRAM 1.3

This program assigns two different sets of characters to the string variable B$.

```
10 B$ = "GEORGE"
20 PRINT B$
30 B$ = "JUDY"
40 PRINT B$
50 PRINT "IT IS NICE TO SEE YOU "; B$
READY
>RUN
GEORGE
JUDY
IT IS NICE TO SEE YOU JUDY
READY
>
```

Observe that at line 50 a sentence can be formed from two strings, the first of which in this case is not a variable.

Note that when a semicolon rather than a comma is used to separate items in a print statement, the items will be printed next to each other on the same line.

REVIEW

1. Write a program that will print the value of Y when X=5 and Y=5X+7

2. Write a program that will produce the following output by using string variables for "HARRY" and "SHERRY", but not for the other words.

```
>RUN
HELLO HARRY
SHERRY IS LOOKING FOR YOU.
READY
>
```

READ, DATA

A variable may be directly assigned its value not only by a statement such as X = 5, but also by a combination of READ and DATA statements.

PROGRAM 1.4

This program uses READ and DATA statements to assign values to numeric variables.

```
10 READ X, Y, Z
20 PRINT 2 * X  +  3 * Y  +  8 * Z
30 DATA 3, 2, 0.5
READY
>RUN
 16
READY
>
```

The READ statement at line 10 instructs the computer to assign numbers to the variables X, Y, Z. The computer finds these numbers in the DATA statement at line 30 and assigns them in the order listed (X = 3, Y = 2, and Z = 0.5).

In a DATA statement only numbers that are expressed in decimal or scientific form are acceptable. For example, the numbers .0032, -5.78, 1050, 2.9E5, and 4.76 E-12 are acceptable. The E stands for "times ten to the power" (e.g., 5.3 E3 = 5300 and 8.72 E-3 = .00872). However, data such as the arithmetic expressions 15/3, 3*5, and 7+2 are not permitted in DATA statements since, unlike PRINT statements, DATA statements allow for no calculations.

GOTO

Suppose that a student has more than one set of values for the variables X, Y, Z in Program 1.4. To introduce the extra values, line 30 can be retyped as follows:

```
>30 DATA 3, 2, 0.5, -7, 2.5, 1E2
>RUN
 16
```

Note that only the first three numbers in the DATA statement are processed, the remaining numbers are not used. To overcome this problem, line 30 could be retyped each time a new set of data is to be run, but this involves unnecessary labor. By including a GOTO statement between lines 20 and 30, the problem can be more easily solved by establishing a loop which allows line 10 to be used over again.

```
>LIST
10 READ X, Y, Z
20 PRINT 2 * X + 3 * Y + 8 * Z
25 GOTO 10
30 DATA 3, 2, 0.5, -7, 2.5, 1E2
READY
>RUN
 16
 793.5
Out of DATA in 10
READY
```

Observe that by typing the command LIST, the computer prints the current version of Program 1.4 including the new line. By running Program 1.4, all of the data presented in line 30 can now be processed. Each time the computer reaches line 25, the GOTO statement causes the computer to return to line 10 where the next set of data is assigned to the variables. On the first pass through the loop X = 3, Y = 2, Z = .5; on the second pass X = -7, Y = 2.5, Z = 1E2. However, on the third attempted pass, no additional data is available for assignment to the variables at line 10 and, therefore, an error message is printed.

The location of the DATA statement within a program is not important. Therefore, it can be placed anywhere. When the computer encounters a READ statement, it makes use of the DATA statement regardless of its location. DATA statements may contain strings as well as numbers and are usually placed at or near the end of a program.

PROGRAM 1.5

This program reads the names and grades of three students and prints the averages of their grades.

```
5 PRINT "NAME", "AVERAGE"
10 READ N$, A, B, C, D
20 X = (A + B + C + D) / 4
30 PRINT N$, X
40 GOTO 10
50 DATA WATERS,83,95,86,80,FRENCH,42,97,66,89,MIKAN,61,83,42,90
READY
>RUN
NAME            AVERAGE
WATERS            86
FRENCH            73.5
MIKAN             69
Out of DATA in 10
READY
>
```

Examine this program carefully since it contains a number of important concepts. Line 5 produces the headings for the columns and is placed at the beginning of the program to insure that the headings will only be printed once. Line 10 assigns a student's name to the string variable N$ and the student's four grades to the numeric variables A, B, C, D. Unless

1.8

the sequence of string variables and numeric variables in the READ statement is the same as the sequence of strings and numbers in the DATA statement, an error will occur. Line 40 returns the program to line 10 to read more data. What would happen if

$$40 \; GOTO \; 5$$

was substituted for the current line 40?

REVIEW

3. Write a program using READ, DATA statements to evaluate Y where Y = 3X +5 and X = 3, 5, 12, 17, 8.

4. Write a program containing the DATA line in Program 1.5 which prints only the name and first grade of each student

```
>RUN
NAME                FIRST GRADE
WATERS                  83
FRENCH                  42
MIKAN                   61
Out of DATA in 10
READY
>
```

INPUT

In many instances it is preferable to introduce data from the keyboard rather than placing it in a DATA statement. To do this an INPUT statement is used in place of the READ, DATA statements. When an INPUT statement is executed, the computer prints a question mark (?) and then waits for data to be entered.

PROGRAM 1.6

Data entered from the keyboard is used to assign a value to the variable X in the following program.

```
10 INPUT X
20 PRINT 5 * X * X  +  3 * X  +  2
30 GOTO 10
READY
```

```
>RUN
? 3
 56
? 6
 200
? 2
 28
?
Break in 10
```

The GOTO statement at line 30 creates a loop which will continue to run until it is interrupted by pressing the BREAK key. This operation halts the run of the program and causes BREAK IN 10 to be printed. If this is not done, Program 1.6 will continue to run until the RESET key is pressed or the computer is shut off.

PROGRAM 1.7

This program is a revision of Program 1.5. Here a student is asked for his or her name and four grades. The computer then prints the name and grade average. It is possible to have the INPUT statement print a question or a remark by enclosing the words to be printed in quotation marks followed by a semicolon and the variable names. Also, note that more than one variable can be entered by using a single INPUT statement.

```
10 INPUT "WHAT IS YOUR NAME"; N$
20 INPUT "WHAT ARE YOUR GRADES"; A, B, C, D
30 X = (A + B + C + D) / 4
40 PRINT N$, X
50 GOTO 10
READY
>RUN
WHAT IS YOUR NAME? TED
WHAT ARE YOUR GRADES? 87, 54, 76, 95
TED              78
WHAT IS YOUR NAME? JOHN
WHAT ARE YOUR GRADES? 98, 96, 47, 84
JOHN              81.25
WHAT IS YOUR NAME? ALBERT
WHAT ARE YOUR GRADES? 100, 95, 31, 60
ALBERT            71.5
WHAT IS YOUR NAME?
Break in 10
READY
>
```

PRINT Formatting

There are a number of ways in which output can be formatted by the use of punctuation. A few of the more important uses of punctuation are demonstrated by the following program.

PROGRAM 1.8

The TRS-80 is capable of printing 64 characters on a single line. This line is divided into four printing zones consisting of 16 characters each. When commas are used in a PRINT statement, the output is printed in successive zones.

```
5 PRINT "N A M E", "G R A D E S", "AVERAGE"
10 READ N$, A, B, C
20 X = (A + B + C) / 3
30 PRINT
40 PRINT N$, A; B; C, X
50 GOTO 10
60 DATA HAYES,90,87,93, GRAHAM,74,98,83, WATSON,53,76,18
READY
>RUN
N A M E            G R A D E S        AVERAGE

HAYES              90  87  93          90

GRAHAM             74  98  83          85

WATSON             53  76  18          49
Out of DATA in 10
READY
>
```

Note the output produced by line 5. Each word begins at the beginning of one of the zones because commas have been used to separate the words. The PRINT at line 30 is used to place a blank line between each of the printed lines. When printing a number, the computer places a single space in front of and behind the number. If the number is negative, the space in front is occupied by the minus (−) sign.

When semicolons (;) are used in place of commas (as in line 40), the output of each variable begins in the next space following the last variable printed.

PROGRAM 1.9

This program demonstrates the difference between commas and semicolons used in a print statement.

```
10 PRINT "ZONE 1", "ZONE 2", "ZONE 3", "ZONE 4"
20 X = -14
30 PRINT "**"; X; "**"
40 T = 42
50 PRINT "**"; T; "**"
60 A$ = "86"
70 PRINT "**"; A$; "**"
80 PRINT X; T; A$; 99
READY
>RUN
ZONE 1             ZONE 2          ZONE 3          ZONE 4
**-14 **
** 42 **
**86**
-14  42 86 99
READY
>
```

Note how the values −14 and 42 were printed by lines 30 and 50, respectively. Line 70 shows that strings are not printed with a leading and trailing space.

REVIEW

5. Write a program in which you input a value of X and have the computer calculate 5*X and X/5. The printout should appear exactly as shown below.

```
>RUN
WHAT IS X? 12
5*X= 60
X/5= 2.4
WHAT IS X? 20
5*X= 100
X/5= 4
WHAT IS X? 64
5*X= 320
X/5= 12.8
WHAT IS X?
Break in 10
```

6. Write a program which allows you to input your name and the name of a friend and then produces the printout as follows:

```
>RUN
WHAT IS YOUR NAME? BRUCE
WHAT IS YOUR FRIEND'S NAME? JUDY
JUDY IS A FRIEND OF BRUCE
```

```
WHAT IS YOUR NAME? DON
WHAT IS YOUR FRIEND'S NAME? SHERRY
SHERRY IS A FRIEND OF DON

WHAT IS YOUR NAME?
Break in 10
```

Immediate Mode

The computer may perform simple tasks using the immediate mode rather than a program. An immediate mode instruction is typed without a line number. When the computer receives a command without a line number, it recognizes that the command is not part of a program but is to be executed immediately. The following are examples of immediate mode statements:

```
>PRINT (3*5) + 4
 19
READY
>
>PRINT 7/9
 .777778
READY
>
>A = 5
READY
>B = 2
READY
>PRINT A + B + 4
 11
READY
>
>A$ = "BETTY"
READY
>PRINT A$; " BOO"
BETTY BOO
READY
>
```

Note that a RUN command was not used in any of the preceding examples. Most commands are permissible in the immediate mode with the notable exception of the INPUT statement. In performing most tasks it is best to write complete programs and to reserve the use of immediate mode for simple calculations.

REM

The REM statement is used in the body of a program to allow the programmer to introduce explanatory remarks. Everything to the right of a REM statement is ignored by the computer when the program is run. For example,

30 REM CALCULATE AREA OF CIRCLE

will be printed only when the program is listed. Remarks placed strategically within a program are useful in explaining the function of various parts of the program.

PART A

1. Write a program which prints the following.

```
>RUN
A
  B
    C
ABCD
```

2. Write a program which makes the following calculations. Check the results by hand computation.

    (a) 8 * (19 - 4)
    (b) 1 * 2 + 2 * 3 + 3 * 4 + 4 * 5
    (c) 1 + 1 / 10 + 1 / 100
    (d) 10 - 20 + 30 - 40 + 50 - 60

3. What is the exact output for the following program?

```
10 A=3
20 PRINT "THE VALUE OF B"
30 B=A+4*4
40 PRINT B
```

4. How many lines of output does the following program produce before an error message appears indicating "Out of DATA in 10"?

```
10 READ A,B,C
20 PRINT (A+B+C)/3
30 GOTO 10
40 DATA 11,32,43,14,25,36,47
50 DATA 58,39,50,61,22,83,94
```

5. Peter Kolodnigork has loused up once again. Here is a program of his which he says "mysteriously doesn't work". Give Peter a hand and correct this monstrosity for him so that the output looks like the following:

THE SUM IS 20
THE SUM IS 14
OUT OF DATA IN 10

```
10 READ A B
20 PRINT THE SUM IS   A+B
30 GOTO 12
40 DATA 12,8,3*3,5
```

6. Write the output, and check by running the program.

```
10 READ A$
20 PRINT A$
30 GOTO 10
40 DATA S,I,X!," 6",6
```

7. Write a program in which the price (P) in cents of a loaf of bread and the number (N) of loaves bought are entered from the keyboard. The total spent for bread is to be printed in dollars and cents.

8. Write a program to enter your weight (W) in pounds and height (H) in inches and which then prints the quotient W/H followed by the words "POUNDS PER INCH".

9. Using an INPUT statement, write a program which produces the following output.

```
>RUN
? 2,4
X= 2            Y= 4            X*Y= 8
? -8,70
X=-8            Y= 70           X*Y=-560
?
```

1.16

10. Predict the output of the following program. Check the answer by running the program.

```
10 P$ = "TOTAL PRICE"
20 P = .89
30 PRINT P$;" = $0";P
```

11. Predict the output, and check by running the program.

```
10 READ A,B,C,D
20 PRINT A,B
30 PRINT C;"   ";D
40 DATA 3E2,510,3E-1,.51
```

12. Use immediate mode to print the following numbers.
   (a) .05
   (b) .005
   (c) 123456789
   (d) 1234567890
   (e) –.065
   (f) 4.62E5
   (g) .086E-3
   (h) –4,900

13. Self-proclaimed computer whiz Cecil Cedric Cenceless has typed the following gibberish in the immediate mode and has challenged anyone to guess the output correctly before he or she presses the RETURN key. Put Cecil in his place and correctly predict the answer.

```
>PRINT"AAA";111,222;"AAA","333";"   ";16-3*2
```

14. Write a program which will add the numbers 3, 5, and 7.

PART B

15. What is the exact output for the following program?

```
10 A$ = "ABCD"
20 B$ = "XYZ"
30 F = 7
40 G = -4
50 PRINT A$;B$
60 PRINT A$;F
70 PRINT F;B$
80 PRINT G;B$
```

16. Write a program to evaluate each of the following expressions for A = 10 and B = 7.

$$(7A + 10B)/2AB \qquad\qquad (1/2)A/(A-B)$$

17. In the first week of the season the cross country team ran the following number of miles each day: 2, 3, 4, 3, 5. Write a program to calculate and print the total mileage for the week.

18. A piece of pizza normally contains about 375 calories. A person jogging one mile uses about 100 calories. Write a program that asks a person how many pieces he or she wishes to eat and then tells him/her how far they must run to burn up the calories they will consume.

```
>RUN
HOW MANY PIECES DID YOU EAT? 4
YOU MUST RUN 15 MILES.
```

19. Have the computer evaluate the expression 12x + 7y for the following data:

x	3	7	12
y	2	9	−4

20. The art of thinking up good insults can be enormously aided by the computer. To test an insult, have a computer program ask for the victim's name and the insulting word which should then be attached to the suffixes "breath" and "head". For example, given "Gary" as the victim's name and "bone" as the insulting word, the program should print:

GARY IS A BONE-HEAD
or
GARY IS A BONE-BREATH

21. Using an INPUT statement, write a program that will compute the volume of a room given its length, width, and height.

22. Write a program to compute the areas (cm²) of circles with radii 5.0 cm., 3.0 cm., and 8.0 cm. Have the output in the form "AREA OF CIRCLE =" with two spaces between each of the printed lines.

23. Just as three-dimensional objects are measured by volume, so four-dimensional objects are measured by tesseracts. Have your program ask for the dimensions of a four-dimensional object, height, width, length, and "presence" and print the object's tesseract.

24. With the equation $E = MC^2$, Einstein predicted that energy could be produced from matter. If the average human hair weighs a tenth of a gram and the town of Woodsylvania uses 2×10^{11} units of energy in a day, find out how many hairs from Einstein's head would be required to supply the town for a day ($C = 3 \times 10^{10}$).

25. Use the computer to calculate your library fines. Enter the number of books you have borrowed and how many days late they are. Have the computer print the amount of your fine if you are charged 10¢ per day per book.

26. The perimeter of a triangle is equal to the sum of the lengths of the three sides of the triangle. The semiperimeter is one-half of the perimeter. A triangle has sides of lengths 13 cm, 8 cm, 11 cm. A second triangle has sides of 21 ft, 16 ft, 12 ft. Write a program that reads these measurements from a DATA statement and then prints the semiperimeter of each triangle showing the correct units. The output should look like this:

SEMIPERIMETER OF FIRST TRIANGLE 16 CM.

SEMIPERIMETER OF SECOND TRIANGLE 24.5 FT.

27. Professional athletes have succeeded in making staggering sums of money through careful negotiations. Of course, the real winner is Uncle Sam who does not negotiate at all. Write a program which asks for a player's name and salary and then prints the player's name, take-home salary, and taxes if the tax rate for his income bracket is 44%.

```
>RUN
WHAT IS THE PLAYERS NAME? JUGGIE RACKSON
WHAT IS JUGGIE RACKSON'S WAGE? 150000
JUGGIE RACKSON WOULD KEEP $ 84000
HE WOULD PAY $ 66000 IN TAXES.
READY
>RUN
WHAT IS THE PLAYERS NAME? DOPEY
WHAT IS DOPEY'S WAGE? 4200
DOPEY WOULD KEEP $ 2352
HE WOULD PAY $ 1848 IN TAXES.
READY
```

28. Sale prices are often deceptive. Write a program to determine the original price of an item, given the sale price and the discount rate.

```
>RUN
SALE PRICE? 3.78
DISCOUNT RATE? 10
THE ORIGINAL PRICE WAS $ 4.2
```

29. The area of a triangle can be found by multiplying one-half times the length of the base times the length of the altitude (A = .5 x base x height). Write a program that allows the user to enter from the keyboard the base and altitude of a triangle and then skips a line before printing out the area of the triangle.

```
>RUN
WHAT IS THE BASE? 10
WHAT IS THE ALTITUDE? 5

THE AREA IS 25
```

30. A state has a 7 percent sales tax. Write a program that will allow you to INPUT the names and prices (before taxes) of different items found in a department store and then print the item, tax, and the price of the item including tax.

```
>RUN
ITEMS NAME? COAT
WHAT IS ITS PRICE? 65.00
COAT HAS A TAX OF $ 4.55 AND COSTS $ 69.55
ITEMS NAME? TENNIS RACKET
WHAT IS ITS PRICE? 23.00
TENNIS RACKET HAS A TAX OF $ 1.61 AND COSTS $ 24.61
ITEMS NAME?
Break in 10
READY
>
```

31. In an election in Grime City, candidate Sloth ran against candidate Graft for mayor. Below is a listing of the number of votes both candidates received in each ward. What total vote did each candidate receive? What percentage of the total vote did each candidate receive?

Candidate	Sloth	Graft
Ward 1	528	210
2	313	721
3	1003	822
4	413	1107
5	516	1700

32. A Susan B. Anthony dollar of diameter 2.6 centimeters rests on a square postage stamp as shown. Have the computer find the area in square centimeters of the part of the stamp not covered by the coin.

33. Given the assumption that you sleep a healthy 8 hours a night, have the computer print the number of hours of your life which you have spent sleeping. Input the date of your birth and today's date in numeric form (e.g., 6, 4, 62). Use 365 days in each year and 30 days in a month.

34. Using an INPUT statement, write a program which averages each of the following sets of numbers: (2, 7, 15, 13); (8, 5, 2, 3); (12, 19, 4); (15, 7, 19, 24, 37). Note that the sets do not contain the same number of elements.

10 Input "Number in the set"; N
20 IF N=3 then input A, B, C : PRINT (A+B+C)/3
30 IF N=4 then input A, B, C, D : PRINT (A+B+C+D)/4
40 Input A, B, C, D, E : PRINT (A+B+C+D+E)/5
50 RUN

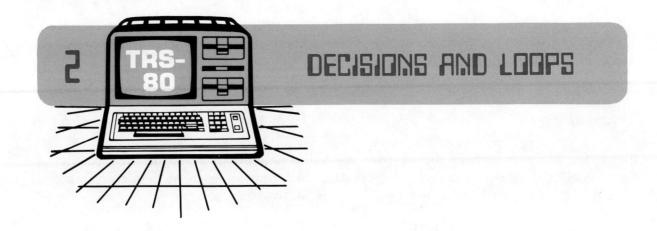

2 TRS-80

DECISIONS AND LOOPS

The statements presented in Chapter One allow the user to perform routine calculations and to print numbers or strings in different formats. The higher capabilities of a computer are not called upon, however, until the computer is used to make decisions or to carry out a process many times. This chapter presents the conditional statement IF . . . THEN . . . ELSE which allows the computer to make simple decisions, and also the statements FOR . . . TO . . . STEP, NEXT which allow loops to be established in a convenient manner.

IF . . . THEN

The statements introduced in Chapter One (GOTO, PRINT, etc.) are called unconditional because the computer will always execute them. In contrast, the IF . . . THEN statement is conditional because the action taken depends upon whether the conditonal statement is found to be true or false.

The simplest form of the IF . . . THEN statement is:

IF <condition> THEN <line number>

The 'condition' portion of the statement compares two quanities which must be separated by one of the symbols indicated in the table below:

SYMBOL	MEANING
=	equal to
>	greater than
<	less than
>=	greater than or equal to
<=	less than or equal to
<>	not equal to

An example of an IF . . . THEN statement is:

$$20 \text{ IF } X>5 \text{ THEN } 60$$

When the condition in line 20 (X is greater than 5) is true, the computer jumps to line 60. When the condition is false, as when X is less than or equal to 5, the computer proceeds to the next line of the program.

PROGRAM 2.1

This program determines whether the value entered for X is the solution to the equation $2X - 18 = 0$. The computer decides which of two messages is to be printed.

```
10 INPUT X
20 IF 2*X-18=0 THEN 50
30 PRINT X;"IS NOT THE SOLUTION"
40 GOTO 10
50 PRINT X;"IS THE SOLUTION"
READY
>RUN
? 15
 15 IS NOT THE SOLUTION
? 4
 4 IS NOT THE SOLUTION
? 9
 9 IS THE SOLUTION
READY
>
```

Note the necessity of line 40. Without it, the program would print "IS THE SOLUTION" even when the solution was not X. The line number sequence that the computer follows when X is the solution is 10, 20, 50; and when X is *not* the solution, it follows the line number sequence 10, 20, 30, 40, 10.

The IF . . . THEN statement can be used to compare two strings. Here the symbols greater than (>), less than (<), equal (=), etc., now refer to an alphabetical rather than a numerical order.

PROGRAM 2.2

The following program determines whether A$ is alphabetically before, the same, or after B$.

2.2

```
10 PRINT
20 INPUT "ENTER TWO STRINGS";A$,B$
30 IF A$=B$ THEN 70
40 IF A$>B$ THEN 90
50 PRINT A$;" IS BEFORE ";B$
60 GOTO 10
70 PRINT A$;" IS EQUIVALENT TO ";B$
80 GOTO 10
90 PRINT A$;" IS AFTER ";B$
100 GOTO 10
READY
>RUN

ENTER TWO STRINGS? A,C
A IS BEFORE C

ENTER TWO STRINGS? TRS,ALL
TRS IS AFTER ALL

ENTER TWO STRINGS? SYSTEM,SYSTEM
SYSTEM IS EQUIVALENT TO SYSTEM

ENTER TWO STRINGS?
Break in 20
READY
>
```

Line 30 directs the computer to line 70 if A$ and B$ are equivalent. Line 40 causes a jump to line 90 if A$ comes after B$ in the alphabet. Line 50 is reached only if both conditions in lines 30 and 40 fail and, therefore, A$ comes before B$ in the alphabet.

Extended Use of the IF . . . THEN Statement, Multiple Statement Lines

In the preceding section the simplest form of the IF . . . THEN statement was given as

IF <condition> THEN <line number>

More flexible usage of IF . . . THEN permits a statement instead of a line number to follow the word THEN. This means that the statement after the condition will be executed only if the condition is true. The form is:

IF <condition> THEN <statement>

The following examples illustrate legal use of the IF . . . THEN statement:

IF X<>0 THEN PRINT X
IF Z>1 THEN PRINT "IT IS LARGER THAN ONE"
IF R<=0 THEN R = X + 2

The computer allows a series of statements to be entered on a single program line if they are separated from each other by colons (:). Multiple statement lines have special meaning when used with IF . . . THEN. *All* statements following THEN will be executed when the condition following IF is true. *No* statements following THEN will be executed when the condition is false. For example,

60 IF X = 5 THEN PRINT "GOOD": GOTO 80

has two statements on one line. If the condition X = 5 is true, then "GOOD" will be printed and program control will be passed to line 80. If the condition is false, neither of these actions is taken. Instead, the program will continue on to the line following line 60. This means either the PRINT "GOOD" and the GOTO 80 statements are executed, or neither is executed. Whichever of the two occurs depends upon whether the condition X = 5 be true or false.

PROGRAM 2.3

Program 2.1 can be shortened by using multiple statement techniques.

```
10 INPUT X
20 IF 2*X-18=0 THEN PRINT X;"IS THE SOLUTION": GOTO 10
30 PRINT X;"IS NOT THE SOLUTION": GOTO 10
READY
>RUN
? 15
 15 IS NOT THE SOLUTION
? 2
 2 IS NOT THE SOLUTION
? 9
 9 IS THE SOLUTION
?
Break in 10
READY
>
```

Note that the statement GOTO 10 in line 20 is executed *only* if the condition in the IF . . . THEN statement is true. Otherwise the program proceeds to line 30. The statement GOTO 10 on line 30 will always be executed if line 30 is reached since it is not preceded by an IF . . . THEN statement on the same line.

IF . . . THEN . . . ELSE

The IF . . . THEN statement can be extended by the use of the modifier ELSE to include an alternate statement if the condition of the IF . . . THEN is false. When the IF condition is true, the statement following THEN is executed; otherwise the statement following ELSE is executed. The general form of the IF . . . THEN . . . ELSE is:

IF <condition> THEN <statement> ELSE <statement>

When the following statement is executed, "LARGER" is printed if X>50; otherwise the program will print "SMALLER OR EQUAL"

40 IF X>50 THEN PRINT "LARGER" ELSE PRINT "SMALLER OR EQUAL"

A line number is also valid following ELSE.

40 IF X>50 THEN PRINT "LARGER" ELSE 100

When IF . . . THEN . . . ELSE is used, only one statement may appear between THEN and ELSE. The following line is *not* valid:

70 IF Y = 3 THEN PRINT "DONE": GOTO 200: ELSE 30

More than one statement may appear after the ELSE; and it will only be executed if the condition of the IF is false. When the statement

80 IF Z<>5 THEN 200 ELSE PRINT "RIGHT": GOTO 20

is executed, the program will jump to line 200 if Z<>5; otherwise "RIGHT" is printed and the program jumps to line 20.

REVIEW

1. Allow two numbers, A and B, to be entered in the computer and then print the two numbers in descending order.

2. Allow two names to be entered and then printed in alphabetical order.

```
ENTER TWO LAST NAMES? PATRICK,GREER
GREER
PATRICK
ENTER TWO LAST NAMES?
Break in 10
READY
>
```

AND, OR

The statement modifiers AND and OR can be used in the IF . . . THEN statement when more than one condition is to be considered. The statement

20 IF X>5 AND Y = 3 THEN 50

will cause a transfer to line 50 only if *both* conditions are true. On the other hand, the statement

$$20 \text{ IF } X > 5 \text{ OR } Y = 3 \text{ THEN } 50$$

will cause program control to be transferred to line 50 if *either or both* conditions are true.

PROGRAM 2.4

The following program uses the OR modifier and reviews much of what has been presented.

```
10 INPUT "WHO ARE YOU";N$
20 IF N$="JAMES BOND" OR N$="007" THEN 50
30 PRINT "THIS MISSION IS NOT MEANT FOR YOU!"
40 PRINT : GOTO 10
50 PRINT "THESE ORDERS ARE FOR YOUR EYES ONLY!"
60 INPUT "ARE YOU ALONE";A$
70 IF A$<>"YES" THEN PRINT "TRY LATER." : GOTO 10
80 PRINT : PRINT " DR. GOODHEAD HAS ESCAPED! YOUR"
90 PRINT "MISSION, SHOULD YOU DECIDE TO ACCEPT"
100 PRINT "IT, IS TO SEEK OUT GOODHEAD AND"
110 PRINT "RETURN HER TO THE TELENGARD PRISON"
READY
>RUN
WHO ARE YOU? BRAVE SIR ROBIN
THIS MISSION IS NOT MEANT FOR YOU!

WHO ARE YOU? JAMES BOND
THESE ORDERS ARE FOR YOUR EYES ONLY!
ARE YOU ALONE? NO
TRY LATER.
WHO ARE YOU? 007
THESE ORDERS ARE FOR YOUR EYES ONLY!
ARE YOU ALONE? YES

 DR. GOODHEAD HAS ESCAPED! YOUR
MISSION, SHOULD YOU DECIDE TO ACCEPT
IT, IS TO SEEK OUT GOODHEAD AND
RETURN HER TO THE TELENGARD PRISON
READY
>
```

Line 10 asks the user for a name. The name entered as N$ is compared with the two names at line 20. If N$ is either 'JAMES BOND' or '007', then the program skips to line 50. Otherwise, a message is printed by line 30, and the program returns to line 10. At line 50, a warning message is printed, while line 60 inquires whether Mr. Bond is alone or not. Note that in line 70, any response other than 'YES' will cause the program to print 'TRY LATER' and jump back to line 10. Otherwise, the mission description is printed by lines 80 through 110.

END

The END statement is used to terminate the run of a program. For example,

$$80 \ \text{END}$$

will cause the run of a program to stop when line 80 is reached. It is possible to place END statements at more than one location within a program, including insertion in an IF . . . THEN statement.

PROGRAM. 2.5

This program uses the END statement to terminate program execution when the name KERMIT is input.

```
10 INPUT "WHAT IS YOUR NAME";N$
20 IF N$="KERMIT" THEN END
30 PRINT "IT'S GOOD TO MEET YOU ";N$
40 PRINT : GOTO 10
READY
>RUN
WHAT IS YOUR NAME? CYNTHIA
IT'S GOOD TO MEET YOU CYNTHIA

WHAT IS YOUR NAME? KERMIT
READY
>
```

REVIEW

3. Write a program that will allow a number N to be entered. If the number is between 25 and 112 then the computer should indicate this; otherwise, the computer should say that the number is out of range.

```
>RUN
ENTER A NUMBER? 14
 14 IS OUT OF RANGE
ENTER A NUMBER? 54
 54 IS BETWEEN 25 AND 112
ENTER A NUMBER? 112
 112 IS OUT OF RANGE
ENTER A NUMBER?
Break in 10
READY
>
```

4. Write a program in which the user enters a string N$. If it comes alphabetically before Garbage or after Trash, then have the computer print "YES"; otherwise print "NO".

2.7

FOR . . . TO . . . STEP, NEXT

The FOR . . . TO . . . STEP, NEXT statements provide a simple way of establishing a loop. A loop is a section of a program designed to be executed repeatedly. The FOR . . . TO . . . STEP, NEXT loops provide a method for generating a large sequence of numbers in a case where each number in the sequence differs from its predecessor by a constant amount. The general form of the FOR . . . TO . . . STEP, NEXT statement is:

```
┌─ FOR <variable> = <starting value> TO <ending value> STEP <increment>
│        •
│        •
│        •
└─ NEXT <variable>
```

Note that the 'variable' after FOR and NEXT must be the same. A string variable cannot be used in a FOR . . . NEXT loop. The STEP portion may be omitted if the increment equals +1.
For example,

```
┌─ 10 FOR X = 2 TO 6
│        •
│        •
│        •
└─ 40 NEXT X
```

```
┌─ 70 FOR H1 = N*2 TO 26 STEP +2
│        •
│        •
│        •
└─ 100 NEXT H1
```

```
┌─ 120 FOR T = 10 TO 0 STEP—1
│        •
│        •
│        •
└─ 180 NEXT T
```

Note that a loop is formed by the FOR . . . TO . . . STEP and NEXT statements. In the example,

```
┌─ 30 FOR N = 3 to 11 STEP 2
│        •
│        •
│        •
└─ 80 NEXT N
```

the variable N starts at line 30 with a value of 3. N retains the value of 3 until the NEXT N statement is encountered at line 80. At this point, N is increased by the STEP value. In this example N changes from 3 to 5 to 7, etc. All the statements in the lines occurring between lines 30 and 80 are executed in sequence during each consecutive pass through the loop. The program continues to return from line 80 to the line immediately following line 30 until N exceeds the specified limit of 11. At this point, the program exits from the loop and moves on to the line following 80.

PROGRAM 2.6

This program uses READ, DATA, while Program 2.7 uses a FOR ... TO ... STEP, NEXT loop to print all integers between 10 and 30, inclusive.

```
10 READ N
20 PRINT N;
30 GOTO 10
40 PRINT "   DONE"
50 DATA 10,11,12,13,14,15,16,17,18
60 DATA 19,20,21,22,23,24,25,26,27
70 DATA 28,29,30
READY
>RUN
  10  11  12  13  14  15  16  17  18  19  20  21  22  23  24  25
  26  27  28  29  30
Out of DATA in 10
READY
```

PROGRAM 2.7

```
10 FOR N=10 TO 30
20     PRINT N;
30 NEXT N
40 PRINT "   DONE"
READY
>RUN
  10  11  12  13  14  15  16  17  18  19  20  21  22  23  24  25
  26  27  28  29  30    DONE
READY
```

Program 2.6 continues to read data until all of it is exhausted. Program 2.7 generates all of the values of N between 10 and 30. Note that the loop in Program 2.7 is completed by a NEXT statement, not a GOTO statement. Unlike Program 2.6, Program 2.7 can therefore proceed to line 40.

PROGRAM 2.8

This program finds solutions to the compound condition 5X + 3<100 and 2X²-1>50 and tests all odd integers from 1 to 25.

```
10 FOR X=1 TO 25 STEP 2
20      IF 5*X+3<100 AND 2*X[2 1>50 THEN PRINT X;
30 NEXT X
40 PRINT " DONE"
50 END
READY
>RUN
 7  9  11  13  15  17  19  DONE
READY
>
```

Note that the symbol ([) is used to denote 'raised to the power' (e.g. X[2 means X*X). The ([) symbol is generated by pressing the uparrow (↑) key. Lines 10 and 30 create a loop for testing the conditions located at line 20. The loop starts at line 10 with X=1. Each time the program reaches the NEXT X statement at line 30, N is incremented by the STEP value which is 2. The program will then return to line 20 unless the value of the loop variable X has exceeded its maximum value of 25, at which point the loop will be exited. Remember that a FOR loop is not completed by a GOTO statement, but by a NEXT statement.

PROGRAM 2.9

The following program illustrates the use of a negative STEP value. The integers from 1 to 10 are printed in descending order.

```
10 FOR X=10 TO 1 STEP -1
20      PRINT X;
30 NEXT X
40 PRINT
50 END
READY
>RUN
 10  9  8  7  6  5  4  3  2  1
READY
>
```

REVIEW

5. Write a program that prints the integers between 1 and 25, inclusive.

6. Using a FOR ... TO ... STEP, NEXT loop, have the computer print the following:

```
>RUN
 20  18  16  14  12  10
READY
>
```

7. Write a program that will allow a number N to be entered. Using N as a STEP value, print numbers between 8 and 20.

```
>RUN
STEP VALUE? 2
  8   10   12   14   16   18   20
READY
>
```

RESTORE

At times the user might find it desirable to employ a set of data more than once. The RESTORE statement makes it possible to read data again starting at the beginning of the data. For example,

40 RESTORE

causes the next READ statement encountered to read data starting with the first item in the first DATA statement.

PROGRAM 2.10

This program searches DATA statements for a specific student and then prints the student's grades. It employs the RESTORE statement so that each time a student's name is entered, a searching process starts at the beginning of the first DATA statement. How would the program run if line 20 is deleted?

```
10 PRINT : INPUT "NAME";B$.
20 RESTORE
30 FOR P=1 TO 6
40     READ N$,A,B,C,D
50      IF N$=B$ THEN 80
60 NEXT P
70 PRINT "STUDENT ";B$;" NOT FOUND": GOTO 10
80 PRINT N$;" HAS THE FOLLOWING GRADES:"
90 PRINT A;B;C;D
100 GOTO 10
110 DATA WATERS,83,75,52,80,PARTRIDGE,74,81,92,76
120 DATA HAYDEN,72,81,63,60,HAYES,99,84,92,87
130 DATA GRAHAM,100,93,82,89,STEHLE,78,93,85,94
140 END
READY
```

```
>RUN

NAME? STEHLE
STEHLE HAS THE FOLLOWING GRADES:
 78   93   85   94

NAME? LYNCH
STUDENT LYNCH NOT FOUND

NAME? HAYDEN
HAYDEN HAS THE FOLLOWING GRADES:
 72   81   63   60

NAME?
Break in 10
READY
>
```

IF THENS
<, >, = comparisons
RESTORE
NESTED LOOP

PART A

1. Write a program to allow two numbers (A and B) to be entered. Have the computer compare them and print a message stating whether A is less than, equal to, or greater than B.

2. Write a program which allows three names to be entered as A$, B$, and C$. Have the computer print the name which is alphabetically last.

3. Allow a string (A$) composed of letters to be entered. Have the computer print A$ if it comes alphabetically after the string "MIDWAY". Use only two line numbers and no colons.

4. Write a program which prints six exclamation marks if BIGWOW is entered for the string X$ but which otherwise prints six question marks. The program is to run until the BREAK key is struck.

5. Use only one line number to enter two strings (A$ and B$) and to print output similar to the following.

```
>RUN
? START,FINISH
START          FINISH
FINISH         START
```

6. Allow a number (X) to be entered. Print the message "NOT BETWEEN" if X is either less than –24 or greater than 17. Only one IF . . . THEN statement is permitted.

7. Allow a string (A$) to be entered. Print the message "A$ IS BETWEEN" if A$ comes between "DOWN" and "UP" alphabetically. Only one IF . . . THEN statement is permitted.

8. Allow a number (X) to be entered. Print "IN THE INTERVAL" if X satisfies the inequality $25 < X < 75$, but otherwise print "NOT IN THE INTERVAL". Only one AND and one IF . . . THEN statement are to be used.

9. Rewrite the program of the preceding exercise, using OR instead of AND.

10. Use only one PRINT statement to produce the following rectangle.

```
>RUN
************
************
************
```

11. Print the cubes of the odd integers from 11 to –11, inclusive, in that order.

12. Print all the integers which end in 4 from 4 to 84, inclusive.

13. Use a loop to print a line of 40 asterisks.

14. Write a one line IMMEDIATE MODE command for each of the following:
    (A) Find the value of 143 x 74.
    (B) Find the average of 53, 72, 81, and 76.
    (C) Find which is larger, X↑Y or Y↑X, when X = 4 and Y = 5.

PART B
15. Print all of the integers in the set 10, 13, 16, 19, . . ., 94, 97.

16. Using a loop have the computer print a letter I as follows:

```
>RUN
*****
 ***
 ***
 ***
 ***
 ***
 ***
*****
```

17. Below is a list of various creatures and the weapon necessary to destroy each.

Creature	Weapon
Lich	Fire Ball
Mummy	Flaming Torch
Werewolf	Silver Bullet
Vampire	Wooden Stake
Medusa	Sharp Sword
Triffid	Fire Hose

Using READ and DATA, have the computer state what weapon is to be used to destroy a given creature. For example:

```
RUN
CREATURE? VAMPIRE
YOU CAN KILL A VAMPIRE WITH A WOODEN STAKE
CREATURE? LICH
YOU CAN KILL A LICH WITH A FIRE BALL
CREATURE? BLOB
CREATURE BLOB NOT FOUND.
CREATURE? MEDUSA
YOU CAN KILL A MEDUSA WITH A SHARP SWORD
CREATURE?
Break in 10
READY
>
```

2.15

18. Menacing Matilda has written the following program using too many GOTO statements and cannot figure out in what order the lines of the program will be executed. Assist her by listing the line numbers in the sequence in which the computer will execute them.

```
10 READ A,B
20 IF A > 4 OR B > 4 THEN 50
30 IF A < 1 AND B < 1 THEN 60
40 GOTO 70
50 X = A + B: GOTO 80
60 X = A * B: GOTO 80
70 X = A / B
80 IF X > 1 THEN PRINT X:GOTO 10
90 DATA 5,3,-1,-2,0,2
```

19. John Doe's brother Jim has been assigned the following program for homework. Jim is not in shape today, so assist him by stating the exact order in which the lines of the following program are to be executed.

```
10 READ A,B,C
20 S = A+B*C
30 IF S = 10 THEN RESTORE : READ S
40 PRINT S,
50 IF S = 14 THEN END
60 GOTO 10
70 DATA 4,2,3,6,0,2,7
```

20. Write a program which asks for a person's age. If the person is 16 years or older, have the computer print "YOU ARE OLD ENOUGH TO DRIVE A CAR". Otherwise, have the computer indicate how many years the person must wait before being able to drive.

```
>RUN
HOW OLD ARE YOU ? 16
YOU ARE OLD ENOUGH TO DRIVE A CAR
```

21. The Happy Holiday Motel has 10 rooms. Have the computer print a label for each room's door indicating the room number. For example:

```
>RUN

-------------------------------------
    HAPPY HOLIDAY MOTEL
         ROOM 1
-------------------------------------
```

22. As candidate for mayor, you are very busy. Use the computer to print thank you letters to 10 people who have contributed money to your election campaign. Be sure to mention the exact amount each person has contributed.

```
>RUN

DEAR RICH BRYBURRY,
    THANK YOU FOR YOUR GENEROUS CONTRIBUTION
OF 25000 DOLLARS TO MY ELECTION CAMPAIGN. MAYBE
NEXT YEAR WE WILL HAVE BETTER LUCK!
                              SINCERELY,

                              SMILEY R. POLITICO
```

23. Write a program which will produce the following table:

```
>RUN
X                 X[2              X[3

2                 4                8
4                 16               64
6                 36               216
8                 64               512
10                100              1000
```

24. The Bored Auto Company has done it again! Some models of their cars may be difficult to drive because their wheels are not exactly round. Cars with model numbers 102, 780, 119, 220, 189, and 195 have been found to have a defect. Write a computer program that allows 10 of their customers to enter the model number of their car to find out whether or not it is defective.

25. Using only two print statements, write a program to print a triangle that is N lines high and N columns wide. For example:

```
>RUN
? 5
*
**
***
****
*****
```

26. Have the computer find all odd integers from 5 to 25 which are simultaneous solutions of the inequalities $X^3 > 500$ and $X^2 + 3X + 2 < 700$. Print only the solutions.

27. The following table contains employee performance data for the Tippecanoe Typing Company.

Employee	Performance
Oakley	69%
Howe	92%
Anderson	96%
Wolley	88%
Goerz	74%

Tippecanoe Typing is suffering from financial difficulties and needs to cut back on its staff. Using READ, DATA and a loop, have the computer print notices of dismissal for any employee whose production performance is below 75%.

```
>RUN

DEAR OAKLEY,
   I AM SO SORRY THAT I MUST FIRE YOU.
YOU HAVE BEEN SUCH A FINE EMPLOYEE
WITH A PERFORMANCE RATING OF 69 %
I'M SURE YOU'LL HAVE NO TROUBLE
FINDING ANOTHER JOB.
                    SINCERELY,

                    GEORGE SHWABB


DEAR GOERZ,
   I AM SO SORRY THAT I MUST FIRE YOU.
YOU HAVE BEEN SUCH A FINE EMPLOYEE
WITH A PERFORMANCE RATING OF 74 %
I'M SURE YOU'LL HAVE NO TROUBLE
FINDING ANOTHER JOB.
                    SINCERELY,

                    GEORGE SHWABB
```

28. Wayne Peber bought stock two years ago and wants to use the computer to calculate his profit or loss. He bought 200 shares of Consolidated Technologies at $85.58 per share and 400 shares of American Amalgamated Securities at $35.60 per share. Today C.T. is worth $70.82 a share and A.A.S. is worth $47.32 a share. What is his profit or loss?

29. The Exploitation Oil Company uses the computer to determine the weekly wages of its employees by inputting the hours worked and the hourly wage for each employee. If the employee works over 40 hours, he or she is paid one and a half times the hourly rate for each additional hour.

```
>RUN
HOURS WORKED? 45
HOURLY WAGE? 10.00
THE WAGE FOR THE WEEK IS $ 475
```

30. The Last Chance Finance Company is charging a rate of 2% per month on all loans it is making. Write a program that allows Last Chance to calculate the monthly payments charged a customer using the following formula.

$$\text{Monthly Payment} = \frac{L*I}{1-(1+I)^{-m}}$$

where L = Amount Loaned
I = Interest (monthly)
m = Number of months to be loaned

```
>RUN
THE AMOUNT OF THE LOAN? 100
LENGTH OF THE LOAN IN YEARS? 5
THE MONTHLY PAYMENT IS 2.88
TOTAL AMOUNT PAID WILL BE   172.61
READY
```

31. You have $200.00 to spend on a buying spree. Write a program that, as you buy merchandise, subtracts the cost and the appropriate sales tax (5%) from your remaining money and shows your present total. The program should prevent you from buying items that cost more than you have.

```
>RUN
HOW MUCH DOES THE ITEM COST? 10.00
YOUR TOTAL IS NOW $ 189.5

HOW MUCH DOES THE ITEM COST? 250.00
YOU DON'T HAVE ENOUGH
HOW MUCH DOES THE ITEM COST? 25.00
YOUR TOTAL IS NOW $ 163.25

HOW MUCH DOES THE ITEM COST? 0
READY
```

Flow Charting

Input 3 numbers
Output in ascending order

Possibilities

ABC
ACB
BAC
BCA

CAB
CBA

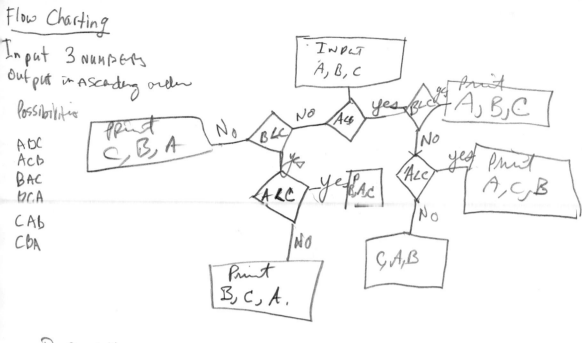

Program

```
10 INPUT A, B, C.
20 IF A<B THEN 100
30 IF B<C then 130
40 PRINT CBA
```

```
100 IF B<C THEN PRINT ABC
110 IF A<C then Print A, C, B
120 PRINT CAB : END
130 IF A<C PRINT BAC
140 Print BCA
```

3 TRS-80 COMPUTER GAMES AND GRAPHICS

This chapter introduces material which should be interesting, practical, and entertaining. In fact, the emphasis will be placed on employing graphics to involve the user in computer games which are often the most enjoyable way to learn computer programming.

RND

In many computer simulations that involve science problems and also in a variety of computer games, the process of generating random numbers becomes essential. The RND function is used to generate random numbers on the computer and it operates in two ways. The statement

$$X = RND(0)$$

will assign X a random six place value such that $0 \leq X < 1$. The statement

$$X = RND(n)$$

will assign X a random integer between 1 and n, inclusive, where n can be a positive integer between 2 and 32767. RND(1) is meaningless and will always return 1.

Sometimes it may be desirable to produce a random number between two values other than 1 and n. The following formula will assign X a random integer between A and B, inclusive:

$$X = RND(B-A+1) + A-1$$

For example, the statement

$$X = RND(26) + 74$$

will assign X a random integer between 75 and 100, inclusive.

PROGRAM 3.1

This program will produce five random numbers between 0 and 1 followed by five random integers between 5 and 14.

```
10 REM Five random floating point values
20 FOR X = 1 TO 5
30      R = RND(0)
40      PRINT R
50 NEXT X
60 REM Five random integers between 5 and 14
70 FOR Y = 1 TO 5
80      PRINT RND(10)+4;
90 NEXT Y
100 PRINT
READY
>RUN
 .536813
 .625858
 .708253
 .71425
 .571674
 14  8  6  5  12
READY
>
```

PROGRAM 3.2

This game program selects a random number between 1 and 100 and then gives the player an unlimited number of chances to guess it. After each guess the computer informs the player whether the guess is too high, too low, or correct.

```
10 PRINT "I'm thinking of a random number between 1 & 100."
20 R = RND(100)
30 INPUT "What is your guess"; G
40 IF G < R THEN PRINT "Too Low!" : GOTO 30
50 IF G > R THEN PRINT "Too High!" : GOTO 30
60 PRINT "That is correct!!!"
READY
```

```
>RUN
I'm thinking of a random number between 1 & 100.
What is your guess? 50
Too High!
What is your guess? 25
Too Low!
What is your guess? 34
Too Low!
What is your guess? 43
Too High!
What is your guess? 40
That is correct!!!
READY
>
```

INT

The statement A = INT(X) sets A to the largest integer that is not greater than X. This function does not round off a positive number but simply truncates its decimals. In the case of a negative number, it takes the next lower negative integer. For example:

$$INT (3.7640) = 3 \qquad\qquad INT (5.9) = 5$$
$$INT (-1.7) = -2 \qquad\qquad INT (-3.01) = -4$$

The process of rounding off a number to the nearest integer is performed by using A = INT(X + .5). For example:

If X = 3.4, then 3.4 + .5 = 3.9, and INT(3.9) = 3.
If X = 3.6, then 3.6 + .5 = 4.1, and INT(4.1) = 4.
If X = −6.2, then −6.2 + .5 = −5.7, and INT(−5.7) = −6.

```
>PRINT INT(3.6 + 0.5)
 4
READY
>PRINT INT(3.1 + 0.5)
 3
READY
>PRINT INT(3.5 + 0.5)
 4
READY
>
```

The INT function is also used to round off numbers to any desired number of decimal places. For example, INT(10*X + .5)/10 will round X to one decimal place. If X = 2.57, then (10*X + .5) = (25.7 + .5) = 26.2 and INT (26.2) = 26. If the 26 is then divided by 10 the result is 2.6, the correct rounded value. Furthermore, INT(100*X + .5)/100 rounds X to two decimal places and INT(1000*X + .5)/1000 to three places and so on. Rounding off a number to the nearest tens place (for example, 257 to 260) is accomplished by using INT(0.1*X + 0.5)/0.1. The general formula for rounding X to N decimal places is:

$$INT(10\uparrow N*X+.5)/10\uparrow N$$

REVIEW

1. Write a program that will generate 2 random integers between 50 and 150 and then find their product.

```
>RUN
 93 multiplied by 123 is 11439
READY
>
```

2. Write a game program similar to Program 3.2 which picks a random number between 1 and 50, inclusive, and gives the player only five attempts to guess it.

```
>RUN
I'm thinking of a random number between 1 & 50.
What is your guess? 25
Too Low!
What is your guess? 37
Too Low!
What is your guess? 43
Too High!
What is your guess? 40
Too Low!
What is your guess? 41
Too Low!
You've had 5 guesses now.
The number was 42
READY
>
```

Summation

If the programmer decides to keep score for the number guessing game (Program 3.2), some technique would have to be devised to keep count of the number of guesses taken. One possible technique is to use a summation statement of the form:

$$30 \; A=A+1$$

The statement A=A+1 makes no sense in mathematics since A can equal A but not A+1. The computer, however, interprets the equal sign to mean "is replaced by" rather than "equal to"; and each time it encounters the statement above, it takes the present value of A, adds 1 to it, and makes that sum the new value of A.

PROGRAM 3.3

This program demonstrates how the summation statement works by printing the values of A until the program is halted with the BREAK key.

```
10 A = A + 1
20 PRINT A;
30 GOTO 10
READY
>RUN
 1  2  3  4  5  6  7  8  9  10  11  12  13  14  15  16  17  18
 19  20  21  22  23  24  25  26  27  28  29
Break in 20
READY
>
```

If line 10 is replaced with

$$10\ A = A + 5$$

then 5 will be added to A each time the statement is encountered.

```
>10 A = A + 5
>RUN
 5  10  15  20  25  30  35  40  45  50  55  60  65  70  75  80
 85
Break in 10
READY
>
```

In this problem the initial value of A is zero for both runs. This is true because the computer sets any undefined numeric variable to zero at the start of the run.

PROGRAM 3.4

Here, Program 3.2 has been modified to record the number of turns required to guess the random number. In this case the variable T acts as a counter, increasing in value by 1 after each guess.

```
10 PRINT "I'm thinking of a random number between 1 & 100."
20 R = RND(100)
30 INPUT "What is your guess"; G
35 T = T + 1
40 IF G < R THEN PRINT "Too Low!" : GOTO 30
50 IF G > R THEN PRINT "Too High!" : GOTO 30
60 PRINT "That is correct!!!"
70 PRINT "That took you"; T; "guesses."
READY
```

```
>RUN
I'm thinking of a random number between 1 & 100.
What is your guess? 50
Too Low!
What is your guess? 75
Too Low!
What is your guess? 86
Too High!
What is your guess? 78
That is correct!!!
That took you 4 guesses.
READY
>
```

Rounding Errors

Because the computer has a finite capacity, any numerical computations involving infinitely repeating decimals cannot be accurate (for example, $1/3 = .3333\ldots$, which the computer truncates to a limited number of digits). Since the computer uses binary numbers (0 and 1), any fraction whose denominator is not an integral power of 2 (e.g., 2, 4, 8, 16) will be an infinitely repeating decimal and therefore will be truncated by the computer. In Chapter Eight binary numbers are examined in greater detail.

PROGRAM 3.5

This program illustrates summation and rounding errors.

```
10 FOR X = 1 TO 1500
20      A = A + (1 / 2)
30      B = B + (1 / 3)
40 NEXT X
50 PRINT "A ="; A
60 PRINT "B ="; B
READY
>RUN
A = 750
B = 500.006
READY
>
```

The final value of A is the result of adding 1/2 1500 times which comes out to be exactly 750. B, however, which is the result of adding 1/3 1500 times does not come out to be exactly 500 because of the rounding error. The computer will sometimes not recognize an equality when one in fact should exist. If the line

70 IF B = 500 THEN PRINT "EQUALS"
ELSE PRINT "NOT EQUAL"

were added to the above program, the computer would print "NOT EQUAL".

3.6

REVIEW

3. Select 50 random integers between 0 and 9, inclusive, and have the computer tell how many of the numbers were from 0-4 and how many were from 5-9.

```
>RUN
There were 18 numbers between 0 and 4.
There were 32 numbers between 5 and 9.
READY
>
```

4. Input ten numbers from the keyboard and have the computer tell how many are odd and how many are even.

```
>RUN
Enter a number? 42
Enter a number? 69
Enter a number? 14
Enter a number? 111
Enter a number? 86
Enter a number? 72
Enter a number? 164
Enter a number? 8218
Enter a number? 2001
Enter a number? 9
 6 Even;   4 Odd
READY
>
```

FORMATTING OUTPUT

The statements presented in this section allow program output to be formatted. For advanced formatting techniques, which are especially useful in producing tables, refer to Appendix D where the PRINT USING statement is presented.

PRINT TAB

The PRINT TAB statement provides an easy way to format output and allows the programmer to begin portions of the printout at specified locations. The left edge of the screen is TAB(0), and the right edge of the screen is TAB(63). The printing of information at TAB positions 13, 25 and 32 is accomplished by:

```
10 PRINT TAB(13); "This"; TAB(25); "is"; TAB(32); "TAB"
READY
>RUN
             This        is      TAB
READY
>
```

It is important to use semicolons (;) in each instance after the TAB parentheses.

PROGRAM 3.6

The substitution of variables for the numbers in the TAB parentheses is permissible provided these variables have previously been assigned values.

```
10 READ X, Y, Z
20 PRINT TAB(X); "This"; TAB(Y); "is"; TAB(Z); "TAB"
30 DATA 13, 25, 32
READY
>RUN
                This            is        TAB
READY
>
```

PROGRAM 3.7

This program draws a triangle on the display screen.

```
10 PRINT TAB(10); "*******"
20 FOR X = 1 TO 5
30     PRINT TAB(X + 10); "*"; TAB(16); "*"
40 NEXT X
50 PRINT TAB(16); "*"
READY
>RUN
          *******
           *     *
            *    *
             *   *
              *  *
               **
                *
READY
>
```

The PRINT TAB statement does not move the cursor to the left, but only to the right. If a TAB position is specified which is to the left of the current TAB position, the cursor will remain where it is and the printing will proceed from there.

```
10 PRINT TAB(10); "##"; TAB(15); "##"
20 PRINT TAB(15); "##"; TAB(10); "##"
READY
>RUN
          ##    ##
               ####
READY
>
```

CLS

The CLS statement is used to clear the entire display screen. This statement is generally used before graphing. CLS may also be used in the immediate mode.

POS

The POS function is used to find the current horizontal position of the cursor. The statement

$$X = POS(0)$$

will assign X a value corresponding to the horizontal position (the current TAB position) of the cursor on the screen. X = 0 for the left edge and 63 for the right edge.

PROGRAM 3.8

The following program demonstrates TAB and POS.

```
10 PRINT TAB(32); "ROCK";
20 PRINT POS(0)
30 PRINT TAB(21); POS(0)
READY
>RUN
                                      ROCK 36
                          21
READY
>
```

PRINT@

The TRS-80 screen can hold 16 lines of 64 characters, or a total of 1024 characters. The PRINT@ statement allows output to begin at any one of these 1024 positions. The general form of PRINT@ is:

PRINT@ <position>, <print list>

where "position" refers to one of the 1024 (numbered 0 to 1023) print positions on the display screen. The top line on the screen contains print positions 0 through 63; the second, 64 through 127, and so on, down to the bottom line, which contains print positions 960 through 1023.

"Print list" is any expression valid in a normal PRINT statement. The statement

PRINT @30, "HERE"

will output the word "HERE" at the middle of the top line on the display screen, while the statement

$$PRINT @409, A\$$$

will print the contents of the string variable A$ in the middle of the screen.

The "position" can be a variable. For instance, if X = 863, then the statement

$$PRINT @X, \text{"CARROTS"};$$

will place the word "CARROTS" at position 863. The trailing semicolon leaves the cursor positioned immediately after "CARROTS." A subsequent PRINT statement will begin output at that point on the screen.

The PRINT@ statement may be extended to print several items at several different locations on the display screen. The statement

$$70 \ PRINT @30, \text{"HERE"}; @442, \text{"THERE"}; @814, \text{"EVERYWHERE"}$$

will print "HERE" at position 30, "THERE" at 442, and "EVERYWHERE" at 814.

PROGRAM 3.9

The following program will print the word "M*A*S*H" and "4077" 14 times in diagonals on the screen using the PRINT@ statement. The output is shown as it appears on the video screen.

```
10 CLS
20 FOR I = 0 TO 13
30    N = I * 67 + 1
40    P = (36 - 3*I) + I*64
50    PRINT @P, "    4077" @N, "M*A*S*H"
60 NEXT I
```

```
M*A*S*H                                          4077
   M*A*S*H                                     4077
      M*A*S*H                               4077
         M*A*S*H                         4077
            M*A*S*H             4077
               M*A*S*H 4077
                  M*A*S*H
               4077M*A*S*H
            4077        M*A*S*H
         4077              M*A*S*H
      4077                    M*A*S*H
   4077                          M*A*S*H
   4077                             M*A*S*H
4077                                   M*A*S*H
READY
>
```

GRAPHICS

The graphics capability of the computer is often used to produce game programs, and the mastery of this skill is the secret to developing most of the entertaining computer games.

The TRS-80 divides the graphing area on the display screen into 48 rows. Each row is subdivided into 128 rectangular areas shaped like 'bricks.' Each brick represents a point and may be shaded either black or white. The origin (0,0) of the 48 by 128 graphing grid is located in the upper-left corner of the display screen.

No special command is needed to enable the graphics capabilities on the TRS-80. In fact, text and graphics may be intermingled on the display screen.

SET-RESET

The SET statement is used to plot a single point or 'brick' on the display screen, and to shade it white. The statement

$$SET(X,Y)$$

will plot a white brick at the coordinates (X,Y). Note that X may range from 0 to 127, and Y may range from 0 to 47, inclusive.

PROGRAM 3.10

The following program will plot 21 bricks on the display screen; 20 at random locations, and 1 at (60,47).

```
10 CLS
20 FOR T = 1 TO 20
30      X = RND(128) - 1
40      Y = RND(48) - 1
50      SET(X,Y)
60 NEXT T
70 SET(60,47)
>RUN
```

The RESET statement functions exactly as the SET statement, except that the point (brick) plotted is shaded black instead of white. The statement

$$RESET(A,B)$$

will plot a black brick at the coordinates (A,B).

The SET and RESET statements can be combined to cause a brick on the screen to appear to blink. This is done by continuously SETting and RESETting a particular point.

PROGRAM 3.11

This program utilizes SET and RESET to blink a brick in the center of the display screen, while plotting 50 random bricks on the screen.

```
10 REM Plot border around edge of screen
20 CLS
30 FOR S = 0 TO 127
40      SET(S,0) : SET(S,47)
50      IF S < 48 THEN SET(0,S) : SET(127,S)
60 NEXT S
100 REM
110 REM Plot 50 random points while simultaneously
120 REM flashing a single point at (60,22)
130 FOR X = 1 TO 50
140     SET(60,22)
150     FOR D = 1 TO 50 : NEXT D : REM Delay Loop
160     RESET(60,22)
170     FOR D = 1 TO 40 : NEXT D : REM Delay again
180     SET(RND(128)-1, RND(48)-1) : REM Random Point
190 NEXT X
>RUN
```

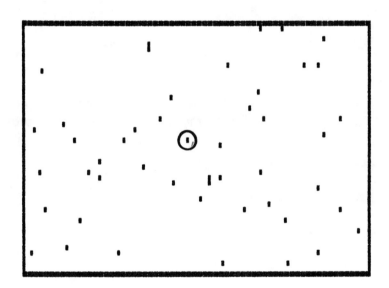

The loops at lines 150 and 170 are needed to slow the rate of flashing of the point circled at (60,22).

REVIEW

5. Write a program that will produce the following figure.

6. Write a program that will move a single brick back and forth across the center of the screen.

POINT

The POINT function is used to test whether a particular brick on the screen is shaded black or white. This function returns a non-zero value if the brick is shaded white, otherwise a zero is returned meaning that the selected brick is shaded black. The line

$$20 \text{ SET}(14,42) : \text{IF POINT}(14,42) <> 0$$
$$\text{THEN PRINT "IVORY" ELSE PRINT "EBONY"}$$

will always print "IVORY" since position (14,42) is SET just prior to the IF ... THEN ... ELSE statement which tests (14,42).

PROGRAM 3.12

This game program plots eight targets at random locations on the display screen. The player's mission is to destroy all eight targets. Each time a shot is fired, the coordinates struck flash momentarily.

```
10 REM    A,B = Coordinates fired at by player
20 REM    L   = Loop variable for plotting random targets
30 REM    C   = # of hits scored
40 REM
50 REM Plot 8 random targets on screen
60 CLS
70 FOR L = 1 TO 8
80      SET(RND(127), RND(41))
90 NEXT L
100 REM
110 REM Get coordinates to shoot at from player
120 PRINT @896, "Coordinates to fire at (1-127,1-47)";
130 INPUT A,B
140 PRINT @896, "                                    "
150 IF POINT(A,B) = 0
        THEN PRINT @896, "Missed..."
        ELSE PRINT @896, "A Hit!!!" : C = C + 1
200 REM
```

3.14

```
210 REM Flash coordinates struck
220 FOR X = 1 TO 8
230     SET(A,B)
240     FOR D = 1 TO 50 : NEXT D : REM Delay loop
250     RESET(A,B)
260     FOR D = 1 TO 50 : NEXT D : REM Delay loop
270 NEXT X
280 IF C < 8 THEN 100
>RUN
```

Coordinates to fire at (1-127,1-47)?

Lines 70 through 90 plot the eight targets on the screen. The player enters the coordinates to fire upon at line 130. Line 150 checks to see if a hit is scored and notifies the player of his results. The variable C is used as a counter. When C = 8, all of the targets have been destroyed and the game is over.

PROGRAM 3.13

The following program is a game similar to Program 3.12, except that the player, instead of battling many, is involved in a one-on-one dogfight. The mission is to align the view sight (+) directly on the target. At that point, the enemy is destroyed.

```
10 REM    P1,P2 = Random target position (P1,P2)
20 REM    S,T,N = Dummy variables for Loops
30 REM    X,Y   = Sight position (X,Y)
40 REM    A,B   = Coordinates entered by player
50 REM    SC    = # of hits scored
100 REM
110 REM Draw border around screen & init variables
120 CLS
130 FOR S = 0 TO 127
140     SET(S,0) : SET(S,38)
150 NEXT S
160 FOR T = 0 TO 38
170     SET(0,T) : SET(127,T)
180 NEXT T
190 SC = 0 : REM Score
```

```
200 X = 63 : Y = 19 : REM Sight position
300 REM
310 REM New random target at (P1,P2)
320 P1 = RND(108) + 8 : P2 = RND(28) + 5
400 REM
410 REM Plot sight centered at (X,Y)
420 FOR N = 1 TO 4
430     SET(X+N-7,Y) : SET(X+N+2,Y)
440     SET(X,Y+N-7) : SET(X,Y+N+2)
450 NEXT N : SET(P1,P2)
460 PRINT @832,"SCORE:";SC; @869,"POSITION: (";X;",";Y;")    "
500 REM
510 REM Did player score a hit?
520 IF POINT(X,Y) THEN SC = SC + 1 : RESET(X,Y) : GOTO 310
600 REM
610 REM Get new coordinates
620 INPUT "NEW COORDINATES (8-118,6-32): ";A,B
700 REM
710 REM Erase old sight
720 FOR N = 1 TO 4
730     RESET(X+N-7,Y) : RESET(X+N+2,Y)
740     RESET(X,Y+N-7) : RESET(X,Y+N+2)
750 NEXT N
800 X = A : Y = B : GOTO 400
>RUN
```

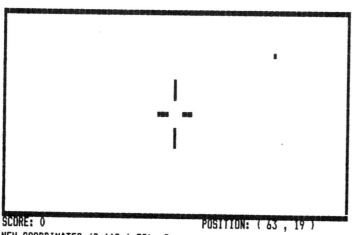

```
SCORE: 0                    POSITION: ( 63 , 19 )
NEW COORDINATES (8-118,6-32): ?
```

Lines 100 through 200 draw a border around the display screen and set up program variables. Line 320 generates a random target for the screen, while lines 400-460 plot the view sight and display the player's current score. A 'hit' is scored only if the center of the view sight is aligned directly on the target (note line 520). The player is prompted for coordinates at line 620. Lines 700-750 erase the view sight so that it may be replotted elsewhere on the screen.

PART A

1. Generate ten random numbers between 0 and 1, but print only those which are greater than 0.5.

2. Generate three random numbers between 0 and 1, and print their sum.

3. Input a number (N). Print it only if it is an integer. (Hint: compare N and INT(N)).

4. Allow a user to guess a random integer between −3 and 4, inclusive. Print whether the guess was correct or not. If the guess was wrong, the correct value is also to be printed.

5. Determine randomly how many coins you find on the street. You are to find from 2 to 5 nickels, 1 to 4 dimes, and 0 to 3 quarters. Lunch costs 99 cents. The program is to report the amount that you found and whether you are able to buy lunch with it.

```
>RUN
YOU FOUND $ .75
SORRY, YOU CAN'T BUY LUNCH
READY
>RUN
YOU FOUND $ 1.25
YOU CAN BUY LUNCH
READY
```

6. Input an integer (N), and print the sum of N random numbers between 0 and 1. Also print N/2 for comparison with the sum.

7. A child puts pennies into a piggy bank once each week for four weeks. The bank already contains 11 pennies in it when the child first receives it. Write a program to allow pennies to be added each week and to print the dollar value of the bank's contents after each addition.

8. Have the computer produce the following output.

```
>RUN
12345678901234567890123456789012345678901234567890

     *        9    ?    --         !    )         *
```

9. Use PRINT@ to draw a straight diagonal line (composed of asterisks) starting at the upper left hand corner and moving 3 spaces over for each space down until the line hits the bottom of the screen.

10. Put a flashing notice on the screen which advertises Uncle Bill's whamburgers for $0.59.

```
TODAY ONLY!
    UNCLE BILL'S
    WHAMBURGERS
        ONLY $0.59
```

PART B

11. Les Brains wrote both of the following programs but has forgotten what their output is. Determine the output, and check your answer by running the program.

    (a)
    ```
    10 FOR Z = 1 TO 4
    20    PRINT TAB(Z);Z
    30 NEXT Z
    40 FOR Y = 1 TO 4
    50    PRINT TAB(Y),Y
    60 NEXT Y
    ```

    (b)
    ```
    10 G = 123.456
    20 PRINT INT (10 * G)/10, INT (10 * G + .5)/10
    30 PRINT INT (100 * G)/100, INT (100 * G + .5)/100
    ```

3.18

12. Write a program that generates 10 random integers between 8 and 25, inclusive, and prints them on the same line. The output should be similar to the following:

17 12 22 25   8 17 19 11 21 23

13. Make a chart showing in their correct order the values taken by the variables X and Y. Circle those values that are printed by the computer. Check by running the program.

```
10 FOR X = 1 TO 3
15    READ Y
20    IF Y > 0 THEN 35
25    Y = Y + X
30    IF X = 2 THEN Y = Y - 1 : GOTO 40
35    PRINT X,Y
40 NEXT X
45 DATA 5,0,-1
```

14. (a) Determine a possible output for the program below.
    (b) Rewrite the program so that the message LEARN THE MULTIPLICATION TABLE is printed if three wrong answers are given.
    (c) Rewrite the program so that five different questions are asked and the message NICE GOING, HOTSHOT is printed if all five questions are answered correctly.

```
10 CLS : PRINT@384,
20 A = RND(10)
30 B = RND(10)
40 PRINT TAB(12);A;"*";B;"=";
50 INPUT C
60 IF C = A * B THEN 90
70 PRINT "YOU ARE WRONG. TRY AGAIN."
80 GOTO 40
90 PRINT TAB(12);"CORRECT"
```

15. Write a program that contains one FOR . . . NEXT loop which finds the sum of all the odd integers from 13 to 147, inclusive. The output should be as follows:

THE SUM = 5440

16. Suzy Fowlup, one of the slower members of the computing class, wrote the following program. It allows the user to enter at the keyboard any integer greater than 1 and to have the computer tell the user whether or not the integer is prime. A prime number is an integer that contains only itself and 1 as factors. The computer tests the integer by repeatedly dividing it by integers smaller than itself but larger than 1 and checking whether the quotient is whole. If so, the integer entered by the user is not prime. The program contains three errors. Find them, rewrite tho program, and run it. The output should look like this:

```
>RUN
INTEGER > 1 PLEASE? 12
THAT INTEGER IS NOT PRIME.
READY
>RUN
INTEGER > 1 PLEASE? 17
THAT INTEGER IS PRIME.
```

- - - - - - - - - - - - - - -

```
20 READ "INTEGER > 1 PLEASE";N
30 FOR X = 2 TO N-1
40     IF N / X = INT(N/X) THEN 70
50 NEXT N
60 PRINT "THAT INTEGER IS PRIME. "
70 PRINT "THAT INTEGER IS NOT PRIME."
```

17. Generate 1000 random integers between 1 and 9, inclusive, and print how many were even and how many were odd. The output should be similar to the following:

```
>RUN
THERE WERE 547 ODD INTEGERS.
THERE WERE 453 EVEN INTEGERS.
```

18. Write a program that allows the user and computer to alternately select integers between 3 and 12, inclusive, keep a sum of all the integers selected, and declare the winner to be the one who selects that integer which makes the sum greater than 100. Have the program ask the user if he or she would like to proceed first or second.

19. A bank pays interest once a year at a yearly rate of 5%. A man deposits $1000 on January 1, 1983 and wishes to leave it there to accrue interest until the balance is at least $2000. Compute the balance on Jan. 1 of each year, starting with 1984 and ending in the year when the balance exceeds $2000. The output should resemble the following:

```
DATE                    BALANCE
JAN 1,  1984            $ 1050
JAN 2,  1985            $ 1102.5
 . . .                   . . .
 . . .                   . . .
 . . .                  $ 1979.93
 . . .                  $ 2078.93
```

20. Input a positive integer N, and print all positive integers that are factors of N. The output should resemble the following:

```
>RUN
A POSITIVE INTEGER, PLEASE? 1.4
YOUR NUMBER WAS NOT AN INTEGER
A POSITIVE INTEGER, PLEASE? 12
  1  2  3  4  6  12
```

21. Print the radius (cm.) of a sphere, given its volume (cm.³). Round off the results to the nearest hundredth.

DATA: 690, 720, 460, 620
Note: Volume = $(4/3)$ (π) R^3, where $\pi = 3.14159$

22. (a) Print twenty random integers between 0 and 100, inclusive.
(b) Change the program so that sixty percent of the twenty integers printed will be less than 25.

23. Write a program that will produce the following triangle. The figure is centered on TAB(15).

```
>RUN
```

24. Modify the answer to Exercise 23 so that the display is done graphically.

25. Using SET, write a program that will draw a football in the middle of the screen. (Hint: use the equation of a circle.)

26. (a) Have the TRS-80 draw the dart board pictured below, and have it fire ten random shots, using SET to indicate the points hit. (The coordinates of the corners are shown). (b) Rewrite program (a) to give the score at the end of a game. A hit in the center rectangle is worth 10 points, the outer rectangle 4 points, and the region outside both −1 points.

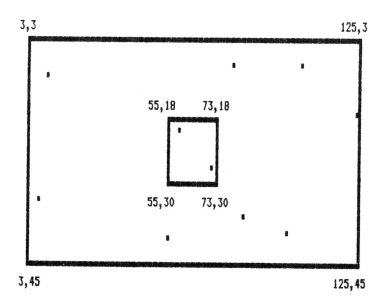

27. Have the computer randomly select a number of quarters (from 0 to 7), dimes (from 0 to 4), and pennies (from 0 to 9) and print the exact number of coins and their total value. The user has ten chances to determine how many quarters, dimes and pennies were selected.

3.22

28. Luke Skywalker needs a simple simulator for his computer so that he can train before his next battle against the Empire. Help Luke by writing a simple Star Wars game. Have the computer plot two points at random positions on the screen. Luke has ten chances to guess the X and Y coordinates of the two enemy points or the rebellion will fail. After each guess, have the computer briefly flash the location of the guess. Use PRINT@ to position the input line each time so that the enemy points are not pushed off the top of the screen during the course of the game.

29. Have the computer draw a solid rectangle with its upper left corner at (19,10), a length of 3 columns, and a height of 2 rows.

30. Have the computer draw a small letter i about an inch high with the dot at (15,18).

31. The following table shows production output per day for each employee of Papa's Pizza Parlor. Plot a bar graph showing the output for the week for each of Papa's employees.

Employee	Pizza Production
Greer	18,12,9,10,16,22,14
McPherson	12,21,19,16,28,20,22
Rady	18,20,14,19,11,16,23
Wyncott	23,27,18,16,21,14,24

32. Allow the user to enter 3 numbers: A, B, and R. Have the computer plot a circle of radius R with its center at (A,B). (Hint: The equation of a circle with center (A,B) and radius R is $(X-A)^2 + (Y-B)^2 = R^2$.)

NESTED LOOPS AND SUBSCRIPTED VARIABLES

We have previously observed that the FOR . . . TO . . . STEP, NEXT statements set up loops. This chapter proceeds further by showing how to combine two or more loops in such a way as to place one loop inside another.

The second part of this chapter deals with subscripted variables which use a fixed variable name in conjunction with a variable subscript (e.g. A(N)), where A is fixed and N varies. This technique enables a program to deal conveniently with a large amount of data. Subscripted variables usually employ FOR . . . NEXT loops to generate the values for the subscripts.

Nested FOR . . . NEXT Loops

The concept of a FOR . . . NEXT loop was presented in Chapter Two. In this chapter, the concept of nested FOR . . . NEXT loops (that is, one loop placed or 'nested' within another) is introduced. For example:

```
10 FOR P = 1 TO 20
20      FOR Q = 3 TO 10
30         NEXT Q
40 NEXT P
```

By definition, nested loops must never cross. One loop must be contained entirely within another, or entirely separate from another. For example, the following arrangement is not permissible because the loops cross each other:

```
10 FOR P = 1 TO 20
20 FOR Q = 3 TO 10
30 NEXT P
40 NEXT Q
```

When this program is run, the following error message will result:

NEXT WITHOUT FOR IN 40

PROGRAM 4.1

This program uses nested loops to print a portion of the multiplication table.

```
10 FOR X = 1 TO 5
20      FOR Y = 1 TO 3
30           PRINT X; "*"; Y; "="; X*Y,
40      NEXT Y
50 PRINT
60 NEXT X
READY
>RUN
 1 * 1 = 1        1 * 2 = 2        1 * 3 = 3
 2 * 1 = 2        2 * 2 = 4        2 * 3 = 6
 3 * 1 = 3        3 * 2 = 6        3 * 3 = 9
 4 * 1 = 4        4 * 2 = 8        4 * 3 = 12
 5 * 1 = 5        5 * 2 = 10       5 * 3 = 15
READY
>
```

Line 10 establishes the outer X loop and starts X with the value 1. X retains this value until it is incremented by the execution of line 60. Line 60 is not executed, however, until the inner Y loop, lines 20-40, has run its entire course. X therefore retains the value 1 while Y changes from 1 to 2 to 3. When the Y loop has finished its cycle of three passes, line 60 is executed, incrementing X to 2. The program returns to line 20 and starts the Y loop over again at its initial value of 1. Whenever a program encounters the FOR . . . TO statement of a loop, the loop variable is reset to its initial value. Since this program does not return to line 10, the X loop is never reset back to 1. Notice that Y will take on its values of 1, 2 and 3 five times. Indentation is used in the above program in order to clarify the program's structure, and the contents of each loop are indented to clarify the boundaries of the loop.

PROGRAM 4.2

This program calculates and prints all possible combinations of coins that add up to fifty cents, using quarters, dimes, and nickels.

```
10 PRINT "Quarters", "Dimes", "Nickels"
20 FOR Q = 0 TO 2 : REM Quarters
30      FOR D = 0 TO 5 : REM Dimes
40           FOR N = 0 TO 10 : REM Nickels
50                IF Q*25 + D*10 + N*5 = 50 THEN PRINT Q, D, N
60           NEXT N
70      NEXT D
80 NEXT Q
READY
```

```
>RUN
Quarters          Dimes          Nickels
   0                0                10
   0                1                8
   0                2                6
   0                3                4
   0                4                2
   0                5                0
   1                0                5
   1                1                3
   1                2                1
   2                0                0
READY
>
```

Q represents the number of quarters, D the number of dimes, and N the number of nickels. There may be anywhere from 0 to 2 quarters in a combination. Similarly, there may be anywhere from 0 to 5 dimes and from 0 to 10 nickels. Using three nested loops, *every* possible combination that *might* work is checked at line 50.

REVIEW

1. Use nested loops to produce the following output. The outer loop runs from 20 to 24, and the inner loop runs from 1 to 3.

```
>RUN
Outer Loop: 20
Inner: 1          Inner: 2          Inner: 3
Outer Loop: 21
Inner: 1          Inner: 2          Inner: 3
Outer Loop: 22
Inner: 1          Inner: 2          Inner: 3
Outer Loop: 23
Inner: 1          Inner: 2          Inner: 3
Outer Loop: 24
Inner: 1          Inner: 2          Inner: 3
READY
>
```

The Need for Subscripted Variables

The following section demonstrates the usefulness of subscripted variables.

PROGRAM 4.3

```
10 FOR X = 1 TO 10
20     Y = RND(20)
30     PRINT Y;
40 NEXT X
READY
>RUN
 5   14   1   16   20   13   20   11   17   17
READY
>
```

4.3

Every time a new value is assigned to Y, it replaces the previous value for Y. Since the previous values of Y are not remembered, it is impossible to prevent repetition by comparing the old values of Y with the new value of Y. If a box analogy is used here, the first two cycles of Program 4.3 would appear as:

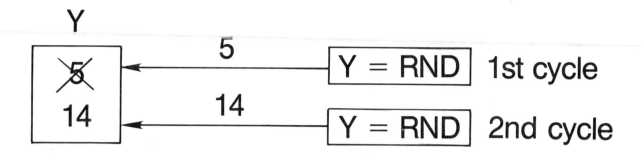

PROGRAM 4.4

This program prints four random numbers between 1 and 20 without any repetition. The technique can be expanded to have the program choose 10 numbers if the user is willing to type the program lines required.

```
10 Y1 = RND(20)
20 PRINT Y1;
30 Y2 = RND(20)
40 IF Y2 = Y1 THEN 30
50 PRINT Y2;
60 Y3 = RND(20)
70 IF Y3 = Y2 OR Y3 = Y1 THEN 60
80 PRINT Y3;
90 Y4 = RND(20)
100 IF Y4 = Y3 OR Y4 = Y2 OR Y4 = Y1 THEN 90
110 PRINT Y4
READY
>RUN
 3  5  17  9
READY
>
```

The similarity between the three sets of lines 30-50, 60-80, and 90-110 is obvious. In each set the first line selects a random number between 1 and 20, while the second line checks to see if the number is a repetition of a number previously chosen. If this is the case, then execution goes back to the first line in the set so that another number may be chosen. Finally, the third line of the set prints the random number selected. The use of subscripted variables will eliminate the need for the repetition of these sets.

Single Subscripted Variables

In mathematics, a set of single subscripted numeric variables (e.g. X_1, X_2, X_3, . . .) is symbolized by a letter and a subscript which is written below the line of the letter. On the computer, the same set of subscripted variables would be referred to as X(1), X(2), X(3), and so on, where the integer enclosed in parentheses is the subscript.

The name for a set of single subscripted numeric variables consists of one of the usual numeric variable names, followed by the parenthesized subscript. For example, A(1), B2(17), and X(8) are all legal subscripted variable names. Similarly, single subscripted string variable names such as Z$(5), Y1$(20), and M$(14) are acceptable.

The subscript variable L(2) is *not* the same as the variable L2. Furthermore, the subscript is a part of the variable name and must not be confused with the value of the variable. For example, in the statement L(5) = 32 the subscript is 5 and the value of L(5) is 32.

PROGRAM 4.5

This program illustrates the difference between the subscript and the value of a subscripted variable.

```
10 L(1) = 7
20 L(2) = 5
30 L(3) = 4
40 PRINT "L(1)="; L(1), "L(2)="; L(2), "L(3)="; L(3)
50 PRINT "L(1 + 2)="; L(1 + 2)
60 PRINT "L(1) + L(2)="; L(1) + L(2)
70 X = 2
80 PRINT "L(X)="; L(X)
READY
>RUN
L(1)= 7          L(2)= 5          L(3)= 4
L(1 + 2)= 4
L(1) + L(2)= 12
L(X)= 5
READY
>
```

Lines 10 through 30 set the value of L(1) through L(3) as follows:

L (1)

L (2)

L (3)

| 7 | 5 | 4 |

Lines 50 and 60 point out the difference between adding two subscripts and adding the values of two variables. L(1 + 2) is identical to L(3) and has a value of 4. L(1) + L(2) calls for the values 7 and 5 to be added, thus producing a total of 12. Since the subscript X equals 2 in line 80, a value of 5 is printed. Thus, as can be seen, it is permissible to use a numeric variable as the subscript of a subscripted variable.

PROGRAM 4.6

Like Program 4.3, this program selects 10 random numbers between 1 and 20 and makes no attempt to prevent repetition. Yet unlike Program 4.3, it stores the numbers chosen in a subscripted variable.

```
10 FOR X = 1 TO 10
20     R(X) = RND(20)
30 NEXT X
40 PRINT "Ten random numbers have been stored in R()."
50 PRINT
60 FOR N = 1 TO 10
70     PRINT "R("; N; ") has a"; R(N); "stored in it."
80 NEXT N
READY
>RUN
Ten random numbers have been stored in R().

R( 1 ) has a 15 stored in it.
R( 2 ) has a 6 stored in it.
R( 3 ) has a 6 stored in it.
R( 4 ) has a 11 stored in it.
R( 5 ) has a 18 stored in it.
R( 6 ) has a 2 stored in it.
R( 7 ) has a 2 stored in it.
R( 8 ) has a 18 stored in it.
R( 9 ) has a 19 stored in it.
R( 10 ) has a 11 stored in it.
READY
>
```

This program has two loops which are not nested but which follow one another. Each loop is executed 10 times. In the first loop, line 20 chooses a random number and stores it in one of the subscripted R() variables. The first time through this loop (X = 1), a random number is stored in R(1); the second time (X = 2), a new number is stored in R(2), and so on 10 times. After the above run of this program, the R() boxes had contents as follows:

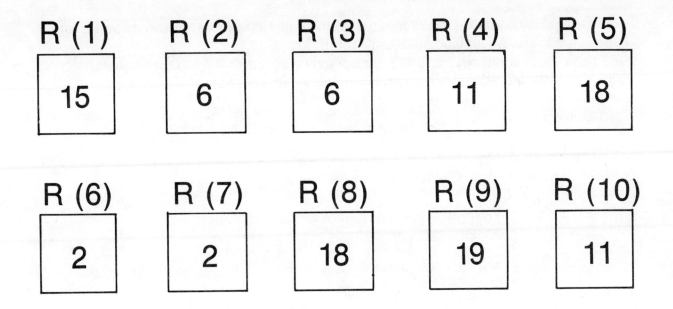

R (1)	R (2)	R (3)	R (4)	R (5)
15	6	6	11	18

R (6)	R (7)	R (8)	R (9)	R (10)
2	2	18	19	11

The second loop (lines 60 through 80) prints the contents stored in the boxes.

The ability to store numbers in this way will allow the writing of a new program to choose 10 random numbers *without* repetition. By checking whether a chosen random number equals any of those previously selected, a program can determine whether to accept the random number chosen or to make another selection.

PROGRAM 4.7

This program uses nested loops and subscripted variables to pick 10 random numbers between 1 and 20 without repetition.

```
10 FOR X = 1 TO 10
20     Y(X) = RND(20)
30     IF X = 1 THEN 70
40     FOR Q = 1 TO X-1
50         IF Y(X) = Y(Q) THEN 20
60     NEXT Q
70     PRINT Y(X);
80 NEXT X
READY
>RUN
  10  12  18  4  1  8  3  20  17  16
READY
>
```

Line 20 selects a random number between 1 and 20 and stores it in one of the subscripts of Y(). Since Y(1) is the first random number, line 30 is included to ensure Y(1) will be printed immediately since it is obviously not a repeat of another number. Lines 40 to 60 constitute a nested loop which determines if a number just chosen, Y(X), is equal to any of the previously chosen numbers, Y(1) through Y(X-1). The X-1 in line 40 ensures that Y(X) is not rejected by being checked against itself. If X rather than X-1 were used, then Q

4.7

would eventually equal X. Line 50 would determine that Y(X) was a repeated number when Q equalled X and would then mistakenly return to line 20.

There is an additional reason for including line 30. When X and Q are equal to 1, Y(X) will equal Y(Q) and without line 30 program flow would continuously jump back to line 20.

PROGRAM 4.8

The following program will randomly read a list of 5 names into a subscripted string variable N$(), without repeating any of the names.

```
10 FOR X = 1 TO 5
20     Y = RND(5)
30      IF N$(Y) <> " " THEN 20
40      READ N$(Y)
50 NEXT X
60 FOR Z = 1 TO 5
70      PRINT N$(Z)
80 NEXT Z
90 DATA TED, JOHN, MARY, KEITH, ANN
READY
>RUN
MARY
ANN
KEITH
TED
JOHN
READY
>RUN
TED
KEITH
JOHN
ANN
MARY
READY
>
```

This program reads the names in the DATA statement in the order of occurrence, but randomly places them in N$(1) to N$(5). Repetition is avoided by checking each new box as it is selected to discover whether it contains a name. If it is full, a new box is tried by selecting a new random number. At line 30 the consecutive double quotes ("") refer to the box being empty. Unassigned subscripted string variables contain an empty space, which is represented on the compuer by ("").

REVIEW

2. Using subscripted variables, write a program in which 3 numbers are input. Then have the computer type them back in reverse order.

```
>RUN
? 4
? 6
? 1
  1
  6
  4
READY
>
```

3. Six words are to be entered from the keyboard. Have the computer randomly select and print four of the words as a "sentence" (which may not make sense). Repetition of words is allowed.

```
>RUN
? JACK
? AND
? JILL
? RAN
? AWAY
? SCREAMING
JACK SCREAMING AWAY AWAY .
```

4. Modify the program of the previous exercise so that words are not repeated.

```
>RUN
? JACK
? AND
? JILL
? RAN
? AWAY
? HAPPILY
AWAY JILL JACK HAPPILY .
```

DIM

Whenever the highest subscript of a subscripted variable exceeds 10, the computer must be informed. The DIM (dimension) statement is used to direct the computer to open enough boxes in its memory to accommodate the anticipated input. Program 4.8 could store 100 names by making the appropriate changes in several lines and by adding the line

5 DIM N$(100)

If the ages of the people were also to be stored, a numeric subscripted variable would have to be added and the DIM statement modified.

5 DIM N$(100), A(100)

It is possible to request more space (i.e. boxes) in memory than the computer can supply. This results in the error message:

SUBSCRIPT OUT OF RANGE

It is a good idea to place DIM statements at the beginning of a program since the DIM statement must be executed before using more than 10 subscripts of a subscripted variable. Though it is possible to have several DIM statements in a program, each subscripted variable may only be dimensioned once. If there are two DIM statements for the same variable or if a DIM statement is executed more than once, the error message

REDIMENSIONED ARRAY

will result.

CLEAR

The computer sets aside a limited amount of space for storing string variables, including subscripted string variables. Storage space for 50 characters of string data is initially set aside by the computer. For many applications this is not sufficient. The CLEAR statement is used to change the amount of space reserved for string variable storage. The line

10 CLEAR 250

will set aside storage space for 250 characters of string data, set all numeric variables to zero, set all string variables to null (""), and cancel the effect of any previous DIM statement. The CLEAR statement should be the first line in a program and should only be preceeded by REM statements. The maximum value that may be CLEARed is 32767, the minimum is 0.

Double Subscripted Variables

The computer can also use double subscripts to name a variable. This is similar to single subscripting except that there are two numbers within the parentheses instead of one. For example,

A(1,5)   B3(7,3)   C$(4,9)

are all double subscripted variables. The computer reserves space in memory for a double subscripted variable by placing them in rows and columns, rather than in a single column (as is the case with a single subscripted variable). This procedure provides a convenient technique for dealing with problems in which the data is two-dimensional in nature, such as the location of seats in a theater.

To understand more clearly how the double subscripted variable operates, the box analogy is again helpful. The first integer in the subscript identifies the row and the second the column in which the variable is located. For example, A(2,3) is located at the second row, third column.

	Col. 1	Col. 2	Col. 3	Col. 4
Row 1	A (1, 1)	A (1, 2)	A (1, 3)	A (1, 4)
Row 2	A (2, 1)	A (2, 2)	A (2, 3)	A (2, 4)
Row 3	A (3, 1)	A (3, 2)	A (3, 3)	A (3, 4)

PROGRAM 4.9

A classroom has 5 rows of seats with 3 seats to a row. The following program randomly assigns a class of 14 students to seats, leaving one seat empty.

4.11

```
10 CLEAR 150
20 DIM N$(5,3)
30 FOR X = 1 TO 14
40      READ A$
50      R = RND(5)
60      C = RND(3)
70      IF N$(R,C) <> "" THEN 50
80      N$(R,C) = A$
90 NEXT X
100 FOR R1 = 1 TO 5
110     FOR C1 = 1 TO 3
120         IF N$(R1,C1) = ""
                THEN PRINT "Empty",
              ELSE PRINT N$(R1,C1),
130     NEXT C1
140     PRINT
150 NEXT R1
160 DATA   ANNE,  DON,  SHERRY,  MAGGIE,  TED,  LIZA,  ROB
170 DATA   MARY,  DAVID,  MARK,  KEVIN,  SUSAN,  WENDELL,  CINDY
>RUN
MARY              ROB             Empty
CINDY             SHERRY          MAGGIE
DAVID             MARK            SUSAN
WENDELL           LIZA            KEVIN
DON               TED             ANNE
READY
>
```

The computer also allows 3, 4, etc., all the way up to 11 dimensions in a subscripted variable (e.g. DIM X(5,5,8,2,3,19)). However, the more dimensions that a subscripted variable has, the smaller each dimension must be. This is due to the limited amount of space available in the computer's memory.

REVIEW

5. Six numbers are to be input from the keyboard as X(K). These are subsequently to be printed in a vertical column, and then a second time, closely spaced on a single line.

```
            RUN
            ? 23
            ? 67
            ? 128
            ? 37
            ? 42
            ? 143
             23
             67
             128
             37
             42
             143

             23   67   128   37   42   143
            READY
            >
```

6. Use the double subscripted variable X$(I,J) for which the row variable I runs from 1 to 5 and the column variable J from 1 to 3. Enter the letters A, B, C as the first row, D, E, F as the second, up to M, N, O as the fifth. Have the program print the following (making the rows become columns). (Hint: Use READ, DATA)

```
>RUN
A  D  G  J  M
B  E  H  K  N
C  F  I  L  O
READY
>
```

Some Final Notes on Subscripted Variables

Subscripted string and numeric variables greatly enhance the programmer's ability to store and deal with large quantities of data within any one program run. It must be remembered, however, that if the program is run again, all of the stored data in the computer's memory is erased. This means that all of the boxes become either null ("") or zero at the start of the next run. A method for permanently storing data is presented in chapters 9 and 10.

Extended Variable Names

Previously, variable names have consisted of a single letter, possibly followed by a digit. As was pointed out in this chapter, these names may also be subscripted. Actually, TRS-80 variable names may be of any length. For example, ALPHABET, HAROLD, SCARE and BLACKBEARD23 are all permissable variable names. There are, however, drawbacks to these names. Nowhere in the name of a variable may any key word occur. For example, SCORE, FORTUNE, SAND and DIMWIT are all unacceptable variable names because they contain the words OR, FOR, AND and DIM in them, respectively. Also, no matter how long the variable name may be, the TRS-80 only considers the first two characters. This means the variable names XMIN and XMAX are considered the same because the both start with XM. Because of these drawbacks, it is recommended that extended variable names not be used except where they are useful in identifying what a variable represents.

PART A

1. Using a nested loop have the computer print a rectangle consisting of eight lines of thirty asterisks each.

2. Show the output of the following program and check by running it. Rerun the program after removing line 50.

```
10 FOR I = 1 TO 5
20    FOR J = 1 TO 2 * I - 1
30       PRINT ".";
40    NEXT J
50    PRINT
60 NEXT I
```

3. Enter values of X(I) for I=1 to 6. Print the values of I and X(I) in two columns with I proceeding in the order 1, 3, 5, 2, 4, 6.

4. Enter 15 letters of the alphabet (not necessarily different), and print them in reverse order as a single block of letters.

5. Have the computer compute the values of A(I,J), where A(I,J)=3*I+J*J, I varies from 1 to 4, and J varies from 1 to 12. The user is to input a number N from 1 to 4 so that all values of A(N,J) can be printed.

4.14

6. Using a DATA statement have the computer enter one letter of the alphabet for each member of A$(I,J), where I runs from 1 to 11 and J from 1 to 3. The letters are first to be printed in the form of an 11 word sentence, with each word consisting of 3 letters. Then, the letters are to be printed again as a 3 word sentence, with each word consisting of 11 letters. The words may or may not make sense.

PART B

7. (a) Les Brains, who has forgotten where the computer is, needs to know the output for the following programs. Predict the output in each case, and check by running the program.

(a)
```
10 FOR L1 = 1 TO 3
20     FOR L2 = 5 TO 6
30         PRINT L1,L2
40     NEXT L2
50 NEXT L1
```

(b)
```
10 FOR X = 10 TO 15 STEP 2
20     FOR Y = 15 TO 10 STEP -2
30         IF Y = X THEN 99
40         IF X < Y THEN PRINT X: GOTO 60
50         PRINT Y
60     NEXT Y
70 NEXT X
99 END
```

(c)
```
10 FOR S = 1 TO 10
20     READ A(S)
30 NEXT S
40 PRINT A(3),A(7),A(10)
50 DATA 23,12,45,2,87,34,89,17,2,35,70
```

8. Suzy Fowlup has done it again and has written another program that will not run properly. Assist her by correcting the program. The output should look like this:

```
>RUN
3        4
4        3
4        4
5        3
5        4
```

_ _ _ _ _ _ _ _ _ _ _ _

```
10 FOR A = 3,5
20     FOR B = 1,4
30         IF A * B <= 10 GOTO 50
40         PRINYAB
50     NEXT A
60 NEXT B
```

9. The following program is designed to print the numbers in the DATA statement in decreasing order. However, there are some errors in the program. Correct and run the program to produce this output:

```
>RUN
  40  37  27  27  16  9  8  5  2  1
READY
```

— — — — — — — — — — — — — — — — —

```
10 FOR X = 40 TO 1
20    FOR Y = 1 TO 10
30       READ N
40        IF N = X THEN PRINT N;
50     NEXT X
60 NEXT Y
70 DATA 5,27,37,16,27,8,2,40,1,9
```

10. What is the exact output for the following program?

```
10 READ B1,B2,B3,B4,B5,B6
20 FOR X = 1 TO 6
30    READ B(X)
40 NEXT X
50 PRINT "B4=";B4;" BUT B(4)=";B(4)
60 PRINT B1 + B2 + B3,B(1) + B(2) + B(3),B(1 + 2 +3)
70 DATA 3,7,4,1,8,12
80 DATA 14,42,69,86,12,111
```

11. The following program is designed to find random integers between 1 and 99, inclusive, until it encounters a duplicate. At that point it should print how many numbers it has found and then print all of them. However, there are a number of errors in the program. Correct them to produce output similar to:

```
>RUN
DUPLICATE AFTER 12 NUMBERS
  3  46  26  7  93  37  14  80  90  96  52  3
READY
```

— — — — — — — — — — — — — — — — — — —

```
20 FOR X = 1 TO 100
30    N(X) = RND(99)
40    FOR Y = 1 TO 100
50       IF N(X) <> N(Y) THEN 70
60       PRINT "DUPLICATE AFTER";X;"NUMBERS"
70        FOR Z = 1 TO X : PRINT N(X); : NEXT Z
80    NEXT Y
90 NEXT X
```

12. Write a program that reads the names, street addresses, town, and zip codes of five people into subscripted variables N$(X), A$(X), T$(X), and Z$(X). The user enters a name, and the program prints the full name and address of that person. If the name is not there, have the program print PERSON NOT FOUND.

13. A Pythagorean Triple is a set of three integers which are the lengths of the sides of a right triangle ($C^2 = A^2 + B^2$). Find all sets of three integers up to C = 50 which are Pythagorean triples. For example, A = 3, B = 4, C = 5 is a solution. (Note that due to rounding errors, it is better to use A*A + B*B = C*C rather than $A \uparrow 2 + B \uparrow 2 = C \uparrow 2$ to check for equalities.)

14. Stan's Grocery Store has 3 aisles and in each aisle there are five items. Write a program that will read 15 items into the subscripted variable I$(X,Y), dimensioned 3x5. Let his customers type in the item they want to buy, and be informed by the computer of the aisle and the item's number.

```
>RUN
WHAT ARE YOU LOOKING FOR ? CHERRIES
YOU WILL FIND CHERRIES IN AISLE # 1   ITEM # 4
WHAT ARE YOU LOOKING FOR ? BREAD
YOU WILL FIND BREAD IN AISLE # 2   ITEM # 1
WHAT ARE YOU LOOKING FOR ? PEPPER
I'M SORRY, WE DON'T HAVE PEPPER
WHAT ARE YOU LOOKING FOR ?
Break in 70
READY
                    /
```

15. Pick 20 random integers between 10 and 99, inclusive. Print the odd integers on one line and the even integers on the next line. The output should look like this:

```
>RUN
ODD INTEGERS: 27   13   55   59   45   33   93   29
EVEN INTEGERS: 52   60   84   46   54   12   34   82   38   52   44   74
READY
```

16. Find the average of four grades for each of five students. The output should give in columns on consecutive lines each student's name, four grades, and average. Each column should have a heading. The last student's average should be underlined and the class average printed below it in the same column.

```
>RUN
STUDENT # 1 ? DON
ENTER FOUR GRADES: ? 42,86,99,99
STUDENT # 2 ? LESTER
ENTER FOUR GRADES: ? 50,55,45,34
STUDENT # 3 ? LIZ
ENTER FOUR GRADES: ? 100,98,99,97
STUDENT # 4 ? ROB
ENTER FOUR GRADES: ? 67,72,71,68
STUDENT # 5 ? SUE
ENTER FOUR GRADES: ? 89,91,93,90
NAME            1     2     3     4      AVE.
DON            42    86    99    99      81.5
LESTER         50    55    45    34      46
LIZ           100    98    99    97      98.5
ROB            67    72    71    68      69.5
SUE            89    91    93    90      90.75
                                        -------
                                         77.25
```

17. Marcus Welby wants you to program the computer to keep track of his busy schedule. (a) Write a program to allow a patient to choose the day and time he or she wants to see the doctor. There are 5 days and 6 time slots for each day. If the desired slot is empty, the patient enters his or her name. If it is full, the program asks for another slot. (b) Add the steps needed to allow Dr. Welby to print his schedule for any particular day.

18. Susie Gossip has 3 skirts—red, green, and purple; 2 pairs of jeans—white and electric purple; 4 blouses—blue, pink, orange, and black; and 2 slightly tight sweaters—yellow

and green. Have the computer print a list of all possible combinations of the articles she can wear (e.g., red skirt and blue blouse, or white jeans and yellow sweater).

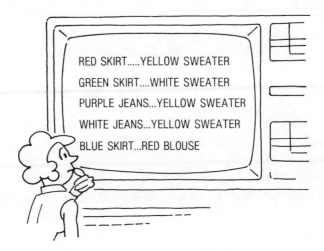

19. Write an extended version of the game high-low. In this game, the computer picks a secret random number between 1 and 100 and gives the player an unlimited number of chances to guess it. For each wrong guess the computer tells whether to guess higher or lower and stores the guess in a subscripted variable. If the player guesses the same number twice, the computer should produce the message WAKE UP! YOU GUESSED THAT NUMBER BEFORE.

20. Betty Bright has written the following two programs to sort data. Read the programs carefully and predict the output.

```
(a)   10  DIM A(10)
      20  FOR B = 1 TO 10
      30      READ A(B)
      40  NEXT B
      50  FOR C = 2 TO 10
      60      FOR D = 1 TO C-1
      70          IF A(D) < A(C) THEN 90
      80          E = A(D): A(D) = A(C): A(C) = E
      90      NEXT D
      100 NEXT C
      110 FOR F = 1 TO 10
      120     PRINT A(F)
      130 NEXT F
      200 REM
      210 DATA 1,3,7,2,4,9,0,2,5,8
```

(b)

```
10 DIM Q$(10)
20 FOR M = 1 TO 10
30    READ Q$(M)
40 NEXT M
50 FOR R = 5 TO 10
60    FOR Z = 5 TO R-1
70       IF Q$(Z) < Q$(R) THEN 90
80       T$ = Q$(Z):Q$(Z) = Q$(R):Q$(R) = T$
90    NEXT Z
100 NEXT R
110 FOR I = 10 TO 1 STEP -1
120    PRINT Q$(I)
130 NEXT I
200 REM
210 DATA DON,FRENCH,LESTER,FAZIOLI,MARY
220 DATA SUSAN,LIZ,ELI,ROB,KIM
```

21. The game Penny Pitch is common in amusement parks. Pennies are tossed onto a checkerboard on which numbers have been printed. By adding up the numbers in the squares on which the pennies fall, a score is accumulated. Write a program which simulates such a game in which ten pennies are to be randomly pitched onto the board shown below.

Have the computer print the board with an X indicating where each penny has landed and then the score. Below is a sample run. Note that more than one penny can land in one square.

```
>RUN
 1   1   X   1   1   X
 1   2   2   2   2   X
 1   2   3   3   2   1
 1   2   X   X   2   X
 X   X   2   2   X   1
 1   1   1   1   1   1

     SCORE =17
```

22. Write a program that rolls two dice 1000 times and prints the number of times each different point total (2, 3, 4, 5, ..., 12) appeared. The output should resemble the following:

```
>RUN
POINT TOTAL      TIMES APPEARING
2                34
3                64
4                66
...              ...
12               33
```

23. Write a program which makes up 15 "words" (i.e. groups of letters, whether pronounceable or not) composed of from one to seven randomly chosen letters, and print them. (Hint: use addition of strings. For example if A$(2)="B" and A$(12)="L" then A$(2)+A$(12)="BL".)

24. Use the computer to play a modified game of Othello. Have it randomly fill an 8x8 subscripted string variable with X's and O's and print the array by row (horizontal) and column (vertical). Examples are below. The X's are for player 1, the O's for player 2. Have the program alternately ask the players for the row and column of the opponent's piece that should be flipped (changed from an X to an O or vice versa). All of the opponent's pieces along the horizontal or vertical line passing through the flipped piece are also flipped. For example, if player 1 flipped the 0 at 1,8, board A would be changed to board B.

```
A     1 2 3 4 5 6 7 8        B       1 2 3 4 5 6 7 8
   1  O O O X X O O O           1     X X X X X X X X
   2  O X O O X X X X           2     O X O O X X X X
   3  X X X O O O X O           3     X X X O O O X X
   4  X O X O O O X O           4     X O X O O O X X
   5  O O X O O O O X           5     O O X O O O O X
   6  X O O X O O O X           6     X O O X O O O X
   7  O X O O O X O X           7     O X O O O X O X
   8  O X X O X X O O           8     O X X O X X O X
```

25. The ancient puzzle 'Towers of Hanoi' uses 5 different sized disks and 3 pegs. The 5 disks are initially stacked on the left peg in order of decreasing size. The object of the game is to move all of the disks to the right peg. Only 1 disk can be moved at a time and a larger disk cannot be placed on top of a smaller disk.

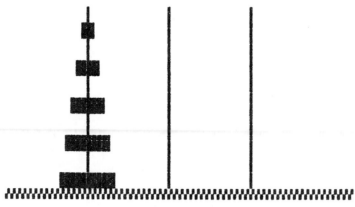

TOWERS OF HANOI

Initial Configuration for Towers of Hanoi

(a) Write a program using graphics that will draw a checkered base with pegs and plot the initial configuration of 5 disks on the left tower.

(b) Expand the program from part A to allow movement of the disks. The user should be able to enter two values (P and Q). This should cause the top disk on tower P to be moved to the top of the stack on tower Q. (Hint: Set up a subscripted variable A(X,Y) with maximum values X=3, Y=5). There are 15 possible slots for disks; 3 towers, 5 slots per tower. When a slot is occupied, the subscripted variable A(X,Y) should contain the disk number occupying that slot (1-5). If the slot is free, the appropriate position in A(X,Y) should contain a zero).

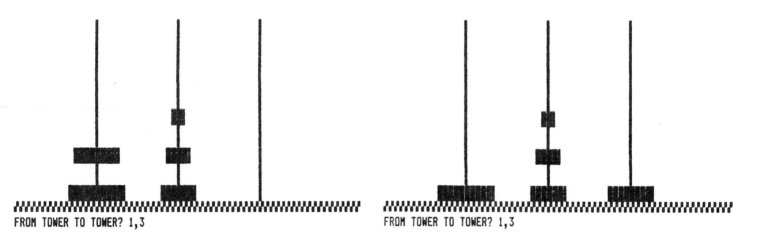

26. Have the computer generate 200 random integers between 1 and 10, inclusive. Using graphics, plot a properly labeled bar graph showing the number of occurrences of each random number.

27. Mr. and Mrs. Charles Windsor want to start a bank account for their newborn son, William. They open the account with $500. At the beginning of each successive year they deposit $60 more. When William is 21, how much money will be in the account? (Assume the interest rate to be 6% compounded quarterly).

5 TRS-80 PROGRAMMING TECHNIQUES

In a well written program the purpose and sequence of each line should be obvious. As a whole, the lines should serve as a clear indication of what the program does and the sequence it must follow.

The term 'code' is used to define the instructions which comprise a program. Each line of a program contains statements referred to as code. If presented in a clear and logical style, the code is less likely to contain errors. Furthermore, a well written program is easily read and understood by another programmer with a minimum of effort.

The first step in writing a program is to understand precisely the problem to be solved. Next, a plan should be developed to break the problem down into a series of smaller units; each can then be programmed as a unit. A common mistake made by many inexperienced programmers is to start writing the code before the problem or its solution is understood. From this, there results a program which is frequently modified by adding or deleting lines of code until the desired output is achieved. The resulting program is usually a "mish-mash" of statements which do not flow logically from one to another. When GOTO and IF . . . THEN statements have to be added to a program to make it work, the sequential top to bottom flow from line-to-line—a sign of good programming—is often destroyed. Therefore, one should plan a program as thoroughly as possible before approaching the computer. As the computer pioneer, R.W. Hamming has declared; "Typing is no substitute for thinking."

Structuring a program

The structure of a program determines the ease with which it can be read and understood. Several techniques which follow help to achieve such a structure.

1. REM statements strategically placed throughout a program can be helpful in explaining how the program works. It is a good practice to use REM statements at the beginning

of a program to indicate what the program does and to list and define the variables used within the program.

2. Indent the lines within FOR . . . NEXT loops to clarify where the loops begin and end and what portions of the program are contained within each loop.

3. Break a program down into separate units in which each unit performs a specific task. It is a good practice to separate each unit from the others by choosing appropriate line numbers. For example, if a program contains three units and each is about 15 lines long, number the lines of the first unit from 100 to 250, the second unit from 300 to 450, and the third from 500 to 650. Separate each unit from the next using blank REM statements and begin each unit with a REM statement which explains the function of that unit.

4. The IF . . . THEN . . . ELSE statement is extremely powerful, and if used properly, it can substantially reduce the amount of code required within a program. Although its structure can be confusing, it may be clarified by being segmented. For example, Program 5.1 will use an IF . . . THEN . . . ELSE statement to cause the program to jump to line 230 if A = X*Y. It will print ANSWER TOO HIGH if A>X*Y, or print ANSWER TOO LOW if A <X*Y.

```
190 IF A = X*Y THEN 230 ELSE IF A>X*Y THEN PRINT "ANSWER TOO HIGH"
ELSE PRINT "ANSWER TOO LOW"
```

With so much of the code all on a single line, it is difficult to determine exactly its function. If this line is structured

```
190 IF A = X*Y
        THEN 230
        ELSE IF A>X*Y
                THEN PRINT "ANSWER TOO HIGH"
                ELSE PRINT "ANSWER TOO LOW"
```

then it is obviously much easier to read. Notice that the line is broken and indented where the THEN and ELSE occur. A line of code can be split by using the downward arrow key (↓) to move the cursor to the next line on the screen and the space bar and backward arrow key (←) to place the cursor where desired. The ENTER key must not be struck until all of the line of code has been entered. Though such a procedure may seem bothersome, the resulting clarity in program format is well worth the effort.

PROGRAM 5.1

The four programming techniques presented above are used here to produce a clear, easy-to-read program. This program tests a student on multiplication and division by giving ten problems of each type, and he or she has five chances to answer each one correctly. If a wrong answer is given, the computer will inform the student whether his or her answer is too high or too low. The student's score is based on receiving five points for a correct answer on the first try, four for a correct answer on the second try, and so on. No points are received if the problem is not answered correctly after five responses.

Read the program carefully, note its structure, and try to predict its output. Many of the programming details are left for the reader to analyze.

```
1 REM      THIS PROGRAM TESTS A STUDENT ON MULTIPLICATION AND
           DIVISION.   THERE ARE TEN PROBLEMS OF EACH TYPE.
2 REM      N = NUMBER OF THE QUESTION (1-10)
3 REM      T = NUMBER OF POINTS AWARDED
4 REM      X,Y = TWO RANDOM NUMBERS USED IN QUESTION
5 REM      A = STUDENT'S ANSWER
6 REM      S = STUDENT'S SCORE
7 REM
8 REM
100 REM    MULTIPLICATION PROBLEMS
110 PRINT "YOU WILL BE ASKED TEN MULTIPLICATION PROBLEMS"
120 PRINT "AND BE GIVEN FIVE CHANCES TO GET EACH CORRECT."
130 FOR N = 1 TO 10
140    X = RND(10)
150    Y = RND(10)
160    FOR T = 5 TO 1 STEP -1
170       PRINT"WHAT DOES ";X;" * ";Y;" = ";
180       INPUT A
190       IF A = X * Y
              THEN 230
              ELSE IF A> X * Y
                      THEN PRINT "ANSWER TOO HIGH"
                      ELSE PRINT "ANSWER TOO LOW"
200    NEXT T
210    PRINT "YOU GOT THE ANSWER WRONG FIVE TIMES, IT IS";X*Y
220    GOTO 240
230    S = S + T
240 NEXT N
250 REM
260 REM
300 REM    DIVISION PROBLEMS
310 PRINT "YOU WILL BE ASKED TEN DIVISION PROBLEMS"
320 PRINT "AND BE GIVEN FIVE CHANCES TO GET EACH CORRECT."
330 FOR N = 1 TO 10
340    X = RND(10)
350    Y = RND(10)
360    FOR T = 5 TO 1 STEP -1
370       PRINT"WHAT DOES ";X;" / ";Y;" = ";
380       INPUT A
390       IF A = X/Y
              THEN 430
              ELSE IF A> X/Y
                      THEN PRINT "ANSWER TOO HIGH"
                      ELSE PRINT "ANSWER TOO LOW"
400    NEXT T
```

```
410     PRINT "YOU GOT THE ANSWER WRONG FIVE TIMES, IT IS";X/Y
420     GOTO 440
430     S = S + T
440 NEXT N
450 REM
460 REM
500 REM    PRINT SCORE
510 PRINT"YOUR SCORE IS =": S
520 END
```

REVIEW

1. Using the techniques discussed in this chapter structure both of the following programs.

```
a). 10  INPUT "ARE YOU COMING OR GOING";A$
    20  IF A$="COMING" THEN PRINT "HELLO" ELSE PRINT "GOOD-BYE"
    30  END
```

```
b).  1 REM    SHELLSORT OF THE LIST OF CLUB MEMBERS
     2 INPUT "HOW MANY NAMES IN THE LIST";N
     3 FOR X=1 TO N
     4 INPUT "MEMBER";M$(X)
     5 NEXT X
     6 S=N
     7 S=INT(S/1.5) : Q=S
     8 F=0
     9 FOR X=1 TO N
    10 Q=X+S
    11 IF Q>N THEN 14
    12 IF M$(X)>M$(Q) THEN T$=M$(X):M$(X)=M$(Q):M$(Q)=T$:F=1
    13 NEXT X
    14 IF S>1 THEN 7
    15 IF F=1 THEN 8
    16 FOR X=1 TO N
    17 PRINT M$(X)
    18 NEXT X
    19 END
```

DEBUGGING

Debugging is the process of locating errors or "bugs" in a program and then correcting them. Obviously, the best approach is to avoid bugs by carefully planning a program, but even the most carefully written program often contains errors.

There are three types of errors which will cause a program to fail in producing proper output.

Syntax Errors

Syntax errors are caused by typing an improper statement. For example,

10 REED X, Y

should be

10 READ X, Y

Happily, the computer detects this type of error and informs the programmer by printing an error message.

Runtime Errors

Runtime errors are detected when a program is run. For example,

10 READ A$, B
20 DATA 35, SMITH

is a format violation since the computer attempts to assign the string "SMITH" to the numerical variable B. Another common runtime error is caused by using two different variables to define a FOR . . . NEXT loop.

10 FOR X = 1 TO 10
20   PRINT X, X[2, X[3
30 NEXT Y

The computer detects a runtime error and prints an appropriate error message.

Logic Errors

Although the computer accepts and runs a program, the output may not reflect the programmer's true intent. Yet if the program does not violate any of the syntax rules of BASIC it is not rejected. The errors in the program may stem instead from the programmer's incorrect analysis of how to develop a logical sequence of statements to achieve the intended goal. These forms of errors—referred to as logic errors—are the most difficult to detect and correct.

PROGRAM 5.2

This program is supposed to print the areas of circles whose radii are integers varying from 1 to 100 except for those whose computed areas are integers (note line 30). The equation $A = \pi R^2$ is used with the value of π taken as 3.1.

```
10 FOR X = 1 TO 10
20    A = 3.1 * X[2
30     IF A = INT(A) THEN 10
40       PRINT A,
50 NEXT X
60 END
READY
>RUN
 3.1          12.4          27.9          49.6
 77.5         111.6         151.9         198.4
 251.1        3.1           12.4          27.9
 49.6         77.5          111.6         151.9
 198.4        251.1         3.1           12.4
 27.9
Break in 40
READY
>
```

Note that the printed areas go as high as 251.1 and then start to repeat. The program actually goes Into an infinite loop, which means that it keeps running until the BREAK key is struck.

A useful technique used for detecting the logic error in Program 5.2 is the placing of an extra PRINT statement in the program in order to print the loop variable X. This extra statement can later be removed when the error has been corrected.

25 PRINT "X ="; X,

```
READY
>RUN
X= 1            3.1             X= 2            12.4
X= 3            27.9            X= 4            49.6
X= 5            77.5            X= 6            111.6
X= 7            151.9           X= 8            198.4
X= 9            251.1           X= 10           X= 1
 3.1            X= 2            12.4            X= 3
 27.9           X= 4            49.6            X= 5
 77.5           X= 6            111.6           X= 7
 151.9          X= 8            198.4           X= 9
 251.1          X= 10           X= 1            3.1
X= 2            12.4            X= 3            27.9
X= 4            49.6            X= 5            77.5
X= 6            111.6           X= 7            151.9
X= 8            198.4           X= 9            251.1
Break in 40
READY
>
```

The output indicates that X only reaches 10 and then starts repeating rather than continuing on to 100 as it should. The problem results from the fact that line 30 should send the program to line 50 rather than to line 10, where it restarts the X loop at one.

In longer programs it is often useful to place additional print statements at a number of locations to check the value of variables and then remove them when the program is operating properly.

Another technique is to place a line in the program to indicate whether it is getting to a certain point as anticipated.

50 PRINT "I'M AT LINE 50 NOW"

The line can later be removed when no longer needed.

Hand Tracing

It is almost impossible to guarantee that a program will run properly for all possible situations that it may encounter, but one technique that creates confidence in the validity of a program is called hand tracing. By using test data, calculations are solved by hand and the results are checked with those produced by the program. If the computer program produces identical answers for the same data, the programmer is then confident that the program at least works for the data that is being tested.

TRON—TROFF

To follow the sequence in which the lines of a program are executed, type the command TRON before typing RUN. Each line number will then be printed as the line is processed by the computer, thus allowing the programmer to easily trace program flow. To stop the line tracing, the command TROFF is typed after the computer completes its run.

PROGRAM 5.3

This program prints the combinations of quarters and dimes which add up to $1.00.

```
1 REM    Q = QUARTERS
2 REM    D = DIMES
3 REM
10 FOR Q = 0 TO 4
20     FOR D = 0 TO 10
30         IF 25*Q + 10*D = 100 THEN PRINT "Q=";Q,  "D=";D
40     NEXT D
50 NEXT Q
60 END
READY
>RUN
Q= 0              D= 10
Q= 2              D= 5
Q= 4              D= 0
READY
>TRON
READY
>RUN
<1><2><3><10><20><30><40><30><40><30><40><30><40><30><40><30><40
><30><40><30><40><30><40><30><40><30>Q= 0            D= 10
<40><50><20><30><40><30><40><30><40><30><40><30><40><30><40><30>
<40><30><40><30><40><30><40><30><40><50><20><30><40><30><40><30>
<40><30><40><30><40><30>Q= 2     D= 5
<40><30><40><30><40><30><40><30><40><30><40><50><20><30><40><30>
<40><30><40><30><40><30><40><30><40><30><40><30><40><30><40><30>
<40><30><40><50><20><30>Q= 4     D= 0
<40><30><40><30><40><30><40><30><40><30><40><30><40><30><40><30>
<40><30><40><30><40><50><60>
READY
>TROFF
READY
>
```

Follow the program flow carefully for both loops. Notice that each time a NEXT statement is executed, it returns the program to the statement following the corresponding FOR . . . TO statement.

STOP and CONT

A useful debugging technique is the halting of a program at certain points by using one or more STOP statements. Upon interruption the values of the program's variables may be examined. Typing CONT will continue program execution from the point at which it was interrupted.

PROGRAM 5.4

```
10 FOR X = 1 TO 100
20    A = 3*X[3 + 2*X[2 + 5
30    B = 7*X[2 + 2*X + 5
40    IF B > A THEN PRINT B;">";A
50 NEXT X
60 END
READY
>RUN
 14 > 10
READY
>
```

When Program 5.4 is run, the computer prints one solution to the condition at line 40 and then gives the appearance of being at rest, until it finally prints READY. Is there only one solution or is there a bug in the program? The values of A and B can be checked when X = 50 by adding the line:

$$45 \text{ IF } X = 50 \text{ THEN STOP}$$

The values of A and B can then be examined when the program is halted by typing PRINT A,B. Typing CONT allows this program to continue on to completion. Since A is much larger than B when X = 50, it is obvious that there will be no other solutions than the first one. Hence there is no bug in the program.

```
READY
>RUN
 14 > 10
Break in 45
READY
>PRINT A,B
 380005          17605
READY
>CONT
READY
>
```

REVIEW

2. Each of the following programs contains a 'bug'. Find it and correct it.

```
a).  10  INPUT A
     20  FOR X=10 TO 1
     30      C=A/X
     40      PRINT INT(C)
     50  NEXT X
```

```
b).  10  INPUT N
     20  IF N < 0 THEN 10 : REM PREVENTS NEGATIVE INPUT
     30  P = N * 5
     40  IF P < 0
             THEN PRINT "THE PRODUCT IS NEGATIVE"
             ELSE PRINT "THE PRODUCT IS POSITIVE"
     50  END
```

1. Each of the following programs contains an error. In each case identify and correct the error(s).

(a)
```
10 READ A,B,C,D
20 E=A*B+C+D
30 PRINT E
40 DATA 2,3,4
50 END
```

(b)
```
10 READ A,B
20 DATA 1,2,3,4
30 PRINT A/B
40 GOTO 20
50 END
```

(c)
```
10 READ A,B,C
20 PRINT A*/B+C
30 PRINT D/F=;D/F
40 DATA 5,6,10
50 END
```

(d)
```
10 READ F,G
20 IF F>5 OR <10 THEN 40
30 GOTO 10
40 PRINT F G
50 DATA 1,10,6,9,11,4
60 END
```

(e)
```
10 FOR X=1 TO 8
20     FOR Y=1 TO 3
30               X=X+Y
40     NEXT X
50 NEXT Y
60 PRINT X
70 END
```

(f)
```
10 READ C,D,F
20 DATA 3,6,9,4,7,10
30 PRINT C+D+F
40 GOTO 20
50 END
```

5.11

2. Trace the following program by hand and determine its output. Use the TRON command to check your results.

```
10 READ N,A,B
20 FOR I=1 TO N
30       FOR J=2 TO N+1
40                 A=2*A+B
50                 B=2*B+A
60       NEXT J
70       PRINT A;B
80 NEXT I
90 DATA 3,-1,2
100 END
```

3. What output is produced by the following program? (Do not run the program.)

```
10 FOR X=1 TO 5 STEP 2
20       READ K1,K2
30       A=A+K1-K2
40       B=B-K1+K2
50 NEXT X
60 PRINT A,B
70 DATA 1,3,2,4,3,5
80 END
```

4. The following simple programs have errors in logic (i.e., the program runs, but the output is illogical). Find and correct the errors.

(a)
```
10 READ A,B,C
20 PRINT A+B+C
30 GOTO 20
40 DATA 1,2,3,4,5,6
50 END
```

(b)
```
10 FOR X=1 TO 10
20       IF X>5 THEN 50
30       PRINT X;"IS GREATER THAN 5"
40       GOTO 60
50       PRINT X;"IS LESS THAN 5"
60 NEXT X
70 END
```

(c)
```
10 READ A,B,C
20 FOR X=1 TO 10
30       Y=(A*B)/(C-X)
40       IF Y<1 THEN 50
50       PRINT "Y<1";Y
60 NEXT X
70 DATA 20,10,5,5,10,20
80 END
```

5. Each of the following programs contains errors which will result in error messages being printed by the computer when the program is run. Find and correct the errors.

(a)
```
10 PRINT "WHAT IS THE FORMULA WEIGHT OF THE ELEMENTS";
20 INPUT FORMULA WEIGHT
30 IF X>20 THEN 50
40 X=X/2
50 PRINT X
999 END
```

(b)
```
15 FOR X=1 TO 2
25       FOR Y=1 TO 3
35              IF Y=X THEN A=A+1 : GOTO 50
45       NEXT Y
55       PRINT "X AND Y ARE EQUAL";A;"TIMES"
65 NEXT X
75 END
```

(c)
```
5 READ B,A,C
10 X1=(B+(SQR(B[2-4*A*C)/2*A)
20 X2=(B-(SQR(B[2-4*A*C)/2*A)
30 IF X1>X2 THEN 50
40 GOTO 5
50 PRINT "X1=";X1; "X2=";X2
60 GOTO 5
70 DATA 1,2,3,4,5,6
80 END
```

(d)
```
10 READ A,B,C
20 X = A * B + C
30 IF X > 200 THEN LINE 10
40 PRINT X
50 DATA 25,26,27,28,29,30
60 END
```

(e)
```
10 FOR X=1 TO 26
20       A$=A$+X
30 NEXT X
40 PRINT A$
50 END
```

(f)
```
10 FOR X=1 TO 26
20       A$=A$+"A"
30 NEXT X
40 PRINT A$
50 END
```

6. The following program is designed to arrange sets of numbers in descending order. If the second number is larger than the first, the computer interchanges the two values. (This occurs in lines 30 and 40.) Explain the output and correct the program to give the desired output.

```
10 READ A,B
20 IF A>B THEN 50
30 A=B
40 B=A
50 PRINT A,B
60 GOTO 10
70 DATA 10,20,20,10
80 END

READY
>RUN
  20                    20
  20                    10
Out of DATA in 10
READY
>
```

7. The area of a square that measures one inch on a side is equal to one square inch. If the computer takes various slices of this same square and sums the areas of the slices, the answer should be one square inch. In the following program 100, 1000, and 1024 slices are used and the output printed below. Explain the results.

```
10 READ N
20 FOR X=1 TO N
30     Y=Y+1/N
40 NEXT X
50 PRINT Y;"SQUARE INCHES FOR";N;"SLICES"
60 Y=0
70 GOTO 10
80 DATA 100,1000,1024
90 END

READY
>RUN
 .999999 SQUARE INCHES FOR 100 SLICES
 .999991 SQUARE INCHES FOR 1000 SLICES
 1 SQUARE INCHES FOR 1024 SLICES
Out of DATA in 10
READY
>
```

8. Structure the following programs by adding spaces and REM statements and by indenting where appropriate and necessary.

(a)
```
1 REM THIS PROGRAM DECIDES WHICH MOVIE WE WILL SEE
2 R=RND(20)+5
3 X=1
4 FORL=1TOR
5 X=X*-1
6 IFL=RTHENPRINT"WEWILLSEE";ELSEPRINT
7 IFX>0THENPRINT"ANNIE"ELSEPRINT"POLTERGEIST"
8 NEXTL
9 END
```

(b)
```
1 DIMJ(10,10)
2 FORX=0TO9
3 PRINT TAB(X*4+5);X+1;
4 NEXTX
5 PRINT
6 FORX=0TO 8
7 PRINTTAB(X*4+6);"--";
8 NEXT X
9 PRINTTAB(42);"--"
10 FORX=1TO10
11 FORY=1TO10
12 J(X,Y)=X+Y
13 IFF=0THENPRINTX;":";
14 PRINTTAB(F*4+5);J(X,Y);
15 F=F+1
16 IFF=10THENPRINT:F=0
17 NEXTY
18 NEXTX
19 END
```

6 TRS-80 MATHEMATICAL FUNCTIONS

This chapter covers the various mathematical functions that the computer can perform. The extent to which they can be useful to any individual depends on his or her mathematical background. Generally speaking, the functions presented here are primarily employed by mathematicians, scientists, and engineers.

Order of Operations

What is the value of 2+20/4? Should the 2 be added first to the 20 and then the division performed afterward, or should the 20 first be divided by 4 and then be increased by 2? The latter procedure is correct because division is carried out before addition. When parentheses are used, the operations in the innermost parentheses are completed first. For example, (2+20)/4 = 22/4 = 5.5.

The computer performs arithmetic operations in the same order as that employed by mathematicians. Quantities in parentheses are evaluated first (starting from the innermost), followed by raising to a power, then by multiplication and division, and finally by addition and subtraction. Operations of equal priority are carried out from left to right. For example:

6/3*2   The result is 4. Although the answer might seem to be 6/6=1, the computer starts at the left and performs the division first, then the result of the division is multiplied by 2.

3*(5 + 6)   The result is 33. The computer first adds 5 and 6 and then multiplies the sum by 3.

5 + (3*(6/2))   The result is 14. The computer first divides 6 by 2, the operation within the innermost parentheses. Next it multiplies that result by 3 and finally adds 5.

12 + 4/0	The result is an error message. The computer does not divide by zero.
2↑3↑2	The result is 64 just as it would be for (2↑3)↑2. Again, the left-to-right rule is in operation. Remember that (↑) is used to raise to a power.

SQR

The SQR function calculates the positive square root of a number.

$$10 \text{ PRINT SQR}(14)$$

The square root of a number N is defined as that value which, when multiplied by itself, gives N. For instance, the square root of 36 is 6 because 6x6=36.

PROGRAM 6.1

This program illustrates the square root function.

```
10 FOR X = 1 TO 4
20     PRINT "The square root of"; X; "is"; SQR(X)
30 NEXT X
READY
>RUN
The square root of 1 is 1
The square root of 2 is 1.41421
The square root of 3 is 1.73205
The square root of 4 is 2
READY
>
```

In the expression SQR(X), SQR is the function name and X is called the argument. With the SQR function, the argument may be any mathematical expression with a non-negative value. For example, SQR(3*X+5) is perfectly acceptable provided that the expression 3*X+5 produces a non-negative value.

Note that the argument of a function must be enclosed in parentheses. In its evaluation of a mathematical function, the computer first evaluates the argument and then the function, using the value previously obtained for the argument. Some functions have a limitation on the value of the argument. Such limitations will be indicated as the functions are introduced.

SGN and ABS

In some situations it may be necessary to know if a variable is positive or negative. The SGN function has only three possible values: 1, 0, and −1.

$$SGN(X) = 1 \qquad \text{if } X>0$$
$$SGN(X) = 0 \qquad \text{if } X=0$$
$$SGN(X) = -1 \qquad \text{if } X<0$$

PROGRAM 6.2

This program finds the SGN (signum) of the numbers from 6 to −6, incrementing by −1.2.

```
10 FOR X = 6 TO -6 STEP -1.2
20      A = SGN(X)
30         PRINT "SGN("; X; ") ="; A
40 NEXT X
READY
>RUN
SGN( 6 ) = 1
SGN( 4.8 ) = 1
SGN( 3.6 ) = 1
SGN( 2.4 ) = 1
SGN( 1.2 ) = 1
SGN( 0 ) = 0
SGN(-1.2 ) =-1
SGN(-2.4 ) =-1
SGN(-3.6 ) =-1
SGN(-4.8 ) =-1
READY
>
```

The ABS function can be used to find the absolute value of a number. The ABS function yields values according to the rule:

$$ABS(X) = X \qquad \text{if } X>=0$$
$$ABS(X) = -1*X \qquad \text{if } X<0$$

This program illustrates the use of the ABS function.

```
10 FOR X = 6 TO -6 STEP -1.2
20      A = ABS(X)
30      PRINT A;
40 NEXT X
READY
>RUN
 6  4.8  3.6  2.4  1.2  0  1.2  2.4  3.6  4.8
READY
>
```

FIX

The FIX function returns the integer portion of a number, that is, it truncates all digits to the right of a decimal point. The statement

$$N = FIX(2.41)$$

will assign N the value 2, truncating the decimal portion .41. Unlike the INT function, the FIX function does not return the next lower value of a number when the number is negative.

INT(5.01) = 5	FIX(5.01) = 5
INT(4.7) = 4	FIX(4.7) = 4
INT(-8.7) = -9	FIX(-8.7) = -8
INT(-6.2) = -7	FIX(-6.2) = -6

The FIX function is useful in determining the fractional portion of a number. The statement

$$N = ABS (X - FIX(X))$$

will assign N the fractional portion of X. For example, if X = 4.237, then N = ABS (4.237 - FIX(4.237)) = 0.237.

REVIEW

1. What is X when X = FIX(ABS(-12 + 6*SGN(-9 +9/3) + 1.8)-18.2)?

2. Write a program that will take a number N and print the fractional portion of N rounded
to two decimal places.

```
>RUN
? 18.648
INPUT: 18.648   OUTPUT: .65
READY
>
```

Trigonometric Functions: SIN, COS, TAN

The computer is able to find the values of several trigonometric functions. The
functions SIN(X), COS(X) or TAN(X) will produce the value of the sine, cosine, or tangent
of the angle X, where X is measured in radians. To convert an angle from degrees to
radians, multiply it by 3.14159265 and then divide the result by 180 (180 degrees equals π
radians).

PROGRAM 6.4

The following program illustrates these functions.

```
10 INPUT "Value"; A
20 X = A * 3.14159 / 180
30 PRINT A; "Degrees equals"; X; "Radians."
40 PRINT "SIN("; A; ") ="; SIN(X)
50 PRINT "COS("; A; ") ="; COS(X)
60 PRINT "TAN("; A; ") ="; TAN(X)
70 PRINT
80 GOTO 10
READY
>RUN
Value? 30
  30 Degrees equals .523598 Radians.
SIN( 30 ) = .5
COS( 30 ) = .866026
TAN( 30 ) = .57735

Value? 45
  45 Degrees equals .785398 Radians.
SIN( 45 ) = .707106
COS( 45 ) = .707107
TAN( 45 ) = .999999

Value?
Break in 10
READY
>
```

Note the rounding error that occurs in the output.

ATN

The only inverse trigonometric function supplied by the computer is the principal arctangent function ATN. The function ATN(X) is used to find the angle whose tangent is X. The value produced by the ATN function is in radians. Thus, the arctangent of 1 is $\pi/4$ radians = .785398163. To convert an angle from radians to degrees, multiply it by 180 and then divide the result by 3.14159265. The ATN function, just like the principal arctangent function in mathematics, gives values only between $-\pi/2$ and $\pi/2$ radians. There is no limitation on the value that the argument may assume.

PROGRAM 6.5

This program finds the angle whose tangent is entered and prints the result in degrees.

```
10 INPUT "Enter a tangent value"; T
20 R = ATN(T)
30 D = R * 180 / 3.14159
40 PRINT "The angle whose Tangent is"; T; "is"; D; "Degrees."
50 PRINT : GOTO 10
READY
>RUN
Enter a tangent value? 1
The angle whose Tangent is 1 is 45 Degrees.

Enter a tangent value? 0
The angle whose Tangent is 0 is 0 Degrees.

Enter a tangent value? 0.57735
The angle whose Tangent is .57735 is 30 Degrees.

Enter a tangent value?
Break in 10
READY
>
```

To find the principal arcsine of a number, it is necessary to use the trigonometric identity:

$$\text{ARCSINE}(X) = \text{ARCTAN}\ \frac{X}{\sqrt{1-X^2}}$$

Therefore, to find the principal angle whose sine is X, the expression ATN(X/SQR(1−X↑2)) is used. This angle will be measured in radians and will be between $-\pi/2$ and $\pi/2$. The value of X, however, must be between −1 and 1, not inclusive.

To find the arccosine of X, use the expression ATN(SQR(1−X↑2)/X). This gives the angle which is between $-\pi/2$ and $\pi/2$ (whose cosine is X). In this expression, X must be between −1 and 1, inclusive, but not equal to 0.

PROGRAM 6.6

This program finds the arcsine and arccosine of X in both radians and degrees.

```
10 INPUT "Value"; X
20 S = ATN(X / SQR(1 - X[2))
30 S1 = S * 180 / 3.14159
40 C = ATN(SQR(1 - X[2) / X)
50 C1 = C * 180 / 3.14159
60 PRINT "The angle whose Sine is"; X; "is"; S; "Radians."
70 PRINT "The angle whose Cosine is"; X; "is"; C; "Radians."
80 PRINT "The angle whose Sine is"; X; "is"; S1; "Degrees."
90 PRINT "The angle whose Cosine is"; X; "is"; C1; "Degrees."
100 PRINT : GOTO 10
READY
>RUN
Value? 0.5
The angle whose Sine is .5 is .523599 Radians.
The angle whose Cosine is .5 is 1.0472 Radians.
The angle whose Sine is .5 is 30 Degrees.
The angle whose Cosine is .5 is 60.0001 Degrees.

Value? 0.877
The angle whose Sine is .877 is 1.06958 Radians.
The angle whose Cosine is .877 is .501214 Radians.
The angle whose Sine is .877 is 61.2826 Degrees.
The angle whose Cosine is .877 is 28.7175 Degrees.

Value?
Break in 10
READY
>
```

Logarithms and the Exponential Function: LOG, EXP

The LOG function can be used to find natural logarithms, that is, logarithms to the base e. To find the natural logarithm of X, LOG(X) is used. Do not confuse the natural logarithm with the common logarithm usually studied in a second year algebra course. The common logarithm, that is, logarithm to base 10, can be found from the natural logarithm by using the formula:

$$\log_{10}(X) = \frac{\ln(X)}{\ln(10)}$$

where ln(x) designates the natural logarithm of X. Therefore, to find $\log_{10}(X)$ simply use LOG(X)/LOG(10). The argument in the LOG function must always be positive.

The function EXP(X) is used to find values of the exponential function, e^x, where e = 2.71828. This number is the same as the base of the natural logarithm function.

PROGRAM 6.7

This program illustrates the use of the above functions.

```
10 INPUT "Enter X"; X
20 PRINT "LN(X) ="; LOG(X)
30 IF X < 87 THEN PRINT "e raised to X ="; EXP(X)
40 T = LOG(X) / LOG(10)
50 PRINT "The common logarithm of"; X; "is"; T
60 PRINT : GOTO 10
READY
>RUN
Enter X? 1
LN(X) = 0
e raised to X = 2.71828
The common logarithm of 1 is 0

Enter X? 0.01
LN(X) =-4.60517
e raised to X = 1.01005
The common logarithm of .01 is-2

Enter X? 10000
LN(X) = 9.21034
The common logarithm of 10000 is 4

Enter X? 0.525
LN(X) =-.644357
e raised to X = 1.69046
The common logarithm of .525 is-.279841

Enter X?
Break in 10
READY
>
```

DEF

Several standard functions, such as SQR, ABS, and LOG, have already been introduced in this chapter. In addition, the programmer can define other functions by using a DEF statement. The major advantage of DEF lies in the fact that the expression for the function need only be written once, even though the function can be evaluated at more than one location within the program. The form of a DEF statement is:

DEF FN <function name> (<variable name>) = <expression>

The function name may be any acceptable numeric variable name (e.g., FNA, FNF, FNG3). The variable name (i.e, the argument) following the function name must always appear within parentheses and may be any appropriate numeric variable.

In the following example,

$$10 \text{ DEF FNP}(X) = X[2 - 2*X - 1$$

P is the function name, X is the variable name, and X^2-2X-1 is the expression used to compute the function's value. For instance, when X = 5, FNP(X) = 14 because $5\uparrow 2 -2*5 -1 = 14$.

PROGRAM 6.8

The following program evaluates the polynomial function FNP(X) several times.

```
10 DEF FNP(X) = X[2 - 2*X - 1
20 PRINT "X", "FNP(X)"
30 FOR A = 1 TO 5
40     PRINT A, FNP(A)
50 NEXT A
60 INPUT X
70 PRINT "The result of FNP("; X; ") is "; FNP(X)
READY
>RUN
X                    FNP(X)
 1                    -2
 2                    -1
 3                     2
 4                     7
 5                    14
? -10
The result of FNP(-10 ) is   119
READY
>
```

When the function is evaluated at line 40, the variable in parentheses is A. When it is evaluated on line 70, the variable is X. The name of the variable in parentheses may be the same as or different from the variable name used in the DEF statement. Note also that if the DEF statement were not used, the formula on line 10 would have to appear twice (lines 40 and 70). Economy results from the fact that though the function is defined only once, it may be evaluated at any place within the program.

Another advantage obtained by the use of the DEF statement is that it can be easily retyped to define a different function. This is illustrated by re-running Program 6.8 with line 10 changed to:

```
>10 DEF FNP(X) = X[3 - 5*X[2 + 1
>RUN
X                 FNP(X)
 1                 -3
 2                -11
 3                -17
 4                -15
 5                  1.00003
? -10
The result of FNP(-10 ) is -1499
READY
>
```

String functions may also be defined using DEF. This technique is handy for simplifying certain string operations such as the addition of strings.

PROGRAM 6.9

This program illustrates how a user defined string function can be implemented.

```
10 DEF FNG$(A$) = A$ + " is yellow"
20 B$ = "The Sun"
30 PRINT FNG$(B$); " and "; FNG$("BIG Mellow"); "."
READY
>RUN
The Sun is yellow and BIG Mellow is yellow.
READY
>
```

Note the output produced by line 30. FNG$() is evaluated twice, first with "The Sun" and then with "BIG Mellow".

User defined functions may have more than one variable within the parentheses. For example, the statement

$$DEF \ FNR(A,B) = RND(B-A+1) + A - 1$$

defines the function FNR(A,B) which returns a random integer between A and B, inclusive. The statement

$$DEF \ FNC\$ \ (X\$,Y\$,Z\$) = X\$ + "," + Y\$ + "," + Z\$$$

defines a function which combines three string variables, and inserts commas between each item.

PROGRAM 6.10

This program illustrates several multivariable user defined functions.

```
10 CLEAR 100
20 DEF FNR(A,B) = RND(B-A+1) + A - 1
30 DEF FNW$(X$,Y$,Z$) = X$ + ", " + Y$ + ", or " + Z$
100 REM
110 REM Print a few random numbers using FNR()
120 FOR K = 1 TO 4
130      S = RND(25) - 12 : T = RND(75) + S
140        PRINT "A random number between "; S; "and "; T;
150        PRINT TAB(35); "is "; FNR(S,T)
160 NEXT K
170 X = 18 : Y = 25
180 PRINT FNR(X,Y), FNR(10,11), FNR(X,X*2), FNR(-5,-2)
200 REM
210 REM Use a string function now...
220 PRINT : PRINT FNW$("This", "That", "The Other Thing")
230 R$ = "KAHN" : V$ = "Mr. Spock"
240 PRINT "Who will defeat: "; FNW$(R$,V$,"a Klingon!")
250 J$ = FNW$("Crystal","Alexis","Blake") + " will move."
260 PRINT J$
READY
>RUN
A random number between  0 and  43 is  8
A random number between -11 and  27 is  21
A random number between  2 and  33 is  17
A random number between -11 and  10 is  6
 21              10              24              -2

This, That, or The Other Thing
Who will defeat: KAHN, Mr. Spock, or a Klingon!
Crystal, Alexis, or Blake will move.
READY
>
```

REVIEW

3. Write a program that will produce the following output. Two user defined functions should be used: one to convert degrees to radians; the other to convert radians to degrees.

```
>RUN
DEGREES? 30
That is .523583 radians.

RADIANS? .785375
That is 45 degrees.
READY
>
```

Shifting and Scaling A Graph

A hand-drawn graph usually includes an X-axis drawn horizontally, a Y-axis drawn vertically, and a continuous curve drawn through a number of plotted points. There are some obvious limitations to graphs produced by the computer (for example, the lack of connection between plotted points). The graphing area on the display screen contains a limited number of points available for plotting. Thus, certain adjustments of the X and Y-axes may be necessary to accommodate functions which produce values that exceed the number of graphing points available. This problem is solved by determining the domain (smallest and largest X values) and the range (smallest and largest Y values) for a function where Y = f(X) and then scaling the axes accordingly. This process is referred to as *shifting* and *scaling*.

Shifting is achieved by subtracting the minimum value of Y from each Y value. For example, if a function has values between −10 and +15, Y minus the minimum value (Y−(−10)) shifts the graph to points between 0 and 25 on the Y-axis. This does not affect the shape of the graph.

Scaling, on the other hand, takes the difference between the largest and smallest values and divides this difference by one less than the number of points available for a particular axis. The one extra space allows the axis to start with the smallest plotted value. For example, if the interval between the largest and smallest Y values for a particular graph is 141 units and the display screen has only 48 vertical points for plotting, the 141 is divided by (48-1) or 47 to produce the proper scale. Every 3 points on the graph's Y axis corresponds to 1 point on the screen.

The 'brick-shaped' points used for graphing on the TRS-80 have a height-width ratio of approximately 1.95 to 1. Thus, scaling is also used to bring shapes into proper proportion as illustrated by Program 6.11.

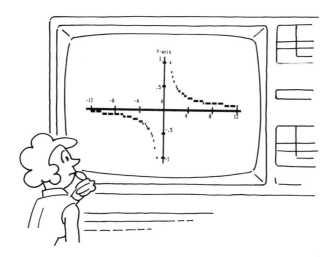

PROGRAM 6.11

The following program illustrates how a figure can be scaled to its proper proportions by plotting two circles side by side, with one scaled and the other unscaled. Here both circles have been derived from the property $X^2 + Y^2 = R^2$.

```
10 REM    XO,YO = Origin of unshifted/unscaled circle
20 REM    X2,Y2 = Origin of shifted/scaled circle
30 REM    R     = Radius of both circles
40 REM    X     = Loop variable
50 REM
60 REM Plot Center of unscaled circle at (XO,YO)
70 CLS : R = 20 : XO = 25 : YO = 25
80 FOR X = XO-R TO XO+R
90      Y = SQR(R[2 - (X-XO)[2)
100     SET(X,YO+Y) : SET(X,YO-Y)
110 NEXT X
120 REM
130 REM Plot Center of scaled circle at (X2,Y2)
140 X2 = 86 : Y2 = 25
150 FOR X = X2-R TO X2+R
160     Y = SQR(R[2 - (X-X2)[2)
170     Y = Y/1.95
180     SET(X,Y2+Y) : SET(X,Y2-Y)
190 NEXT X
>RUN
```

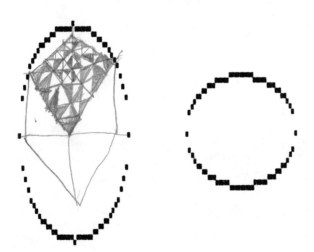

The circle on the left is unscaled and therefore appears elongated, but the circle on the right is scaled to proportion by line 170 of the program. Line 140 moves the origin of the second circle so that the two circles can be plotted next to each other.

PROGRAM 6.12

This program plots the function Y = 1/X on the display screen. Note how the graph has been shifted and scaled.

```
10 REM    XO,YO = Origin of graph on screen
20 REM    X,Y   = Function variables
30 REM    X1,Y1 = Shifted/Scaled X & Y values
40 REM    T     = Loop variable for setting up axes
50 REM
60 XO = 64 : YO = 25 : REM Origin (0,0)
70 REM
80 REM Draw and label X-axis
90 CLS : FOR T = 0 TO 127 : SET(T,YO) : NEXT T
100 FOR T = 4 TO 124 STEP 20
110     SET(T,YO-1) : SET(T,YO+1)
120     READ N : REM Read a label from DATA statement
130     IF N > 0
            THEN PRINT@(574 + INT(T/2)), N;
            ELSE PRINT@(446 + INT(T/2)), N;
140 NEXT T
150 REM
160 REM Draw and label Y-axis
170 FOR T = 3 TO 47 : SET(XO,T) : NEXT T
180 FOR T = 5 TO 45 STEP 10
190     SET(XO-1,T) : SET(XO+1,T)
200 NEXT T
210 PRINT @94,"1";  @993,"-1";  @349,".5";
            @737,"-.5";  @29,"Y-axis";
220 REM
230 REM Plot function Y = 1/X
240 FOR X = -12 TO 12 STEP 0.25
250     IF X<>0 THEN Y = 1/X ELSE Y = 0
260     REM
270     REM Shift/Scale X & Y to display screen
280     X1 = XO + X * (120/24)
290     Y1 = YO - Y * (40/2)
300     IF (X1 > 0 AND Y1 > 0)
            THEN IF (X1 < 128 AND Y1 < 48)
                THEN SET(X1,Y1)
310 NEXT X
320 DATA -12, -8, -4, 0, 4, 8, 12
```

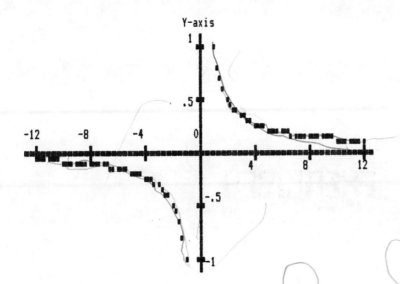

The analysis of this program is left as an exercise for the reader.

PART A

1. When a number is input have the computer generate the following output. Be sure to prevent a negative input.

```
>RUN
? 4
N = 4                    SQUARE ROOTS = + OR - 2
```

2. Write a program which prints the integers from 121 to 144, inclusive, and their respective square roots. Label each column of the output.

3. Perform each of the following computations on paper. Check your results by using immediate mode on the computer.

   (A) 3↑2↑3   (B) 5 - 4↑2
   (C) 3*(5 + 16)   (D) 5 + 3 * 6/2
   (E) 640/10/2 * 5   (F) 5 + 3 * 4 - 1
   (G) 2↑3↑2   (H) 2↑(3↑2)
   (I) 64/4 * 0.5 + ((1 + 5) * 2↑3) * 1/(2 * 4)

4. Input a number N. If N is zero, print 0. Otherwise, print ABS(N)/N. What does the program do?

5. Input a number N, and print the product of SGN(N) and N. What does this program do?

6. Input a number N, square it, and print the square root of the result. What should the program produce?

7. Print a table consisting of 2 columns with headings showing each angle in radians and degrees. The angles in radians are to be 0, .25, .5, .75, . . ., 3.0. Remember that 180° = 3.14159 radians.

8. Input an angle in degrees and convert it to a fraction of a revolution (1 rev. = 360°) and to radians.

9. Input an angle in degrees. Of the three functions sine, cosine, and tangent, print the value of the one which has the greatest value.

10. For angles from 0° to 180° (at intervals of 10°) print the angle in degrees, the sine, the cosine, and the sum of their squares in columns with headings. What patterns emerge?

11. Input two numbers (A, B). Print the quantity F(B)-F(A), given that $F(X) = 9X^3 - 7X^2 + 4X - 1$.

12. Input a number N. Print the values of F(N) and F(F(N)), where F(X) = 20 * SQR (ABS(X))—10 * SGN (X) + 5 * INT (X).

13. Print a table (with headings) of X, the natural logarithm of X, and the exponential function of X for X = 1 to 15.

14. Print a table (with headings) of X, the logarithm of X to the base 10, and 10 raised to the power X for X = 1 to 15.

PART B
15. What is the exact output for the following program? Check by running the program.

```
10 READ A,B,C,D
20 PRINT SQR(A),INT(B),SQR(INT(C)),INT(SQR(D))
30 DATA 25,-3.4,9.7,24
```

16. Print the square roots of the integers from 50 to 60, inclusive.

17. What is the exact output for the following program? Check by running the program.

```
10 DEF FNF(N) = 3 * N - 6
20 FOR X = -4 TO 6 STEP 2
30    IF FNF(X) > 0 THEN PRINT "FNF(";X;") IS POSITIVE"
40    IF FNF(X) = 0 THEN PRINT "FNF(";X;") IS ZERO"
50    IF FNF(X) < 0 THEN PRINT "FNF(";X;") IS NEGATIVE"
60 NEXT X
```

18. Input a number, and print the square root, sign, log, and sine of the number. For example:

```
>RUN
? 16
SQR( 16 ) = 4
SGN( 16 ) = 1
LOG( 16 ) = 2.77259
SIN( 16 ) = -.287903
```

19. What is the exact output for the following program? Check by running the program.

```
10 FOR X = -3 TO 4
20    READ A
30    PRINT SGN(X) * ABS(X)
40 NEXT X
50 DATA 3,-5,1,6,-2,4,-9,5
```

20. Using three user-defined functions, have the computer evaluate the following for the integers from -10 to 10.

$$X^2 + 3X + 2$$

$$LOG(X^2 + 1) - X$$

$$ATN(SIN(X))$$

21. Write a program to convert from polar to rectangular coordinates (i.e., from (r,θ) to (X,Y)).

22. If two functions, f and g, are inverse to each other, the following relations hold:
f(g(x)) = x and g(f(x)) = x.

(a) Tabulate the values of the following quantities for X = -5 to 10: X, EXP(X), LOG(EXP(X)).
(b) Print a table for X = 1 to 151 of X, LOG(X), EXP(LOG(X)), using STEP 10.
(c) Do EXP and LOG appear to be inverse to each other?

23. Produce your own sequence of random numbers without using the RND command. To do this let X vary from 1 to 100 in steps of 1. Obtain SIN(X) and multiply this by 1000, calling the absolute value of the product Y. Divide INT(Y) by 16, and let the remainder R serve as your random number. Hint: the remainder of A ÷ B is A/B—INT (A/B).

24. Six year old Dennis the Menace has decided to invest 50¢ in the Last Chew Bubble Gum Company. Starting with the 11th year, he withdraws 5¢ at the beginning of each year. His money earns 8% interest compounded continually. The formula for interest compounded continually is $P = P_0 e^{it}$, where t is the elapsed time in years, P_0 is the initial deposit, P is the amount at time t, and i is the interest rate. In this case the formula would be $P = P_0 e^{.08t}$. How much is Dennis's deposit worth after 50 years?

25. Use the SIN function to generate the following:

```
                        SHAZAM!
                         SHAZAM!
                          SHAZAM!
                           SHAZAM!
                            SHAZAM!
                             SHAZAM!
                              SHAZAM!
                               SHAZAM!
                               SHAZAM!
                               SHAZAM!
                              SHAZAM!
                             SHAZAM!
                            SHAZAM!
                           SHAZAM!
                          SHAZAM!
                         SHAZAM!
                        SHAZAM!
                       SHAZAM!
                      SHAZAM!
                     SHAZAM!
                    SHAZAM!
                   SHAZAM!
                  SHAZAM!
                 SHAZAM!
                 SHAZAM!
                 SHAZAM!
                 SHAZAM!
                  SHAZAM!
                   SHAZAM!
                    SHAZAM!
                     SHAZAM!
                      SHAZAM!
```

26. (a) Write a program which will solve a triangle (compute the unknown sides and angles) if two sides and the included angle are input. Modify the program to solve for the unknown sides and angles for the following situations:
    (b) input two angles and any side,
    (c) input three sides.

27. Print a graph of $Y = SIN(n \pi X)$, where n is chosen by the user from the set $(-1,1,1/2,1/4)$. The units of length for the X and Y axes need not be the same. The periodic nature of the sine function should be indicated on your graph.

28. Produce the following graphs with numbered X and Y axes and the origin properly centered. (Hint: see Program 6.12).

    (A) Print a graph of $Y = SGN(X)$
    (B) Print a graph of $Y = ATN(X)$
    (C) Print a graph of $Y = INT(X)$

7 TRS-80 SUBROUTINES AND ERROR HANDLING

Writing long, complex programs may require special programming techniques. It is often helpful to divide these programs into sections, called subroutines. Subroutines are useful because they perform a specified task and may be accessed from anywhere in the program. A long program may be divided into a main section and a series of subroutines. The main section directs the order in which the subroutines do their specialized jobs. This type of organization usually reduces the size of a program because the lines needed to perform a certain task have only to be placed once in a program, even though the task may be performed several times.

GOSUB-RETURN

In the case of programs whose various portions are repeated at different places, it may be efficient to use a subroutine. A subroutine is entered by the statement GOSUB <line number> and exited by the statement RETURN. For example:

```
10  ........
20  GOSUB 200
30  ........
40  ........
200 ........ ⌉
210 ........ |
220 ........ ⌋
230 RETURN
999 END
```

The skeleton program illustrates the use of a subroutine. At line 20 the program jumps to the subroutine which begins at line 200, executes the subroutine, and then returns from line 230 to the body of the program at line 30. It is legal to use more than one RETURN statement within a subroutine. You should remember that the computer always returns to the first statement after the GOSUB statement which caused the subroutine to be executed. The only difference between GOSUB and the GOTO statement is that GOSUB permits the use of RETURN whereas GOTO does not. Subroutines are usually placed towards the bottom of a program. They may be written so that one subroutine can access another.

PROGRAM 7.1

Given the numbers of pennies, nickels, dimes, and quarters as input, this program will output the total amount of money represented by these coins. One subroutine processes and reports the amount of money involved for each of the four types of coins.

```
10 A$ = "PENNIES": V = 1
20 GOSUB 200
30 A$ = "NICKELS": V = 5
40 GOSUB 200
50 A$ = "DIMES": V = 10
60 GOSUB 200
70 A$ = "QUARTERS": V = 25
80 GOSUB 200
90 PRINT "THE TOTAL VALUE WAS $";T/100
100 END
200 REM    SUBROUTINE
210 PRINT "NUMBER OF ";A$;
220 INPUT N
230 PRINT N;A$;" =";N*V;"CENTS"
240 T = T + N*V
250 RETURN
READY
>RUN
NUMBER OF PENNIES? 4
 4 PENNIES = 4 CENTS
NUMBER OF NICKELS? 9
 9 NICKELS = 45 CENTS
NUMBER OF DIMES? 3
 3 DIMES = 30 CENTS
NUMBER OF QUARTERS? 6
 6 QUARTERS = 150 CENTS
THE TOTAL VALUE WAS $ 2.29
READY
```

Line 10 assigns the type (A$) and value (V) of the first coin. Line 20 causes a jump to the subroutine, which begins at line 200 where the number of coins is input. Line 210 prints information about the particular coin being considered, and line 240 adds its contribution to the previous total value of all coins up to this point. Line 250 returns the program back to the line following the most recently used GOSUB statement. This entire process, beginning at line 200, repeats itself three more times, and then the dollar total is printed. What would happen if line 100 were deleted?

REVIEW

1. Write a program where names are input and then printed. If DONALD is input use a subroutine to underline the name.

```
>RUN
NAME? MARY
MARY
NAME? SUE
SUE
NAME? DONALD
DONALD
XXXXXXX
NAME?
Break in 10
READY
```

ON—GOTO

The GOTO statement allows a program to jump to a single specified line. The ON—GOTO statement allows jumps to one of several lines, depending on the value of a numeric variable at the time the statement is encountered. This statement takes the form:

ON <variable> GOTO <list of line numbers>

For example:

50 ON X GOTO 100, 120, 140, 160

If X = 1, the program jumps to line 100; if X = 2, it jumps to line 120, and so on. Note that X should not be less than one or greater than the number of line numbers in the list.

PROGRAM 7.2

This program simulates the random path taken by a mouse through the following maze:

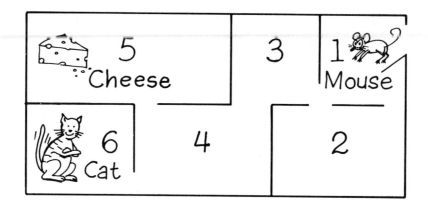

Once the mouse enters the maze, the door is shut. The mouse wanders about until it either finds the cheese or stumbles upon the cat.

```
100 PRINT 1,
110 X = RND(2)
120 ON X GOTO 200,300
200 PRINT 2,
210 X = RND(2)
220 ON X GOTO 100,300
300 PRINT 3,
310 X = RND(3)
320 ON X GOTO 100,200,400
400 PRINT 4,
410 X = RND(3)
420 ON X GOTO 300,500,600
500 PRINT 5
510 PRINT "THE MOUSE IS GORGING ITSELF!"
520 END
600 PRINT 6
610 PRINT "THE CAT HAS BEEN AWAKENED BY ITS LUNCH."
READY
>RUN
 1               3               1               3
 2               3               4               6
THE CAT HAS BEEN AWAKENED BY ITS LUNCH.
READY
```

At line 100, the program prints a 1 to indicate that the mouse is in room #1. Line 110 randomly picks either the number 1 or the number 2. The ON GOTO statement at line 120 sends program execution to line 200 if X = 1, and to 300 if X = 2; lines 200 and 300 correspond to rooms 2 and 3, respectively. Once in one of the other rooms, the program prints the room number and decides where the mouse will go from there. Execution continues until the mouse finds itself either in room 5 or room 6.

REVIEW

2. Write a program to draw five cards from a deck. The computer picks two random numbers, the first is between 1 and 4 inclusive, and the second between 1 and 13 inclusive. An ON GOTO statement should use the first number to pick each suit. The second represents the card's value within the suit.

```
READY
>RUN
CARD 1 IS THE 9 OF HEARTS
CARD 2 IS THE 1 OF HEARTS
CARD 3 IS THE 9 OF DIAMONDS
CARD 4 IS THE 4 OF DIAMONDS
CARD 5 IS THE 12 OF HEARTS
READY
>_
```

ON—GOSUB

The ON—GOSUB statement operates in much the same way as the ON—GOTO statement. If there are a number of subroutines in a program, they can be called using the ON—GOSUB statement.

$$50 \text{ ON X GOSUB } 300, 400, 500$$

If X = 1, the program jumps to the first subroutine at line 300; if X = 2, to the second subroutine at line 400; and if X = 3, to the third subroutine at line 500. When the subroutine is completed, the RETURN statement directs the program back to the first statement after line 50.

Using Subroutines to Structure Programs

Subroutines are useful both in reducing the amount of code required to write a program and in breaking a program down into its separate functions to help clarify its structure.

PROGRAM 7.3

This program tests a student on addition, subtraction, multiplication and division. Without the use of subroutines much of the code would have to be repeated four times.

```
10    PRINT "YOU WILL BE ASKED 2 QUESTIONS ON ADDITION (1),"
12    PRINT "SUBTRACTION (2), MULTIPLICATION (3), OR DIVISION (4),"
14    PRINT "AND BE GIVEN 2 TRIES TO GET EACH ONE CORRECT.  YOU"
16    PRINT "CAN CHOOSE WHICH TYPE OF QUESTION YOU WANT BY"
18    PRINT "RESPONDING WITH THE APPROPRIATE NUMBER."
19    REM
20    INPUT "WHAT TYPE DO YOU WANT";N
30    FOR X = 1 TO 2
40       A = RND(10)
50       B = RND(10)
60       ON N GOSUB 200,300,400,500
70       FOR Y = 1 TO 2
80          INPUT "YOUR ANSWER IS";D
90          IF D = C THEN PRINT "CORRECT": GOTO 130
100         PRINT "YOUR ANSWER IS WRONG"
110      NEXT Y
120      PRINT "YOU ARE WRONG FOR A SECOND TIME, THE ANSWER IS";C
130      PRINT
140   NEXT X
150   GOTO 20
160   REM
170   REM
200   REM    ADDITION
210   PRINT "WHAT DOES";A;"+";B;"="
220   C = A + B
230   RETURN
240   REM
250   REM
300   REM    SUBTRACTION
310   PRINT "WHAT DOES";A;"-";B;"="
320   C = A - B
330   RETURN
340   REM
350   REM
400   REM    MULTIPLICATION
410   PRINT "WHAT DOES";A;"*";B;"="
420   C = A * B
430   RETURN
440   REM
450   REM
500   REM    DIVISION
510   PRINT "WHAT DOES";A;"/";B;"="
520   C = A / B
530   RETURN
```

```
>RUN
YOU WILL BE ASKED 2 QUESTIONS ON ADDITION (1),
SUBTRACTION (2), MULTIPLICATION (3), OR DIVISION (4),
AND BE GIVEN 2 TRIES TO GET EACH ONE CORRECT.  YOU
CAN CHOOSE WHICH TYPE OF QUESTION YOU WANT BY
RESPONDING WITH THE APPROPRIATE NUMBER.
WHAT TYPE DO YOU WANT? 3
WHAT DOES 1 * 10 =
YOUR ANSWER IS? 10
CORRECT

WHAT DOES 9 * 1 =
YOUR ANSWER IS? 10
YOUR ANSWER IS WRONG
YOUR ANSWER IS? 91
YOUR ANSWER IS WRONG
YOU ARE WRONG FOR A SECOND TIME, THE ANSWER IS 9

WHAT TYPE DO YOU WANT? 2
WHAT DOES 6 - 7 =
YOUR ANSWER IS? -1
CORRECT

WHAT DOES 7 - 3 =
YOUR ANSWER IS? 4
CORRECT

WHAT TYPE DO YOU WANT? 1
WHAT DOES 3 + 9 =
YOUR ANSWER IS? 12
CORRECT

WHAT DOES 8 + 1 =
YOUR ANSWER IS? 9
CORRECT

WHAT TYPE DO YOU WANT?
Break in 20
READY
```

ON ERROR GOTO and RESUME

If an error can be anticipated before a program is run, it is possible to "trap" the error by using the ON ERROR GOTO statement which allows the program to continue execution. When an error is encountered, this statement suppresses the printing of an error message and causes the program to jump to the specified line. For example,

30 ON ERROR GOTO 60

sends the program to line 60 *when* an error occurs.

Examples of two frequently encountered errors are that of dividing a number by zero or of taking the square root of a negative number. To trap these errors the ON ERROR GOTO statement must be placed in the program before the error occurs. Then, if there is an error, the program will jump to the specified line.

The RESUME statement performs two functions after an error has been trapped. It returns the program to the point where the error occurred and resets the error trap so that new errors may be trapped. If the RESUME statement is not used, the program will continue from the point where it was sent by the ON ERROR GOTO statement and will therefore be unable to trap any future errors. It is important to correct an error, before executing the RESUME statement; otherwise, the error may occur again and may put the program into an infinite loop.

PROGRAM 7.4

This program allows the user to input two numbers, the first to be divided by the second.

```
1 REM     N,D = NUMERATOR AND DENOMINATOR
2 REM
3 REM
10 ON ERROR GOTO 100
20 INPUT "NUMERATOR AND DENOMINATOR";N,D
30 PRINT N/D
40 GOTO 20
100 PRINT "DIVISION BY ZERO ATTEMPTED"
110 N=1 : D=1
120 RESUME
130 END
READY
>RUN
NUMERATOR AND DENOMINATOR? 5,3
 1.66667
NUMERATOR AND DENOMINATOR? 2,0
DIVISION BY ZERO ATTEMPTED
 1
NUMERATOR AND DENOMINATOR? 8,9
 .888889
NUMERATOR AND DENOMINATOR?
Break in 20
READY
>
```

Note that if an error occurs, the program will assign a value of one to N and D and then resume.

$$RESUME \; <line \; number>$$

instructs the computer to continue execution at the specified line. Changing line 120 to

$$120 \; RESUME \; 20$$

and deleting line 110 eliminates the need of reassigning N and D values before resuming.

$$RESUME \; NEXT$$

instructs the computer to continue execution at the statement immediately following the one where the error occurred. In Program 7.4, the line

$$120 \; RESUME \; NEXT$$

will send the program to line 40 when executed.

ERR and ERL

Program 7.4 has the drawback of handling all errors alike whether they are anticipated or not. The ERR and ERL functions allow the program to be more discriminating in handling errors.

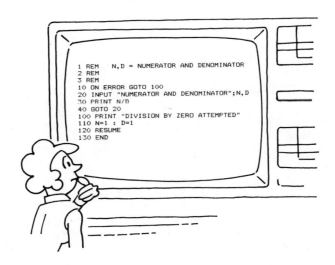

```
1 REM      N,D = NUMERATOR AND DENOMINATOR
2 REM
3 REM
10 ON ERROR GOTO 100
20 INPUT "NUMERATOR AND DENOMINATOR";N,D
30 PRINT N/D
40 GOTO 20
100 PRINT "DIVISION BY ZERO ATTEMPTED"
110 N=1 : D=1
120 RESUME
130 END
```

ERR returns a number that identifies the specific error that has occurred.

$$20 \text{ PRINT ERR}/2 + 1$$

will return a number corresponding to an error listed below. The need to divide ERR by two and add one is an idiosyncrasy of the computer.

Code	Explanation
1	NEXT without FOR
2	Syntax error
3	RETURN without GOSUB
4	Out of data
5	Illegal function call
6	Overflow
7	Out of memory
8	Undefined line
9	Subscript out of range
10	Redimensioned array
11	Division by zero
12	Illegal direct
13	Type mismatch
14	Out of string space
15	String too long
16	String formula too complex
17	Can't continue
18	No RESUME
19	RESUME without error
20	Undefined error
21	Missing operand
22	Bad file data
23	Disk BASIC feature

ERL returns a number equal to the line number where the most recent error occurred. For example,

$$30 \text{ PRINT ERL}$$

PROGRAM 7.5

This program can respond correctly to two different types of errors—division by zero and the square root of a negative number.

```
10 ON ERROR GOTO 100
20 INPUT "FIRST AND SECOND NUMBER";N1,N2
30 PRINT N1;"/";N2;"=";N1/N2
40 PRINT "SQUARE ROOT OF";N1;"=";SQR(N1)
50 PRINT "SQUARE ROOT OF";N2;"=";SQR(N2)
60 END
70 REM
80 REM
100 IF ERR/2+1 = 11
        THEN PRINT "DIVISION BY ZERO AT LINE";ERL
        ELSE IF ERR/2+1 = 5
                THEN PRINT "IMAGINARY ROOT AT LINE";ERL
110 INPUT "NEW NUMBERS";N1,N2
120 RESUME
READY
>RUN
FIRST AND SECOND NUMBER? 10,2
 10 / 2 = 5
SQUARE ROOT OF 10 = 3.16228
SQUARE ROOT OF 2 = 1.41421
READY
>RUN
FIRST AND SECOND NUMBER? 10,0
 10 / 0 =DIVISION BY ZERO AT LINE 30
NEW NUMBERS? 10,-2
 10 /-2 =-5
SQUARE ROOT OF 10 = 3.16228
SQUARE ROOT OF-2 =IMAGINARY ROOT AT LINE 50
NEW NUMBERS?
Break in 110
READY
>
```

The statement

25 ON ERROR GOTO 0

nullifies any previous ON ERROR GOTO statement. If this line were included in Program 7.5 the errors would no longer be trapped.

PART A

1. Have the computer produce the printout below. Use a subroutine to print out "PART"
   and the appropriate number.

```
>RUN

PART 1
*************************************************
PART 2
!                     !                     !
PART 3
ABABABABABABABABABABABABABABABABABABABABABABABAB
READY
>
```

2. Have the computer pick a random integer from 1 to 4 which will determine whether the prize to be awarded will be a ball, balloon, toy car, or candy bar.

3. Input an integer from 1 to 4. The integer should cause one of the following four suggestions to be printed.

DON'T LET YOUR COMPUTER TURN TO TRASH.
DON'T LET BUGS GET IN YOUR TRASH.
STUDY HARD AND YOU WON'T NEED A TRUSS.
NEVER PLAY WITH TRASH.

4. What is the exact output for the following program?

```
10 READ X
20 ON X GOTO 30,40,50,60,70,80,100
30 PRINT "MERRILY, ";:GOTO 10
40 PRINT "ROW, ";:GOTO 10
50 PRINT "YOUR BOAT": GOTO 10
60 PRINT "GENTLY DOWN THE STREAM": GOTO 10
70 PRINT "LIFE IS BUT A DREAM": GOTO 10
80 PRINT : GOTO 10
90 DATA 2,2,2,3,4,1,1,1,1,6,5,7
100 END
```

5. (a) Give the exact order in which the lines of the following program are executed.
   (b) If line 80 is changed to:

$$80 \text{ DATA } 3,0,4,-5,-1,-8,1,5,999$$

what will be the output?

```
10 READ X
20 IF X=999 THEN 90
30 ON SGN(X)+2 GOSUB 50,60,70
40 GOTO 10
50 N=N+1: RETURN
60 Z=Z+1: RETURN
70 P=P+1: RETURN
80 DATA 6,-1,0,999
90 PRINT "N=";N,"Z=";Z,"P=";P
100 END
```

6. (a) Give the exact order in which the lines of the following program are executed.
   (b) If line 90 were changed to:

$$90 \text{ DATA } 1,8,-2,5,-3,-6,2,4,-7,0$$

what would the output be?

```
10 READ X
20 IF X=O THEN 95
30 GOSUB 60
40 T=T+X
50 GOTO 10
60 IF X<O THEN 80
70 P=P+X
80 RETURN
90 DATA 5,2,-9,0,3,5
95 PRINT "T=";T,"P=";P
100 END
```

7. Write a program which reads the dimensions of a triangle from a DATA statement and prints its area and perimeter if it is a right triangle. The program should call a subroutine to check whether the triangle is a right triangle or not.

8. Let X and Y be the coordinates of a point in a plane. Write a program which randomly picks X and Y, each as an integer from -5 and 5, inclusive. The user of the program is to guess X and Y, with the guesses being called X1 and Y1. A subroutine must be used to print the distance between the guessed point and the actual point after each guess. The user is to be given 3 guesses and, if unsuccessful, is then to be given the value of X as well as 2 more tries to guess Y.

9. Isolated in his ski-lodge in the Swiss Alps, Bjorn Rich oftens gets his mail late. As a result the statements from his Swiss bank account rarely arrive on time. To solve this problem, write a program to assist Bjorn in keeping his account up to date. Have three subroutines which take care of deposits, withdrawals, and the interest (5¾% compounded quarterly).

```
>RUN
WITHDRAWAL(1),DEPOSIT(2), OR CALCULATE INTEREST(3)? 2
HOW MUCH WOULD YOU LIKE TO DEPOSIT? 500.00
YOUR BALANCE NOW STANDS AT 500 DOLLARS.
WITHDRAWAL(1),DEPOSIT(2), OR CALCULATE INTEREST(3)? 3
HOW MANY MONTHS SINCE LAST CALCULATION? 5
YOUR BALANCE NOW STANDS AT 507.188 DOLLARS.
WITHDRAWAL(1),DEPOSIT(2), OR CALCULATE INTEREST(3)? 1
HOW MUCH WOULD YOU LIKE TO WITHDRAW? 175.50
YOUR BALANCE NOW STANDS AT 331.688 DOLLARS.
WITHDRAWAL(1),DEPOSIT(2), OR CALCULATE INTEREST(3)? 3
HOW MANY MONTHS SINCE LAST CALCULATION? 1
TOO SOON
YOUR BALANCE NOW STANDS AT 331.688 DOLLARS.
WITHDRAWAL(1),DEPOSIT(2), OR CALCULATE INTEREST(3)?
Break in 10
READY
>
```

10. The area of any triangle may be found from Hero's formula;

$$AREA = \sqrt{S\,(S{-}A)\,(S{-}B)\,(S{-}C)}$$

where A, B, and C are the length of each side of the triangle and S is the semiperimeter. S = (A+B+C)/2. Write a program that uses Hero's formula in a subroutine to calculate the area of a triangle.

11. Write a program that prints all the results of 10 divided by all integers between -5 and 5 inclusive. Your program should trap the error that occurs when you try calculating 10/0.

12. Write a program that uses the Quadratic Formula: $\dfrac{-b\pm\sqrt{b^2-4ac}}{2a}$

to find the roots of an equation. Input a,b,c and have the computer print the two roots. Your program should have an error trap for the error that might occur when the computer attempts to take the square root of a negative number. When this situation arises have the computer print "roots are imaginary."

8 TRS-80

STRING FUNCTIONS AND DATA TYPES

Modern computers have resulted from the union of the binary number system with the principles of electricity. The binary number system uses only two digits, 0 and 1, and can therefore be represented by the two states of an electric circuit, off or on. This concept has made digital computers possible, since they operate by reducing all data to a binary code. How different types of data can be reduced to a binary system is explained in this chapter.

Binary Code

The most familiar number system, the decimal system, uses ten digits: 0,1,2,3, 4,5,6,7,8,9 and is therefore considered to be base ten. In contrast, the binary system, which uses only the digits 0 and 1, is base two.

In the base ten system, columns are used to represent powers of ten with the first column left of the decimal point representing 10^0, the second 10^1, the third 10^2, and so on. For example, in the numeral 458, 8 represents 8×10^0, 5 represents 5×10^1 and 4 represents 4×10^2. The numeral itself represents the sum: $4 \times 10^2 + 5 \times 10^1 + 8 \times 10^0$.

The base two system works identically *except the columns represent powers of two* instead of ten. For example, in the numeral 101, the 1 on the right represents 1×2^0, the 0 represents 0×2^1, and the 1 on the left represents 1×2^2. The numeral itself represents the sum $1 \times 2^2 + 0 \times 2^1 + 1 \times 2^0$, which is known as five in the base ten system.

Base Two		Base Ten
$11 = 1 \times 2^1 + 1 \times 2^0$		$= 3$
$1011 = 1 \times 2^3 + 0 \times 2^2 + 1 \times 2^1 + 1 \times 2^0$		$= 11$
$11001 = 1 \times 2^4 + 1 \times 2^3 + 0 \times 2^2 + 0 \times 2^1 + 1 \times 2^0$		$= 25$

To convert a number from base ten to base two, we must find which powers of two add up to the number. Since 13 = 8 + 4 + 1, the base two representation for 13 is 1101 (1x8 + 1x4 + 0x2 +1x1).

Base Ten		Base Two
$6 = 4 + 2 = 1x2^2 + 1x2^1 + 0x2^0$		$= \quad 110$
$29 = 16 + 8 + 4 + 1\ 1x2^4 + 1x2^3 + 1x2^2 + 0x2^1 + 1x2^0$		$= 11101$
$52 = 32 + 16 + 4 = 1x2^5 + 1x2^4 + 0x2^3 + 1x2^2 + 0x2^1 + 0x2^0$		$=110100$

Computer Memory and Processing

The computer is composed of a solid-state electronic memory which stores information and a central processing unit (CPU) which performs calculations, makes decisions, and moves information.

Because electricity has two basic states, ON and OFF, it is ideal for expressing binary numbers. A circuit (called a "flip-flop") when on stands for a "1", and when off stands for a "0". By designing computers to contain millions of simple flip-flop circuits, huge quantities of information can thus be stored.

A single binary digit (0 or 1) is called a "bit", and eight of these bits constitute a "byte". Single characters require one byte and integers two bytes of memory for storage. The memory stores both instructions for the CPU and data as binary digits.

The power of a computer is vastly increased when it is capable of storing letters and special characters as well as numbers. In order to do this, a code has been established to translate letters and special characters into numbers which can then be stored in binary form. This code has been standardized by the computer industry as the American Standard Code for Information Interchange (ASCII). In this code, each letter of the alphabet, both upper case and lower case, each symbol, and each control function used by the computer is represented by a number. For example, the name JIM is translated by the computer into ASCII numbers 74,73,77. In turn these numbers are then stored by the computer in binary form.

$$J = 74 = 01001010$$
$$I = 73 = 01001001$$
$$M = 77 = 01001101$$

In order for the computer to store a name such as JIM, or any piece of non-numeric information, it must be entered in the form of a string, converted character by character into ASCII numbers, and then stored in memory as binary numbers. The following is a table of the ASCII character codes available on the computer.

The following is a table of the ASCII character codes.

Decimal Value	ASCII Character	Usage	Decimal Value	ASCII Character	Usage	Decimal Value	ASCII Character	Usage
0	NUL	FILL character	43	+		86	V	
1	SOH		44	,	COMMA	87	W	
2	STX		45	-		88	X	
3	ETX	CTRL/C	46	.		89	Y	
4	EOT		47	/		90	Z	
5	ENQ		48	0		91	[	
6	ACK		49	1		92	/	Back-slash
7	BEL	BACKSPACE	50	2		93	]	
8	BS		51	3		94	^ or ↑	
9	HT	HORIZ. TAB	52	4		95	_ or ←	
10	LF	LINE FEED	53	5		96	`	Grave accent
11	VT		54	6		97	a	
12	FF		55	7		98	b	
13	CR	CAR. RET	56	8		99	c	
14	SO		57	9		100	d	
15	SI		58	:		101	e	
16	DLE		59	;		102	f	
17	DC1		60	<		103	g	
18	DC2		61	&		104	h	
19	DC3		62	>		105	i	
20	DC4		63	?		106	j	
21	NAK		64	=		107	k	
22	SYN		65	A		108	l	
23	ETB		66	B		109	m	
24	CAN		67	C		110	n	
25	EM		68	D		111	o	
26	SUB		69	E		112	p	
27	ESC		70	F		113	q	
28	FS		71	G		114	r	
29	GS		72	H		115	s	
30	RS		73	I		116	t	
31	US		74	J		117	u	
32	SP	SPACE	75	K		118	v	
33	!		76	L		119	w	
34	*		77	M		120	x	
35	#		78	N		121	y	
36	$		79	O		122	z	
37	%		80	P		123	{	
38	&		81	Q		124	|	Vertical Line
39	'	APOSTROPHE	82	R		125	}	
40	(		83	S		126	~	Tilde
41	)		84	T		127	DEL RUBOUT	
42	*		85	U				

Data Types

When information is entered into the computer, it can take one of three forms: ASCII characters, integers, or floating point numbers. An integer is a number without decimal places, while a floating point number has either a decimal point or an implied decimal point and decimal places. For example, the number 29 could be either integer or floating point, but 29.73 is definitely floating point.

Floating point numbers on the computer can be specified to be either single precision or double precision. A single precision floating point number is internally accurate to seven significant figures, but rounded to six when printed. A double precision floating point number is internally accurate to seventeen significant figures but rounded to sixteen when printed.

Storage of an integer requires 16 bits, a floating point number either 32 or 64 bits, depending on whether it is single or double precision, and an ASCII character 8 bits. Because of storage requirements it is important to distinguish between the several forms. When files are presented in Chapters 9 and 10, the significance of this factor in planning efficient storage of data will become apparent.

The four data types employ different symbols to inform the computer which is being used. Strings of ASCII characters employ the familiar symbol ($) for string variable names (e.g., G$, B3$). Integers, which have the disadvantage of being restricted to the range −32768 to 32767 are denoted by a percent sign (%). For example, B% and Z% are variable names for integers. While integers have a severe range limitation, they are processed fastest by the computer. Single precision floating point variables are denoted by an exclamation mark (!); (e.g., C!, Hl!). Double precision floating point variables are denoted by a number sign (#); (e.g., G7#, D#). While they are more accurate, calculations involving double precision numbers are the slowest.

The precision of constants as well as variables can be declared and will then determine the precision of the calculations in which they are used. For example,

$$PRINT\ 2/3$$

produces

$$.666667$$

while

$$PRINT\ 2\#/3\#$$

produces

$$.6666666666666667$$

Variables and constants not specifically declared otherwise are assumed to be single precision floating point.

ASCII Code—ASCII Character Conversions

Earlier in this chapter, the ASCII code was described as a method by which the computer converts information in the form of strings into numbers. Commands exist to convert strings into ASCII values and vice versa.

Function Format	Operation
X = ASC(P$)	Converts only the first character of the string P$ to its ASCII code number.
P$ = CHR$(X)	Assigns the character with the ASCII code number of X to P$, which now contains only one character.
P$ = STRING$(X, Y)	Generates a string, P$, of length X composed of characters all having the ASCII code number Y.

PROGRAM 8.1

This program demonstrates the use of the ASCII character conversions.

```
1 REM     C$ = CHARACTER INPUT
2 REM     A = ASCII VALUE OF C$
3 REM     K$ = NEW STRING
4 REM     Y$ = INDICATOR
5 REM
6 REM
10 INPUT "ANY CHARACTER";C$
20 A = ASC(C$)
30 PRINT "THE ASCII VALUE OF '";C$;"' IS";A
40 K$ = STRING$(17,A)
50 PRINT "'";CHR$(A);"' REPEATED 17 TIMES LOOKS LIKE THIS: ";
60 PRINT K$
70 INPUT "WOULD YOU LIKE TO RUN THIS AGAIN";Y$
80 IF ASC(Y$) = 89 THEN 10
READY
>RUN
ANY CHARACTER? R
THE ASCII VALUE OF 'R' IS 82
'R' REPEATED 17 TIMES LOOKS LIKE THIS: RRRRRRRRRRRRRRRRR
WOULD YOU LIKE TO RUN THIS AGAIN? N
READY
>
```

1. Write a program that will allow the user to input a letter. Have the computer print that letter's ASCII code and then print the letter that comes two letters after it in the alphabet. If Y or Z is the letter input, then A or B should be returned respectively.

```
>RUN
A LETTER FROM THE ALPHABET PLEASE? R
THE ASCII OF 'R' IS 82
TWO LETTERS AFTER 'R' IS 'T'
A LETTER FROM THE ALPHABET PLEASE? Y
THE ASCII OF 'Y' IS 89
TWO LETTERS AFTER 'Y' IS 'A'
A LETTER FROM THE ALPHABET PLEASE?
Break in 10
READY
```

String Manipulation Functions

Strings can be manipulated with the following functions:

Function	Operation
I$ = INKEY$	Assigns I$ a one character string which is not printed when entered. The ENTER key need not be struck to input the character.
L$ = LEFT$(A$,N)	Assigns L$ a substring of the string A$ from the leftmost character to and including the Nth character.
L = LEN(A$)	Assigns L a value equal to the number of characters in the string A$, including blank spaces.
M$ = MID$(A$,N)	Assigns M$ a substring of the string A$ from the Nth character to the rightmost character of the string.
M$ = MID$(A$, N1, N2)	Assigns M$ a substring of the string A$, starting with the character N1 and being N2 characters long.
MID$(A$, N1, N2) = R$	Replaces N2 characters of A$, starting at character N1, with the first N2 characters of R$.
R$ = RIGHT$(A$,N)	Assigns R$ a substring of the string A$ consisting of the rightmost N characters.
S$ = STR$(X)	Converts X into a string of numeric characters and assigns it to S$.
T$ = TIME$	Assigns T$ a string representing the current date and time.
V = VAL(A$)	Converts the first set of numeric characters in the string A$ into a numeric value that is assigned to V. Non-numeric characters are ignored.

PROGRAM 8.2

This program will input a ten character string without an ENTER and manipulate it to show the use of string functions.

```
1 REM    I$ = STRING INPUT
2 REM    T$ = TARGET STRING
3 REM
4 REM
100 REM    STRING INPUT SECTION USING INKEY$
110 I$ = INKEY$
120 IF I$ = "" THEN 110
130 T$ = T$ + I$
140 PRINT I$;
150 IF LEN(T$) < 10 THEN 110
160 REM
170 REM
200 REM    STRING MANIPULATION SECTION
210 PRINT
220 PRINT "'";T$;"' BACKWARDS IS: ";
230 FOR X = 10 TO 1 STEP -1
240    PRINT MID$(T$,X,1);
250 NEXT X
260 PRINT
270 PRINT "THE VALUE OF '";T$;"' IS:";VAL(T$)
280 PRINT "'";T$;"' HALVED AND FLIPPED IS: ";
290 PRINT RIGHT$(T$,5);LEFT$(T$,5)
300 PRINT "'";VAL(T$);"' BACKWARDS IS: ";
310 FOR X = LEN(STR$(VAL(T$))) TO 1 STEP -1
320    PRINT MID$(STR$(VAL(T$)),X,1);
330 NEXT X
READY
>RUN
145RTLMJDQ
'145RTLMJDQ' BACKWARDS IS: QDJMLTR541
THE VALUE OF '145RTLMJDQ' IS: 145
'145RTLMJDQ' HALVED AND FLIPPED IS: LMJDQ145RT
' 145 ' BACKWARDS IS: 541
READY
>
```

Unlike INPUT, INKEY$ does not wait for data from the keyboard. When INKEY$ is executed, the computer checks immediately to see if a key is being pressed. If not, the computer proceeds to the next program line. Line 120 checks to see if INKEY$ returned a character. If not, the program returns to line 110.

PART A

1. Write a program in which you input a name and then have the computer print the ASCII number for each letter in the name.

2. Input three letters, add their ASCII numbers, find the INT of one third of their sum, and print the character corresponding to the result. Is there any meaning to this process?

3. Using properly selected ASCII numbers on a DATA line, print the sentence "ASCII DID THIS!"

4. Using ASCII numbers 45 and 46 and the PRINT TAB statement, print the following figure.

5. Enter the string THREE!@#$%STRING!@#$%FUNCTIONS. Use LEFT$, MID$, and RIGHT$ to print the phrase "THREE STRING FUNCTIONS".

6. Enter a string A$ of any length. Print the length of A$ and the ASCII number of its first and last characters.

7. Enter a string A$, and use a loop to print the ASCII number of each of its characters.

8. Let A$="2598". Have the computer apply VAL to those parts of A$ whose sum is 123.

9. Enter the words "QUEEN", "LENGTH", and "REMEMBER". Print each word with all E's removed.

10. Use the computer or a hand calculator to find the binary equivalents of the decimal values given below.

    89, 74, 80, 107, 255, 129, 28, 39, 29, 24, 43

11. Use the computer or a hand calculator to find the decimal equivalents for the binary values given below.

    1011, 10100, 1111, 1110, 1010011, 110011, 1011100,
    1101111, 11000000, 10000111

12. Input a string A$ which consists of the digits 0 to 9, inclusive, each to be used only once (e.g., 1956472038). Use string functions to obtain from A$ two numbers N1 and N2, N1 being the number represented by the first three digits of A$ and N2 the number represented by the last three digits. Print the sum of N1 and N2.

13. Let A$ consist of the first twelve letters of the alphabet. Using A$, construct the right triangle shown at the right.

```
READY
>RUN
A
AB
ABC
ABCD
ABCDE
ABCDEF
ABCDEFG
ABCDEFGH
ABCDEFGHI
ABCDEFGHIJ
ABCDEFGHIJK
ABCDEFGHIJKL
READY
>
```

14. As a young boy Franklin Roosevelt signed his letters to his mother backwards: TLEVESOOR NILKNARF. Write a program that accepts a person's name and prints it backwards.

15. Using the ASCII chart given in the text, determine the output for the following program. Check by running the program.

```
10 FOR A=1 TO 4
20      READ A$
30      PRINT ASC(A$)
40 NEXT A
50 DATA "W","H","7","625"
60 END
```

16. The output of the following program is Foxy Moxie's message to Jimmy Band. What is the message? Check by running the program.

```
10 FOR W=1 TO 6
20      READ A$,B$,C$
30      PRINT LEFT$(A$,1);MID$(B$,2,2);RIGHT$(C$,1)
40 NEXT W
50 END
60 REM    DATA SECTION
70      DATA FGT,LOXK,NTY
80      DATA SFJ,DAYT,GES
90      DATA HWT,QELM,BIP
100     DATA WJM,WILS,WZL
110     DATA CDE,HOMV,PSE
120     DATA SOA,AOOC,TZN
```

17. Choose fifteen random integers from 65 to 90, inclusive, to serve as ASCII code numbers. Convert these fifteen integers to the fifteen characters for which they stand, and print the results.

18. Write a program which produces a sentence containing twenty nonsense words. Each word can contain from two to five letters. Use random numbers and the ASCII code to produce the words.

```
>RUN
YFXS ZVFHR RVL IALIR BK LBN ELS WBLWN ELBKX QB KQD HQDD RSGQ SWK
EP QJAC NSZ IONO AU OPM OY
READY
>
```

```
YFXS ZVFHR RVL IALIR BK LBN
ELS WBLWN ELBKX QB KQD
HQDD RSGQ SWK EP QJAC NSZ
IONO AU OPM OY
```

19. Using random numbers and the ASCII code numbers from 32 to 126, inclusive, have the computer generate a string of 100 characters, allowing repetitions. Tabulate how many characters are letters, numbers, or miscellaneous characters. Print the results.

20. Using string functions, write a program to play a word guessing game. Ask the player to guess a secret word. Search through each guess to see if the guess contains any correct letters. If any letter is correct, have the computer print the ones that are. If the entire word is guessed, type "YOU GUESSED IT!!"

```
>RUN
GUESS A WORD? SUE
GUESS A WORD? HARRIET
H IS IN THE WORD
A IS IN THE WORD
GUESS A WORD? BASEBALL
A IS IN THE WORD
A IS IN THE WORD
GUESS A WORD? GRUMP
G IS IN THE WORD
M IS IN THE WORD
GUESS A WORD? HANGMAN
YOU GUESSED IT
READY
>
```

21. You are a spy who will use the computer to produce a secret code.

(a) Input a short message, and have the computer type back what appears to be nonsense words. To produce the coded words, convert each letter of the original message into its corresponding ASCII code number, add two to each number, and convert to characters to produce the message. Keep all spaces between the words in their original places, and understand that the letters Y and Z are to be converted to A and B.

(b) Write a program that will decode the message.

22. When the following program is run the output is:

A = 1500   B = 999.977

Explain in a clear, brief manner why the value of B is not exactly 1000, and why the value of A is exactly 1500.

```
10 FOR X=1 TO 3000
20     A=A+1/2
30     B=B+1/3
40 NEXT X
50 PRINT "A=";A;"B=";B
60 END
```

23. Often, literary critics argue over the true identity of the author of some ancient manuscript. To resolve such disputes, it is helpful to show similarities between the anonymous text and a text by a known author. Write a program which tabulates the occurrences of each article ("a", "an", and "the"), each adverb (check for "ly"), and of each mark of punctuation (".", ",", "!", "?", ";", ":").

24. Create bizarre "sentences" by having the computer print the words of a real sentence in reverse order. Your program should NOT reverse the order of the letters in each word.

25. Last night you were informed that your aunt had left you several million dollars. You decide to start your own corporation. In the tradition of DEC, GTE, RCA, IBM, and other great corporate conglomerates, you want your corporate name to be composed of as many initials as you like, each standing for a word (e.g., Radio Corporation of America becomes RCA). Write a program which accepts up to ten words and then prints a block of letters composed of the first letters of each word. For example, given "WE AWAIT SILENT TRYSTERO'S EMPIRE", the program should return "WASTE".

26. Write a program which prints a triangle made up of parts of the word "triangle". The triangle should be obtuse, and the program should ask for its height, how far to indent the bottom edge, and where the bottom edge ends.

```
>RUN
A,B,AND C? 18,24,36
 T
  RI
   AN
    NGL
     GLET
      ETRI
       TRIAN
        RIANGL
         ANGLET
          NGLETRI
           GLETRIAN
            ETRIANGL
             TRIANGLET
              RIANGLETRI
               ANGLETRIAN
                NGLETRIANGL
                 GLETRIANGLET
                  ETRIANGLETRI

READY
>
```

27. Enter a positive integer N$ as it would be expressed in binary form. That is, enter a string of ones and zeros. Have the computer print the equivalent of N$ as it is expressed in the decimal system.

9 TRS-80

SEQUENTIAL FILES

A computer file is analagous to a filing cabinet which stores information that can be recalled and cross referenced. As such, the computer file provides the means for storing large quantities of data indefinitely.

The computer utilizes two different file types: sequential and random-access. The sequential file is best adapted to situations requiring data to be recalled in the same order as it was originally stored in the file. Proceeding line-by-line from the beginning, the computer reads the file sequentially until all the desired information has been retrieved. If information is to be retrieved from a random location in the file (for example, a single entry in a mailing list), random-access files are better suited. Since they are more difficult to use, random-access files will be discussed separately in the next chapter.

It is suggested that before proceeding to learn the use of files, the programmer should first read Appendix B in order to become familiar with the special aspects of Disk BASIC.

OPEN

The OPEN statement establishes a line of communication between a program and a file and prepares the file for use. The OPEN statement must include the name of a file, and a channel designator; it also must specify the mode of access desired. A file name is a unique label used by the computer to identify each file and program stored on a disk. A channel designator is an integer from 1 to 15, and not larger than the number of files specified when the system was initialized. It indicates the channel to be used as a line of communication between the program and the file.

The four modes of access are:

O: Sequential Output. The computer will output data to the file starting at the beginning. If the file does not already exist, it will automatically be created, otherwise the new data will be *written over any previously existing data* stored in the file.

I: Sequential Input. The computer will input data from the file to the computer starting at the beginning. If the file does not already exist, it will print FILE NOT FOUND.

E: Sequential Output at End of File. The data will be output from the computer and appended to the end of the file. Previously stored data will be added to, not lost. If it does not already exist, the file will be created.

R: Random Input and Output. This option is discussed in Chapter 10.

The general format for the OPEN statement is:

OPEN "<mode>", <channel>, "<file name>"

It is important to note that the mode and file name must be enclosed in quotation marks. For example,

10 OPEN "I", 2, "PAYROLL/TXT"

will open a file named PAYROLL/TXT for sequential input on channel 2. Remember that files and programs must not have the same name.

CLOSE

Any file previously opened must be closed. This procedure is necessary in order to break the line of communication between a program and a file that was originally established by the OPEN command. A file is closed by using the command CLOSE followed by the channel designator that was specified when the file was opened. For example,

100 CLOSE 2

will close the file previously opened on channel two. Closing a file insures that all its information is properly retained. One should never remove a disk from a drive on which files are open. There is no way to guarantee that all of the data has been written to the file until it is closed, thus removing a disk prematurely may result in loss of data.

PRINT

While the OPEN statement establishes a line of communication between a program and a file, the PRINT# command is used to place data in the file. Its form is:

PRINT #<channel>, <variable>; ","; <variable> . . .

Information contained in the variables mentioned in the PRINT# statement will be placed in the file associated with the specified channel. It is necessary to place commas within quotation marks between the variables so that they too will be placed in the file. The commas act as markers so that the computer can tell the different items of data apart when reading them from the file.

PROGRAM 9.1

This program, named CREATE/BAS, opens a sequential file named WORK/TXT on the disk in drive one. In it are stored the names of four employees, their hourly wages and the number of hours they have worked. Note the structure of line 60.

```
1 REM      N$ = EMPLOYEE NAME
2 REM      W = WAGE
3 REM      H = HOURS WORKED
4 REM
5 REM
10 OPEN "O",1,"WORK/TXT:1"
20 FOR X = 1 TO 4
30     INPUT "NAME";N$
40     INPUT "WAGE";W
50     INPUT "HOURS WORKED";H
60     PRINT #1, N$;",";W;",";H
70     PRINT
80 NEXT X
90 CLOSE 1
READY
>RUN
NAME? LESTER WATERS
WAGE? 4.45
HOURS WORKED? 39

NAME? JULIE COOK
WAGE? 4.75
HOURS WORKED? 42

NAME? ELI HUROWITZ
WAGE? 5.10
HOURS WORKED? 36.75

NAME? DIANE BARRY
WAGE? 4.95
HOURS WORKED? 27.5

READY
>
```

REVIEW

1. Write a program named CALENDAR/BAS that will create the sequential file MONTHS/TXT containing the names of the months of the year.

INPUT

The INPUT# statement is used to read information from a sequential file. Its format is similar to the PRINT# statement.

INPUT #<channel>, <variable>, <variable> . . .

Note that the commas between the variable names mentioned in the INPUT statement are not enclosed in quotation marks. It is necessary that the order in which the variables are listed in the INPUT# statement be the same as the order of the PRINT# statement that created the file. For example, a program that reads the data from WORK/TXT created by Program 9.1 would have to input the data in the order N$, W, H. After the file has been closed the same channel designator need not be used to access it at a later time. For example, a program accessing the file created by Program 9.1 might use channel 3.

PROGRAM 9.2

This program, named SHOW/BAS, will open the file WORK/TXT created by Program 9.1 and print the names and hours worked for the four employees.

```
1 REM     N$ = EMPLOYEE NAME
2 REM     W = WAGE
3 REM     H = HOURS WORKED
4 REM
5 REM
10 OPEN "I",2,"WORK/TXT:1"
20 PRINT "NAME","HOURS WORKED"
30 FOR X = 1 TO 4
40     INPUT #2, N$,W,H
50     PRINT N$,H
60 NEXT X
70 CLOSE 1
READY
>RUN
NAME               HOURS WORKED
LESTER WATERS      39
JULIE COOK         42
ELI HUROWITZ       36.75
DIANE BARRY        27.5
READY
>
```

9.4

Note that line 10 specifies the access mode as "I" because the program will input data from the file to the computer.

The data in the file WORK/TXT appears as follows:

LESTER WATERS, 4.45 , 39
JULIE COOK, 4.75 , 42
ELI HUROWITZ, 5.1 , 36.75
DIANE BARRY, 4.95 , 27.5

Notice that the variable W is read in the input line but is not printed. The computer has an internal pointer that indicates the next item of information that is to be transferred from the file by the INPUT# statement. When the INPUT# statement is executed, the pointer is moved across the data line as each item is read. To insure that the data in the file is read in the correct sequence, it is important that all of the necessary variables be included in the INPUT# statement, even if some of them are not used by the program.

REVIEW

2. Write a program named RETRIEVE/BAS that will retrieve the name of a selected month of the year from the file MONTHS/TXT.

Updating Sequential Files

Specifying the (E)xtend mode allows the user to append new information to the end of an existing file. When an OPEN command is executed with either the (O)utput or the (I)nput mode, the computer opens the file and prepares either to write to it or read from it starting at the beginning of the file. If a programmer uses the (O)utput mode, the new information added will be written over that which was at the beginning of the file, thus destroying the old information. To avoid this loss of data, the "E" mode instructs the computer to write new information at the end of the file.

PROGRAM 9.3

This program, named UPDATE/BAS, will update the old WORK/TXT file created by Program 9.1 so that it includes information on two new employees just hired.

```
1 REM     N$ = EMPLOYEE NAME
2 REM     W = WAGE
3 REM     H = HOURS WORKED
4 REM
5 REM
10 OPEN "E",1,"WORK/TXT:1"
20 FOR X = 1 TO 2
30      INPUT "NAME";N$
40      INPUT "WAGE";W
50      INPUT "HOURS WORKED";H
60      PRINT #1, N$;",";W;",";H
70      PRINT
80 NEXT X
90 CLOSE 1
READY
>RUN
NAME? ERMA MCCONNELL
WAGE? 4.60
HOURS WORKED? 44.25

NAME? JEREMY LEADER
WAGE? 4.80
HOURS WORKED? 41.5

READY
>
```

After changing the FOR. . .NEXT loop in Program 9.2 the program can be re-run to show that the new information is now in the file WORK/TXT.

```
>RUN
NAME             HOURS WORKED
LESTER WATERS    39
JULIE COOK       42
ELI HUROWITZ     36.75
DIANE BARRY      27.5
ERMA MCCONNELL   44.25
JEREMY LEADER    41.5
READY
>
```

There is no single command that will remove or alter outdated information in a sequential file. To change such a file, the information to be kept must be transferred to a new file along with the new or corrected information. After the transfer, the old file can be deleted and the new file given an appropriate name.

PROGRAM 9.4

When an employee retires, this program named REMOVE/BAS will remove the employee's name from the file WORK/TXT. All of the data is read sequentially from WORK/TXT and the information that is to be retained is placed in the file WORK/TMP. After the program has finished, the programmer can delete the old WORK/TXT and rename WORK/TMP as WORK/TXT by using the RENAME command.

```
1 REM    N$ = EMPLOYEE NAME
2 REM    W = WAGE
3 REM    H = HOURS WORKED
4 REM    R$ = RETIRED EMPLOYEE'S NAME
5 REM
6 REM
10 INPUT "WHO HAS RETIRED";R$
20 OPEN "I",1,"WORK/TXT:1"
30 OPEN "O",2,"WORK/TMP:1"
40 FOR X = 1 TO 6
50    INPUT #1, N$,W,H
60    IF N$ = R$ THEN 80
70    PRINT #2, N$;",";W;",";H
80 NEXT X
90 CLOSE 1,2
100 PRINT "THE INFORMATION ON ";R$;" HAS BEEN REMOVED."
READY
>RUN
WHO HAS RETIRED? JEREMY LEADER
THE INFORMATION ON JEREMY LEADER HAS BEEN REMOVED.
READY
>CMD"S"
TRSDOS Ready
KILL WORK/TXT
Killing WORK/TXT
TRSDOS Ready
RENAME WORK/TMP WORK/TXT
WORK/TMP ----> WORK/TXT
TRSDOS Ready
BASIC
```

This program works well in this limited example, but the technique it uses is not always practical. The FOR. . .NEXT loop between lines 40 and 80 prevents the program from attempting to read past the end of the data file. However, this method was used because the length of the file WORK/TXT was known. Otherwise, a loop using a GOTO statement must be used to insure that the entire file is read. The file will then be sequentially read until the program comes to the file's end. At this point an INPUT PAST END error will occur, and the program will be halted. If this occurs, files will be left open and important data may be lost. To prevent this error, the EOF function is used.

EOF

The EOF function has the form

$$EOF (<channel>)$$

It returns a logical true (-1) when the end of the file has been reached, otherwise a logical false (0) is returned.

PROGRAM 9.5

This program, named REMOVE2/BAS, is a revision of Program 9.4 which allows the file WORK/TXT to be of any length.

```
1 REM    N$ = EMPLOYEE NAME
2 REM    W = WAGE
3 REM    H = HOURS WORKED
4 REM    R$ = RETIRED EMPLOYEE'S NAME
5 REM    T = FLAG TO TEST FOR DATA
6 REM
7 REM
10 T = 0
20 INPUT "WHO HAS RETIRED";R$
30 OPEN "I",1,"WORK/TXT:1"
40 OPEN "O",2,"WORK/TMP:1"
50 IF EOF(1) THEN 90
60    INPUT #1, N$,W,H
70    IF N$ = R$
          THEN T = -1
          ELSE PRINT #2, N$;",";W;",";H
80 GOTO 50
90 CLOSE 1,2
100 IF T = -1
       THEN PRINT "THE INFORMATION ON ";R$;" HAS BEEN REMOVED."
       ELSE PRINT "THERE IS NO ";R$;" ON THE PAYROLL."
READY
>RUN
WHO HAS RETIRED? SANDRA COOK
THERE IS NO SANDRA COOK ON THE PAYROLL.
READY
>
```

Program 9.5 demonstrates two major improvements over Program 9.4. First, the program informs the user if a name has been entered that is not in the file. The variable T is used as an indicator. If the name is in the file, T becomes -1; if not, it remains 0. Second, the EOF function and a GOTO loop are utilized to read the entire file. This technique is recommended for reading most sequential files.

LINE INPUT

Since the files created up to this point use commas to separate data, they cannot be used to store data that contains embedded commas. For example, a text file that contains a letter would probably have many commas used for punctuation. Fortunately, there is another method for separating data within a file that does not use commas. The computer stores the carriage return struck at the end of an input line in a file. Therefore, carriage returns can be employed to separate data so long as the data is input to the file a line at a time. This requires that the data be entered into the file using only a single variable. For example,

20 PRINT A$

A$ may contain embedded commas since a carriage return will separate each entry of A$ from the previous entry.

When inputting data from the keyboard that contains embedded commas the INPUT statement cannot be used since it recognizes all commas as data separators. Instead, the LINE INPUT statement is used which allows data containing embedded commas to be used. Its form is:

LINE INPUT <string variable>

PROGRAM 9.6

This program, named LETTER/BAS, can be used to build a series of files containing form letters used by a publishing company. Each file has a name corresponding to the type of letter it contains.

```
1 REM    L$ = FORM LETTER
2 REM    N = NUMBER OF LINES IN LETTER
3 REM    I$ = INPUT TEXT
4 REM
5 REM
10 CLEAR 150
20 INPUT "WHICH LETTER WILL THIS BE"; L$
30 L$ = L$ + "/TXT:1"
40 OPEN "O",1,L$
50 INPUT "HOW MANY LINES WILL THIS BE"; N
60 FOR L = 1 TO N
70     LINE INPUT I$
80     PRINT #1, I$
90 NEXT L
100 CLOSE 1
READY
>RUN
WHICH LETTER WILL THIS BE? REJECT
HOW MANY LINES WILL THIS BE? 6
     THANK YOU FOR YOUR MANUSCRIPT, "BELLING THE MOUSE". IT
WAS VERY GOOD, BUT WE ALREADY HAVE OVER TWO HUNDRED WORKS WITH
THAT TITLE. WE ARE SORRY, BUT YOUR MATERIAL DOES NOT FILL OUR
CURRENT NEEDS.

                         FILTHY RAG PUBLISHERS
READY
>
```

LINE INPUT

When a file using carriage returns rather than commas is read, the LINE INPUT# statement rather than the INPUT# statement must be used, since LINE INPUT# does not recognize commas as data separators. Instead, it will read data until a carriage return or the 255th character is reached. Its general form is

LINE INPUT # <channel>, <string variable>

PROGRAM 9.7

This program, named MAIL/BAS, will read one of several form letters and personalize it for mailing to several people.

```
1 REM     N = NUMBER OF LETTERS
2 REM     N$() = RECIPIENT'S NAME
3 REM     L$ = FORM LETTER
4 REM
5 REM
100 REM     INPUT DATA
110 CLEAR 250
120 INPUT "WHICH LETTER";L$
130 L$ = L$ + "/TXT:1"
140 INPUT "HOW MANY RECIPIENTS";N
150 DIM N$(N)
160 FOR A = 1 TO N
170     PRINT "RECIPIENT #";A;
180     INPUT N$(A)
190 NEXT A
200 REM
210 REM     PRODUCE LETTERS
220 FOR B = 1 TO N
230     PRINT
240     OPEN "I",1,L$
250     PRINT "DEAR ";N$(B);","
260     IF EOF(1) THEN 300
270        LINE INPUT #1, A$
280        PRINT A$
290     GOTO 260
300     CLOSE 1
310     PRINT
320 NEXT B
READY
>RUN
WHICH LETTER? REJECT
HOW MANY RECIPIENTS? 2
RECIPIENT # 1 ? MR. STEINBECK
RECIPIENT # 2 ? MS. CHRISTIE

DEAR MR. STEINBECK,
     THANK YOU FOR YOUR MANUSCRIPT, "BELLING THE MOUSE".  IT
WAS VERY GOOD, BUT WE ALREADY HAVE OVER TWO HUNDRED WORKS WITH
THAT TITLE.  WE ARE SORRY, BUT YOUR MATERIAL DOES NOT FILL OUR
CURRENT NEEDS.

                         FILTHY RAG PUBLISHERS


DEAR MS. CHRISTIE,
     THANK YOU FOR YOUR MANUSCRIPT, "BELLING THE MOUSE".  IT
WAS VERY GOOD, BUT WE ALREADY HAVE OVER TWO HUNDRED WORKS WITH
THAT TITLE.  WE ARE SORRY, BUT YOUR MATERIAL DOES NOT FILL OUR
CURRENT NEEDS.

                         FILTHY RAG PUBLISHERS


READY
>
```

```
>RUN
WHICH LETTER? REJECT
HOW MANY RECIPIENTS? 2
RECIPIENT # 1 ? MR. STEINBECK
RECIPIENT # 2 ? MS. CHRISTIE

DEAR MR. STEINBECK,
      THANK YOU FOR YOUR MANUSCRIPT, "BELLING THE MOUSE". IT
WAS VERY GOOD, BUT WE ALREADY HAVE OVER TWO HUNDRED WORKS WITH
THAT TITLE. WE ARE SORRY, BUT YOUR MATERIAL DOES NOT FILL OUR
CURRENT NEEDS.

                      FILTHY RAG PUBLISHERS

DEAR MS. CHRISTIE,
      THANK YOU FOR YOUR MANUSCRIPT, "BELLING THE MOUSE". IT
WAS VERY GOOD, BUT WE ALREADY HAVE OVER TWO HUNDRED WORKS WITH
THAT TITLE. WE ARE SORRY, BUT YOUR MATERIAL DOES NOT FILL OUR
CURRENT NEEDS.

                      FILTHY RAG PUBLISHERS
READY
>
```

Demonstration Programs

The following programs illustrate applications for the material covered in this chapter. They consist of a series of examples concerning the record keeping process of a sporting goods manufacturer.

PROGRAM 9.8

This program, named ACME/BAS, will produce a file named SALES/TXT that contains the sales records of all salespeople working for the Acme Sporting Goods Company. Each salesperson sells baseball bats, balls and helmets.

```
1 REM      P = NUMBER OF SALESPERSONS
2 REM      N$ = NAME OF SALESPERSON
3 REM      B1,B2,H = BATS, BALLS AND HELMETS SOLD
4 REM
5 REM
10 OPEN "O",1,"SALES/TXT:1"
20 INPUT "HOW MANY SALESPERSONS DO YOU HAVE";P
30 PRINT
40 FOR E = 1 TO P
50     INPUT "SALESPERSON";N$
60     INPUT "BATS SOLD";B1
70     INPUT "BALLS SOLD";B2
80     INPUT "HELMETS SOLD";H
90     PRINT #1, N$;",";B1;",";B2;",";H
100    PRINT
110 NEXT E
120 CLOSE 1
130 PRINT "THE INFORMATION IS IN THE FILE."
READY
>RUN
HOW MANY SALESPERSONS DO YOU HAVE? 5

SALESPERSON? AUSTIN WILMERDING
BATS SOLD? 32
BALLS SOLD? 17
HELMETS SOLD? 23

SALESPERSON? DON KIDDER
BATS SOLD? 4
BALLS SOLD? 10
HELMETS SOLD? 5

SALESPERSON? FIONA L'HUILLIER
BATS SOLD? 29
BALLS SOLD? 34
HELMETS SOLD? 52

SALESPERSON? ROBERT OAKLEY
BATS SOLD? 45
BALLS SOLD? 17
HELMETS SOLD? 39

SALESPERSON? CYNTHIA GARFILED
BATS SOLD? 26
BALLS SOLD? 32
HELMETS SOLD? 12

THE INFORMATION IS IN THE FILE.
READY
>
```

PROGRAM 9.9

This program, named ACME2/BAS, will update the sales records for an individual salesperson.

```
1 REM     N$ = NAME OF SALESPERSON
2 REM     B1,B2,H = BATS, BALLS AND HELMETS SOLD
3 REM     C$ = PERSON WHOSE SALES HAVE CHANGED
4 REM
5 REM
10 OPEN "I",1,"SALES/TXT:1"
20 OPEN "O",2,"SALES/TMP:1"
30 INPUT "WHOSE SALES HAVE CHANGED";C$
40 IF EOF(1) THEN 90
50    INPUT #1, N$,B1,B2,H
60    IF N$ = C$ THEN INPUT "NEW SALES";B1,B2,H
70    PRINT #2, N$;",";B1;",";B2;",";H
80 GOTO 40
90 CLOSE 1,2
100 PRINT C$;"'S RECORDS HAVE BEEN UPDATED."
110 PRINT "PLEASE KILL 'SALES/TXT' AND RENAME 'SALES/TMP'";
120 PRINT " AS 'SALES/TXT'."
READY
>RUN
WHOSE SALES HAVE CHANGED? CYNTHIA GARFILED
NEW SALES? 30,38,22
CYNTHIA GARFILED'S RECORDS HAVE BEEN UPDATED.
PLEASE KILL 'SALES/TXT' AND RENAME 'SALES/MP' AS 'SALES/TXT'.
READY
>CMD"S"
TRSDOS Ready
KILL WORK/TXT
Killing WORK/TXT
TRSDOS Ready
RENAME WORK/TMP WORK/TXT
WORK/TMP ----> WORK/TXT
TRSDOS Ready
BASIC
```

When the computer has found the right salesperson (at line 60) it prompts the user for data from the keyboard. The new information is then placed in the new file SALES/TMP at line 70.

PROGRAM 9.10

This program, named ACME3/BAS, will write a personalized letter of congratulations to all salespersons who have sold 75 units or more.

```
1 REM     N$ = NAME OF SALESPERSON
2 REM     B1,B2,H = BATS, BALLS AND HELMETS SOLD
3 REM     T = INDICATOR TO SEE IF ANYONE QUALIFIED
4 REM
5 REM
10 OPEN "I",1,"SALES/TXT:1"
20 T = 0
30 IF EOF(1) THEN 160
40    INPUT #1, N$,B1,B2,H
50    IF B1 + B2 + H >= 75 THEN GOSUB 80
60 GOTO 30
70 PRINT
80 PRINT "DEAR ";N$;","
90 PRINT "      CONGRATULATIONS, YOU ARE ONE OF OUR TOP"
100 PRINT "SALESPERSONS.  YOUR BONUS CHECK IS IN THE MAIL."
110 PRINT
120 PRINT "                              YOUR BOSS"
130 PRINT
140 T = T + 1
150 RETURN
160 CLOSE 1
170 IF T <> 0
        THEN PRINT T;"SALESPERSONS WILL RECEIVE A BONUS."
        ELSE PRINT "NO ONE SOLD ENOUGH.  THEY NEED A PEP TALK."
READY
>RUN
DEAR FIONA L'HUILLIER,
      CONGRATULATIONS, YOU ARE ONE OF OUR TOP
SALESPERSONS.  YOUR BONUS CHECK IS IN THE MAIL.

                    YOUR BOSS

DEAR ROBERT OAKLEY,
      CONGRATULATIONS, YOU ARE ONE OF OUR TOP
SALESPERSONS.  YOUR BONUS CHECK IS IN THE MAIL.

                    YOUR BOSS

DEAR CYNTHIA GARFILED,
      CONGRATULATIONS, YOU ARE ONE OF OUR TOP
SALESPERSONS.  YOUR BONUS CHECK IS IN THE MAIL.

                    YOUR BOSS

 3 SALESPERSONS WILL RECEIVE A BONUS.
READY
>
```

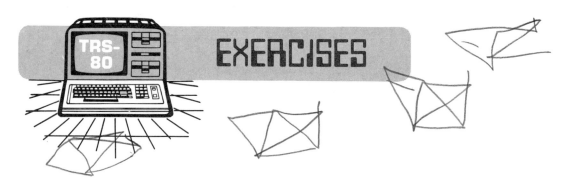

 1. Store 50 random numbers between 0 and 20 in a sequential file. Use a second program to retrieve the numbers, add them, and print the sum.

2. Store in a sequential file the names and prices of five different desserts served at MADGE'S DINER. With a second program add two additional desserts. Have a third program retrieve and print the information.

3. (a) Establish a sequential file name SEQ which contains the members of the following sequence: 1001, 1002, 1003, . . . 1128.
   (b) Write a program to retrieve any member of the sequence from SEQ and print it when its place in the sequence (i.e. third number, eighth number, etc.) is inputted.

4. Store ten different first names of friends in a sequential file. A second program is to print all the names in the file which begin with the letters D, E, F, G and H or a message if none are found.

5. (a) Write a program that will create a sequential file FRAT which contains the names, fraternities, and ages of thirty college students.
   (b) Write a program that will access FRAT and create a Sequential file SIGMA which contains the names and ages of only students who live in Sigma Chi.
   (c) Write a program that accesses the file FRAT and randomly selects twenty-five

students for seats in a classroom of five rows, five seats to a row. Have the computer print the seating plan for the class, placing each student's name at the correct seat location.

6. (a) Create a sequential payroll file called PAY to store each of ten person's names (last name first), his or her hourly pay rate, the number of dependents, and deductions for medical and life insurance for each week. Supply appropriate data.
   (b) Use PAY to prepare the payroll data sheet (supply the number of hours (H) each person worked during the week). The sheet should list the name, hours worked, gross pay, three deductions, and net pay. Assume a tax rate of 25%, with 2% being subtracted from this rate for each dependent.

```
>RUN
MENACE DENNIS
------------------------
HOURS WORKED                          40
GROSS PAY:                         $  40
TAX:                               $  10
MEDICAL INSURANCE:                 $   2
LIFE INSURANCE:                    $  14
NET:                               $  27

BEAVER LEAVEITTO
------------------------
HOURS WORKED                        37.1
GROSS PAY:                         $  83.48
TAX:                               $  20.87
MEDICAL INSURANCE:                 $   1
LIFE INSURANCE:                    $  17
NET:                               $  60.61
```

9.17

7. (a) Two persons, NIT and WIT, measured the Fahrenheit temperature (F) outside on Feb. 12 at various times (T) during a ten hour period. Their results are recorded here. Set up two sequential files, one for each person's data, naming each file after that person.

NIT	T	F	WIT	T	F
	0.0	18.1		1.0	20.9
	2.1	24.0		1.9	23.3
	3.8	27.2		3.5	26.1
	6.0	29.3		6.0	28.8
	8.0	26.6		8.2	26.2
	9.0	16.1		10.0	16.0

(b) Write a program that will merge the two files into one sequential file named MERGE. The times should be sequentially in order. However, when a value of (T) occurs both in NIT and WIT, the average of the two values of (F) should be placed in MERGE.

(c) Retrieve and print the contents of MERGE.

8. There are twenty seats (numbered 1-20) in a classroom which will be used to administer the College Board Examination. The computer is to select seats randomly for each student taking the examination and store the student's name in a Sequential file named SEATS.

(a) Write a program that will create and zero (place a blank space in for each name) the Sequential file SEATS.

(b) Write a program that will randomly assign a seat to each of twenty students whose names are in a data statement and then store the name in SEATS with the appropriate seat number. Make sure no repeats occur.

(c) List the contents of the file SEATS.

9. (a) The Drama Club has decided to use the computer to print out tickets for a play it will perform in the school's auditorium. To reserve a seat a student runs a program called DRAMA, and types in the name and the row and seat number he would like. There are ten rows with five seats to a row. His ticket will appear as below. Write the program DRAMA and open a file named SHOW which stores the seat assignments. Make sure that a seat may not be chosen more than once.

```
DRAMA SHOW CLUB
MICHAEL JONES HAS
RESERVED ROW 4
SEAT 3 FOR
JULY 4, 1983
```

(b) Write a program which will list the empty seats giving their row and seat numbers.

(c) Write a program that will print a seating plan giving the names of the seat holders in their correct location.

RANDOM-ACCESS FILES

A random-access file is structured like a collection of drawers in a filing cabinet, each holding a block of data that may be accessed individually. This filing system offers advantages to the one "drawer" structure of sequential files. To read the last line of data in a sequential file, every line of data preceding it must be read in sequence. However, any "drawer" in a random-access file can be opened without opening any of the others. Updating a random-access file is easier than updating a sequential file since the contents of one "drawer" can be updated without accessing the rest of the file. Unlike a sequential file, which is opened for a specific mode, a random-access file can be both written to and read from simultaneously.

In the random-access file each "drawer", called a record, consists of space reserved to store information. The length of a record, i.e. the amount of information it can hold, is specified when a random-access file is created. The user may define records to be of any length up to 256 characters, but all of the records within a given file must be of the same length.

A single record need not hold simply one item of data but many pieces, as long as they do not require more space than the specified size of the record.

To utilize the potential offered by random-access files, it is necessary to understand how the computer stores information. For file processing, the computer could have been designed to put each small item of information on the disk as soon as that information was made available. Since accesssing the disk is time consuming, however, it is more efficient to transfer information to the disk in complete records. This requires the computer to have a temporary storage space called a buffer, where information is stored until a record is complete.

With sequential files the user has no control over the interaction between the buffer and the disk. Instead, the computer automatically determines when the buffer is full and then transfers its contents to the disk. Random-access files, however, give the user complete control over both the structure of the buffer's contents and its transfer to the disk.

The process of transferring data between a program and a random-access file involves the following series of steps:

1. Using the OPEN statement, the file must be created, opened, and a buffer made ready to receive data.

2. Using the FIELD statement, the buffer must be partitioned to fit the structure of each record.

3. Data has to be transferred from the program to the buffer using the LSET and RSET commands.

4. Data has to be transferred from the buffer to the file using the PUT command.

5. To retrieve data from the file for use in the program, the GET command is used.

Each of these steps is presented separately and should be read carefully so that the reader understands how each interacts with the others.

OPEN

Like sequential files, random-access files use the OPEN statement. The format for opening random-access files is

$$\text{OPEN "R", <channel>, "<file name>", <record length>}$$

For example,

$$\text{20 OPEN "R", 3, "KAZOO", 50}$$

will open a file named KAZOO for random-access on channel three, with each record in the file containing fifty characters, and will assign it a buffer.

FIELD

Unlike sequential files, random-access files store all information as strings. This requires numeric data to be converted to strings before being stored. The commands used in performing these conversions are discussed later in this chapter.

After the OPEN statement assigns a buffer to a file, the FIELD statement is used to organize the buffer so that data can be sent through it from the program to the file and vice versa. The FIELD statement partitions the buffer into regions where each holds a string and is referenced by a specific string variable. Its simplest form is

$$\text{FIELD <channel>, <length> AS <string variable>}$$

For example,

$$10 \text{ OPEN "R", 2, "DATA", 50}$$
$$20 \text{ FIELD 2, 50 AS A\$}$$

After the file has been opened at line 10, the FIELD statement at line 20 reserves the entire fifty characters in the buffer for the string variable A$. It is possible to partition the buffer to hold more than one string.

$$20 \text{ FIELD 2, 20 AS A\$, 30 AS B\$}$$

will reserve the first twenty characters of the buffer for the contents of A$ and the last thirty characters for the contents of B$.

LSET and RSET

The FIELD statement reserves a certain number of spaces for string variables in a buffer, but it does not transfer the strings to the buffer. To do this, it is necessary to use the LSET and RSET commands. The form for both is

LSET
  or   <string variable defined in FIELD> = <string to be transferred to buffer>
RSET

For example,

$$20 \text{ FIELD 1, 24 AS N1\$}$$
$$30 \text{ LSET N1\$ = "TWENTY-FOUR CHARACTERS!!"}$$

or

$$20 \text{ FIELD 1, 24 AS N1\$}$$
$$30 \text{ RSET N1\$ = "TWENTY-FOUR CHARACTERS!!"}$$

Besides transferring strings to the buffer, these commands also change the strings to make sure that they properly fit the space allotted in the FIELD statement. For example, if N1$ contains 15 characters, 9 blank characters have to be added to bring the total to 24. If N1$ contains more than 24 characters, it must be truncated to 24. These operations are performed by either the LSET or RSET commands.

The LSET command left justifies a string by adding needed blank characters to the right end of the string. If N1$ contains 15 characters, LSET will add 9 blank characters on the right end. RSET justifies by adding the 9 blank characters on the left end. Both LSET and RSET will truncate excess characters from the right end of a string which is larger than the space specified in the FIELD statement.

PROGRAM 10.1

This program demonstrates how LSET and RSET change strings to ready them for storage in a random-access file.

```
10 OPEN "R",1,"SUNSET:1",30
20 FIELD 1, 5 AS A$, 10 AS B$, 5 AS C$, 10 AS D$
30 LSET A$ = "ABCDEFG"
40 LSET B$ = "ABCDEFG"
50 RSET C$ = "ABCDEFG"
60 RSET D$ = "ABCDEFG"
70 PRINT "THIS IS HOW THE 30 CHARACTERS APPEAR IN THE"
80 PRINT "BUFFER, EXCLUDING THE PARENTHESES:"
90 PRINT TAB(3);"A$";TAB(12);"B$";TAB(22);"C$";TAB(31);"D$"
100 PRINT "(";A$;")(";B$;")(";C$;")(";D$;")"
110 CLOSE 1
READY
>RUN
THIS IS HOW THE 30 CHARACTERS APPEAR IN THE
BUFFER, EXCLUDING THE PARENTHESES:
   A$         B$          C$          D$
(ABCDE)(ABCDEFG    )(ABCDE)(    ABCDEFG)
READY
>
```

Notice that the FIELD statement at line 20 has set aside 5 characters for A$, but since the string in line 30 is longer than 5 characters, the LSET command in line 30 has truncated the last two. Since 10 characters were set aside for B$, the LSET command in line 40 has added 3 spaces to the right of the string to make it 10 characters long. As only 5 spaces were allotted to C$, the RSET command in line 50 truncated the excess characters from the right. The RSET command in line 60 has added 3 spaces to the left of B$ so that it fills up the space allotted by the FIELD statement.

PUT

The LSET and RSET commands only transfer information from the program to the buffer, but do not transfer the contents of the buffer to the disk. The PUT statement is used to transfer the data in the buffer to a record in the file. Each record is numbered sequentially, from one to the number of records in the file.

The form of the PUT statement is:

PUT <channel>, <record number>

If the record number is not specified, the data is transferred to the record immediately following the last record accessed by the program. For example,

20 PUT 2, 4

instructs the computer to transfer the contents of the buffer to the fourth record of the file open on channel 2. It is important to note that if the next PUT statement executed after the above example does not specify a record number, the data in the buffer will be transferred to the fifth record in the file.

PROGRAM 10.2

This program, named PEOPLE/BAS, creates the file ADDRESS/TXT and will allow the names and addresses for five people to be placed in the file.

```
1 REM    N$,N1$ = NAME (15 CHARACTERS)
2 REM    A$,A1$ = ADDRESS (25 CHARACTERS)
3 REM
4 REM
10   CLEAR 100
20   OPEN "R",1,"ADDRESS/TXT:1",40
30   FIELD 1, 15 AS N$, 25 AS A$
40   FOR X = 1 TO 5
50      INPUT "NAME";N1$
60      INPUT "ADDRESS";A1$
70      LSET N$ = N1$
80      LSET A$ = A1$
90      PUT 1
100     PRINT
110 NEXT X
120 CLOSE 1
READY
>RUN
NAME? C. MAHAN
ADDRESS? 186 BLUE SPRUCE DR.

NAME? G. MANDEL
ADDRESS? 338 OPOSSUM AVE.

NAME? R. MACPHERSON
ADDRESS? 116 FRANKLIN CORNER RD.

NAME? C. JENKINS
ADDRESS? 12 NEWPORT RD.

NAME? D. RIMMER
ADDRESS? 1 SANDBURG DR.

READY
>
```

The variable names used in the INPUT statements and in the FIELD statements must not be the same if the program is to transfer data correctly to the file.

REVIEW

1. Write a program, named CALEN2/BAS, that will create a random-access file MONTHS/TXT and will place the name of each month of the year in order in a separate record.

GET a clue George!

The GET statement performs the opposite function of the PUT statement. It is used to transfer information in a record on the disk to the buffer associated with the file. Again, a FIELD statement must be employed in order to partition the buffer for the data that is to be transferred into it. The form of the GET statement is:

GET <channel>, <record number>

Like the PUT statement, the GET statement will transfer data from the record following the last record accessed if no record number is specified. For example,

20 GET 3, 12

will transfer the contents of record number 12 to the buffer associated with channel 3.

PROGRAM 10.3

This program, named PEOPLE2/BAS, will retrieve and print the name and address of any person stored in the file ADDRESS/TXT.

```
1 REM    N$ = NAME (15 CHARACTERS)
2 REM    A$ = ADDRESS (25 CHARACTERS)
3 REM    R = RECORD NUMBER
4 REM
5 REM
10 PRINT "ENTER A NEGATIVE NUMBER TO STOP THE PROGRAM"
20 OPEN "R",2,"ADDRESS/TXT:1",40
30 FIELD 2, 15 AS N$, 25 AS A$
40 INPUT "WHICH RECORD";R
50    IF R < 0 THEN 100
60    GET 2, R
70    PRINT N$ : PRINT A$
80    PRINT
90 GOTO 40
100 CLOSE 2
READY
```

```
>RUN
ENTER A NEGATIVE NUMBER TO STOP THE PROGRAM
WHICH RECORD? 3
R. MACPHERSON
116 FRANKLIN CORNER RD.

WHICH RECORD? 1
C. MAHAN
186 BLUE SPRUCE DR.

WHICH RECORD? -1
READY
>
```

REVIEW

2. Write a program, named LOOKUP/BAS, that will retrieve the name of a selected month from the file MONTHS/TXT.

Converting Numbers Into Strings

Since random-access files can only store strings, it is necessary to convert numeric data into a string before it is stored. The following functions perform this operation:

Function	Operation
N$ = MKI$(N%)	Converts an integer (N%) into a two character string (N$).
N$ = MKS$(N!)	Converts a single-precision number (N!) into a four character string (N$).
N$ = MKD$(N#)	Converts a double-precision number (N#) into an eight character string (N$).

Converting Strings Into Numbers

When converted numeric data is retrieved from a random-access file, it may be converted back to numeric data using the following functions:

Function	Operation
N% = CVI(N$)	Converts a two character string (N$) into an integer (N%).
N! = CVS(N$)	Converts a four character string (N$) into a single-precision number (N!).
N# = CVD(N$)	Converts an eight character string (N$) into a double-precision number (N#).

LOC and LOF

The LOC and LOF functions are useful when working with random-access files. The LOC function returns the record number used in the last GET or PUT executed on a particular channel. The statement

$$N = LOC(3)$$

will assign to the variable N the record number used in the last GET or PUT operation performed on channel 3. The LOC function will return zero until a GET or PUT is executed.

The LOF function returns the length of a file currently open on a particular channel, that is, the number of records contained in that file. The statement

$$T = LOF(2)$$

will assign to the variable T the number of records contained in the file currently open on channel 2. This value is useful in determining where a new record should be PUT when adding new information to a previously created file.

PROGRAM 10.4

This program illustrates LOC and LOF.

```
1 REM    N,Q = NUMBER OF RECORDS IN FILE
2 REM    B$,D$ = DATA (32 CHARACTERS)
3 REM
4 REM
10   REM    CREATE FILE 'STUFF' AND ALLOW USER TO
20   REM    PLACE DATA IN THAT FILE
30   OPEN "R", 1, "STUFF:1", 32
40   FIELD 1, 32 AS B$
50   INPUT "HOW MANY RECORDS DO YOU WANT TO PLACE IN THE FILE";N
60   FOR T = 1 TO N
70      INPUT "ENTER DATA"; D$
80      LSET B$ = D$ : PUT 1, T
90      PRINT "THAT WAS PLACED IN RECORD"; LOC(1); "OF STUFF"
100 NEXT T
110 CLOSE 1 : PRINT
180 REM
190 REM
200 REM    READ FILE 'STUFF'
210 OPEN "R", 3, "STUFF:1", 32
220 FIELD 3, 32 AS B$ : Q = LOF(3)
230 PRINT "THE FILE STUFF CONTAINS"; Q; "RECORDS."
240 FOR T = 1 TO Q
250     GET 3
260     PRINT "RECORD"; LOC(3); "CONTAINS:"
270     PRINT B$
280 NEXT T
290 CLOSE 3 : PRINT
READY
>RUN
HOW MANY RECORDS DO YOU WANT TO PLACE IN THE FILE? 3
ENTER DATA? HOW'S THIS FOR DATA?
THAT WAS PLACED IN RECORD 1 OF STUFF
ENTER DATA? O.K. LET'S PUT THIS IN # 2
THAT WAS PLACED IN RECORD 2 OF STUFF
ENTER DATA? THAT'S ALL FOLKS
THAT WAS PLACED IN RECORD 3 OF STUFF

THE FILE STUFF CONTAINS 3 RECORDS.
RECORD 1 CONTAINS:
HOW'S THIS FOR DATA?
RECORD 2 CONTAINS:
O.K. LET'S PUT THIS IN # 2
RECORD 3 CONTAINS:
THAT'S ALL FOLKS

READY
>
```

REVIEW

3. Write a program, named SIZE/BAS, that will determine the length of the file MONTHS/TXT and place that information in the first record of a new file called LENGTH/TXT.

Demonstration Programs

The following series of programs establishes a file named GRADES/TXT which contains the names and grades of a number of students and then demonstrates how the file can be used.

PROGRAM 10.5

This program, named SCHOOL/BAS, will store students' names and the course names and grades for four courses in which they are enrolled in a file named GRADES/TXT. In each case the student's I.D. number is used as the record number.

```
1 REM     N$,NM$ = STUDENT'S NAME (20 CHARACTERS)
2 REM     C$,C1$,C2$,C3$,C4$ = COURSE NAMES (20 CHARACTERS EACH)
3 REM     G,G1$,G2$,G3$,G4$ = GRADES (2 CHARACTERS EACH)
4 REM     ID = STUDENT'S ID NUMBER
5 REM
6 REM
10   CLEAR 250
20   OPEN "R",1,"GRADES/TXT:1",108
30   FIELD 1, 20 AS N$, 20 AS C1$, 2 AS G1$, 20 AS C2$,
          2 AS G2$, 20 AS C3$, 2 AS G3$, 20 AS C4$, 2 AS G4$
40   INPUT "NUMBER OF STUDENTS";S
50   FOR ID = 1 TO S
60      INPUT "STUDENT'S NAME";NM$ : LSET N$ = NM$
70      INPUT "COURSE NAME";C$ : LSET C1$ = C$
80      INPUT "GRADE";G : LSET G1$ = MKI$(G)
90      INPUT "COURSE NAME";C$ : LSET C2$ = C$
100     INPUT "GRADE";G : LSET G2$ = MKI$(G)
110     INPUT "COURSE NAME";C$ : LSET C3$ = C$
120     INPUT "GRADE";G : LSET G3$ = MKI$(G)
130     INPUT "COURSE NAME";C$ : LSET C4$ = C$
140     INPUT "GRADE";G : LSET G4$ = MKI$(G)
150     PRINT "THAT STUDENT HAS BEEN ASSIGNED ID #";ID
160     PUT 1
170     PRINT
180 NEXT ID
190 CLOSE 1
READY
```

```
>RUN
NUMBER OF STUDENTS? 10
STUDENT'S NAME? APRIL BARRY
COURSE NAME? ENGLISH
GRADE? 87
COURSE NAME? PSYCHOLOGY
GRADE? 83
COURSE NAME? ART HISTORY
GRADE? 96
COURSE NAME? EUROPEAN HISTORY
GRADE? 79
THAT STUDENT HAS BEEN ASSIGNED ID # 1

STUDENT'S NAME? DAVID GELLER
COURSE NAME? PHYSICS
GRADE? 82
COURSE NAME? CALCULUS
GRADE? 78
COURSE NAME? ENGLISH
GRADE? 80
COURSE NAME? DRAFTING
GRADE? 73
THAT STUDENT HAS BEEN ASSIGNED ID # 2
```

(A COMPLETE RUN IS NOT SHOWN.)

PROGRAM 10.6

This program, named REPORT/BAS, will read and print a particular student's grades and computed grade average. Note the use of LOF in line 60 to check for nonexistent I.D. numbers.

```
1 REM    N$,NM$ = STUDENT'S NAME (20 CHARACTERS)
2 REM    C$,C1$,C2$,C3$,C4$ = COURSE NAMES (20 CHARACTERS EACH)
3 REM    G,G1$,G2$,G3$,G4$ = GRADES (2 CHARACTERS EACH)
4 REM    ID = STUDENT'S ID NUMBER
5 REM
6 REM
10  PRINT "ENTER A NEGATIVE NUMBER TO STOP"
20  CLEAR 250
30  OPEN "R",1,"GRADES/TXT:1",108
40  FIELD 1, 20 AS N$, 20 AS C1$, 2 AS G1$, 20 AS C2$,
        2 AS G2$, 20 AS C3$, 2 AS G3$, 20 AS C4$, 2 AS G4$
50  INPUT "STUDENT'S ID#";ID
60    IF ID > LOF(1) THEN PRINT "BAD ID#" : GOTO 50
70    IF ID < 0 THEN 130
80    GET 1, ID
90    A = (CVI(G1$) + CVI(G2$) + CVI(G3$) + CVI(G4$))/4
100   PRINT TAB(5);CVI(G1$);TAB(10);CVI(G2$);TAB(15);CVI(G3$);
110   PRINT TAB(20);CVI(G4$);TAB(30);"AVE. =";A
120 GOTO 50
130 CLOSE 1
READY
```

```
>RUN
ENTER A NEGATIVE NUMBER TO STOP
STUDENT'S ID#? 7
      84    80    78    81          AVE. = 80.75
STUDENT'S ID#? 4
      83    76    82    90          AVE. = 82.75
STUDENT'S ID#? -1
READY
>
```

PROGRAM 10.7

This program, named CORRECT/BAS, will allow a teacher to correct a mistake in a student's grades.

```
1 REM    N$ = STUDENT'S NAME (20 CHARACTERS)
2 REM    C1$,C2$,C3$,C4$ = COURSE NAMES (20 CHARACTERS EACH)
3 REM    G,G1$,G2$,G3$,G4$ = GRADES (2 CHARACTERS EACH)
4 REM    ID = STUDENT'S ID NUMBER
5 REM
6 REM
10   PRINT "ENTER A NEGATIVE NUMBER TO STOP"
20   CLEAR 250
30   OPEN "R",1,"GRADES/TXT:1",108
40   FIELD 1, 20 AS N$, 20 AS C1$, 2 AS G1$, 20 AS C2$,
        2 AS G2$, 20 AS C3$, 2 AS G3$, 20 AS C4$, 2 AS G4$
50   INPUT "STUDENT'S ID#";ID
60      IF ID > LOF(1) THEN PRINT "INVALID ID#" : GOTO 50
70      IF ID < 0 THEN 210
80      GET 1, ID
90      PRINT "ENTER NEW GRADES"
100     PRINT C1$,
110     INPUT G : LSET G1$ = MKI$(G)
120     PRINT C2$,
130     INPUT G : LSET G2$ = MKI$(G)
140     PRINT C3$,
150     INPUT G : LSET G3$ = MKI$(G)
160     PRINT C4$,
170     INPUT G : LSET G4$ = MKI$(G)
180     PUT 1, ID
190     PRINT "THE RECORDS ON ";N$;" HAVE BEEN UPDATED."
200 GOTO 50
210 CLOSE 1
READY
```

```
>RUN
ENTER A NEGATIVE NUMBER TO STOP
STUDENT'S ID#? 5
ENTER NEW GRADES
PHYSICS                             ? 87
AMERICAN HISTORY                    ? 75
INDEPENDENT STUDY                   ? 78
STATISTICS                          ? 84
THE RECORDS ON LESTER WATERS        HAVE BEEN UPDATED.
STUDENT'S ID#? -1
READY
>
```

PROGRAM 10.8

This program, named NEWKIDS/BAS, allows new students to be added to the file by creating new records at the end of the file.

```
1 REM     N$,NM$ = STUDENT'S NAME (20 CHARACTERS)
2 REM     C$,C1$,C2$,C3$,C4$ = COURSE NAMES (20 CHARACTERS EACH)
3 REM     G,G1$,G2$,G3$,G4$ = GRADES (2 CHARACTERS EACH)
4 REM     ID = STUDENT'S ID NUMBER
5 REM
6 REM
10  CLEAR 250
20  OPEN "R",1,"GRADES/TXT:1",108
30  FIELD 1, 20 AS N$, 20 AS C1$, 2 AS G1$, 20 AS C2$,
        2 AS G2$, 20 AS C3$, 2 AS G3$, 20 AS C4$, 2 AS G4$
40  INPUT "NUMBER OF STUDENTS";S
50  FOR ID = LOF(1) + 1 TO LOF(1) + S
60      INPUT "STUDENT'S NAME";NM$ : LSET N$ = NM$
70      INPUT "COURSE NAME";C$ : LSET C1$ = C$
80      INPUT "GRADE";G : LSET G1$ = MKI$(G)
90      INPUT "COURSE NAME";C$ : LSET C2$ = C$
100     INPUT "GRADE";G : LSET G2$ = MKI$(G)
110     INPUT "COURSE NAME";C$ : LSET C3$ = C$
120     INPUT "GRADE";G : LSET G3$ = MKI$(G)
130     INPUT "COURSE NAME";C$ : LSET C4$ = C$
140     INPUT "GRADE";G : LSET G4$ = MKI$(G)
150     PRINT "THAT STUDENT HAS BEEN ASSIGNED ID #";ID
160     PUT 1, ID
170     PRINT
180 NEXT ID
190 CLOSE 1
READY
```

```
>RUN
NUMBER OF STUDENT'S? 2
STUDENT'S NAME? SHERRY FRENCH
COURSE NAME? ENGLISH
GRADE? 87
COURSE NAME? PHILOSPHY
GRADE? 83
COURSE NAME? ASTRONOMY
GRADE? 71
COURSE NAME? AMERICAN HISTORY
GRADE? 78
THAT STUDENT HAS BEEN ASSIGNED ID # 11

STUDENT'S NAME? LISA HUROWITZ
COURSE NAME? CHEMISTRY
GRADE? 81
COURSE NAME? STATISTICS
GRADE? 82
COURSE NAME? ENGLISH
GRADE? 77
COURSE NAME? BOTONY
GRADE? 78
THAT STUDENT HAS BEEN ASSIGNED ID # 12

READY
>
```

PROGRAM 10.9

This program, named EXTRA/BAS, creates a random-access file named ACTIVI-TY/TXT which will contain the extracurricular activities and athletic teams in which students are involved.

```
1 REM    A1$,A2$ = ACTIVITIES (20 CHARACTERS EACH)
2 REM    T$ = ATHLETIC TEAM (15 CHARACTERS)
3 REM    ID = STUDENT'S ID#
4 REM    I$ = INPUT
5 REM
6 REM
10  PRINT "ENTER STUDENT ID#, TWO ACTIVITIES AND ATHLETIC TEAM"
20  PRINT "ENTER A NEGATIVE NUMBER TO STOP"
30  CLEAR 250
40  OPEN "R",1,"ACTIVITY/TXT:1",55
50  FIELD 1, 20 AS A1$, 20 AS A2$, 15 AS T$
60  INPUT "ID#";ID
70     IF ID < 0 THEN 140
80     INPUT "FIRST ACTIVITY";I$ : LSET A1$ = I$
90     INPUT "SECOND ACTIVITY";I$ : LSET A2$ = I$
100    INPUT "ATHLETIC TEAM";I$ : LSET T$ = I$
110    PUT 1, ID
120    PRINT
130 GOTO 60
140 CLOSE 1
READY
>RUN
ENTER STUDENT ID#, TWO ACTIVITIES AND ATHLETIC TEAM
ENTER A NEGATIVE NUMBER TO STOP
ID#? 1
FIRST ACTIVITY? THEATER
SECOND ACTIVITY? GLEE CLUB
ATHLETIC TEAM? TENNIS

ID#? 2
FIRST ACTIVITY? DEBATING CLUB
SECOND ACTIVITY? CHESS CLUB
ATHLETIC TEAM? FOOTBALL
```

(A COMPLETE RUN IS NOT SHOWN.)

Accessing Multiple Files

It is possible to work with two or more random-access files simultaneously within a single program. When this is done the programmer should not confuse the variables associated with each specific file. Note how the channel numbers are used to keep the information in each file separate within the program.

PROGRAM 10.10

This program, named FOOTBALL/BAS, opens the files GRADES/TXT and ACTIVI-
TY/TXT and prints the names and grade averages for each member of the football team.
The same record number indicates the same student in both files.

```
1 REM     N$ = STUDENT'S NAME (20 CHARACTERS)
2 REM     C1$,C2$,C3$,C4$ = COURSE NAMES (20 CHARACTERS EACH)
3 REM     G1$,G2$,G3$,G4$ = GRADES (2 CHARACTERS EACH)
4 REM     A1$,A2$ = ACTIVITIES (20 CHARACTERS EACH)
5 REM     T$ = ATHLETIC TEAM (15 CHARACTERS)
6 REM     ID = STUDENT ID NUMBER
7 REM
8 REM
10  CLEAR 250
20  OPEN "R",1,"GRADES/TXT:1",108
30  OPEN "R",2,"ACTIVITY/TXT:1",55
40  FIELD 1, 20 AS N$, 20 AS C1$, 2 AS G1$, 20 AS C2$,
         2 AS G2$, 20 AS C3$, 2 AS G3$, 20 AS C4$, 2 AS G4$
50  FIELD 2, 20 AS A1$, 20 AS A2$, 15 AS T$
60  FOR ID = 1 TO LOF(2)
70     GET 2, ID
80     IF LEFT$(T$,8) <> "FOOTBALL" THEN 130
90     GET 1, ID
100    A = (CVI(G1$) + CVI(G2$) + CVI(G3$) + CVI(G4$))/4
110    PRINT N$,A
120    PRINT
130 NEXT ID
140 CLOSE 1,2
READY
>RUN
DAVID GELLER                    78.25

ERIC SLAYTON                    80.75

JEREMY LEADER                   85.5

READY
>
```

1. Store the 26 letters of the alphabet in a random-access file in order. Have a program pick five random numbers from 1 to 26 and use these numbers to put together a five letter "word".

2. Store titles of ten books in a random-access file. Use this file to make a sequential file for all the titles beginning with letters from N to Z, inclusive.

3. (a) Establish a random-access file named SAYING which is to consist of wise sayings. Each sage remark is to consist of up to 128 characters. The number of such utterances is to be determined by the user.
   (b) Write the program required to retrieve and print any one of the wise sayings in SAYING.

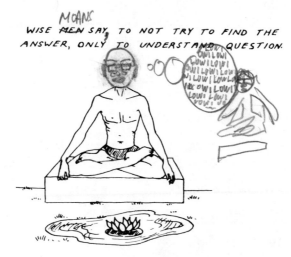

4. (a) Create a random-access file named ACCOUNTS that will contain the customer name and current balance for twenty-five savings accounts.
   (b) Write a program that will update the file ACCOUNTS whenever an individual makes a deposit or withdrawal.
   (c) Write a program using the file ACCOUNTS that sends a letter of warning to the holders of all overdrawn accounts, or a letter of congratulations to the holders of accounts with $500 or more informing them that they will be receiving a toaster in the mail.

5. (a) Create a random-access file named CARS to record how many full-sized, mid-sized and compact cars a dealer sells each month for a twelve month period.
(b) Write a program that will retrieve information from the file CARS for a specific month and then print a bar graph comparing the sales of the three sizes of cars for that month.

6. (a) Write a program that will create a random-access file FRAT which contains the names, fraternities, and ages of thirty college students.
(b) Write a program that will access FRAT and create a sequential file SIGMA which contains the names and ages of the students who live in Sigma Chi.
(c) Write a program that accesses the file FRAT and randomly selects fifteen students for seats in a classroom of three rows, five seats to a row. Have the computer print a seating plan for the class, placing each student's name at the correct seat location.

7. Open four separate random-access files named NAME, SALARY, AGESEX, and AUTO, and store in them the data listed. All information is stored under a person's identification number, assumed for convenience to run from 1 to 10.

File 1 (NAME)

NAME	ADDRESS	STATE
1. BOWMAN	CANAAN	CONN.
2. BROOKS	SYOSSET	N.Y.
3. CHRISTIAN	HARDWICK	VT.
4. CUMMINGS	TRENTON	N.J.
5. EDWARDS	MONTGOMERY	ALA.
6. HALEY	WESTFIELD	N.J.
7. HALPERN	NEW YORK	N.Y.
8. REYNOLDS	HOUSTON	TEX.
9. SCOTT	SHERIDAN	WYO.
10. WALKER	NEWARK	N.J.

File 2 (SALARY)

SALARY	SAVINGS
1. 18,000	4,200.
2. 27,000	3,600.
3. 59,000	2,200.
4. 78,000	500.
5. 25,000	7,800.
6. 45,000	12,000.
7. 9,000	400.
8. 21,000	3,200.
9. 33,000	4,700.
10. 40,000	3,900.

File 3 (AGESEX)

AGE	SEX
1. 48	M
2. 39	F
3. 46	M
4. 71	M
5. 29	M
6. 38	F
7. 51	M
8. 62	F
9. 22	F
10. 32	M

File 4 (AUTO)

AUTO	YR
1. BUICK	79
2. OLDS	72
3. CHEV	80
4. CHEV	73
5. FORD	70
6. CHEV	76
7. FORD	73
8. CAD	74
9. VW	79
10. FORD	69

By performing the correct file searches, find the following:

(a) Names and addresses of men over 30 years old who own a Ford and have an income over twenty thousand dollars a year.

(b) Names of men and women who drive a Chevrolet, Ford, or Volkswagen and have a salary above fifteen thousand dollars a year and savings below two thousand dollars.

(c) The F.B.I. is looking for a young man (under 35) who drives a Ford with New Jersey plates. Have the computer print his name and address.

8. (a) Write a program that will create a random-access file named SAVE that can be used by a bank to store information about ten depositors. Each depositor's name, social security number, complete address (number and street, city, state, and zip code), and account balance are to be included. The file SAVE is structured as shown below.

Variable	Variable name	Space allotment
Name	N$	20
Social Security Number	SS$	11
Street Address	A$	25
City	C$	15
State	S$	2
ZIP Code	Z$	5
Balance	B$	4

(b) Write a single program which allows any of the information, including the balance of the account, to be changed or updated.

```
>RUN
DEPOSITOR'S ACCOUNT NUMBER? 2
NAME: MARY ANN WILSON
                (1) CHANGE NAME
                (2) CHANGE SOCIAL SECURITY NUMBER
                (3) CHANGE ADDRESS
                (4) CHANGE BALANCE

OPTION? 4
OLD BALANCE: 134.58
NEW BALANCE? 159.58
READY
>
```

(c) The bank gives its depositors 1/2% interest per month compounded monthly. Write a program which is run at the end of each month to add 1/2% to the balance of each account.

9. The computer is to be used to store information on charge account customers at the Buy Low Department Store in a random access file named CHARGE/TXT. The information on each customer is to be stored in a single record with the record number serving as the customer's charge account number.

(a) Create the file CHARGE/TXT and store in it the name, street address, city, state, zip code, and total unpaid balance for each of ten charge customers.

(b) Write a program that will daily update the balances as new charges are made and bills are paid.

```
>RUN
ENTER A NEGATIVE NUMBER TO STOP THE PROGRAM
ACCOUNT #? 2
CHARGE (C) OR PAYMENT (P)? C
AMOUNT? 48.95
TRANSACTION RECORDED

ACCOUNT #? -1
READY
>
```

(c) Write a program that will send each customer a bill at the end of each month. If the total due exceeds $800, the message YOUR ACCOUNT EXCEEDS YOUR CHARGE LIMIT, PAY IMMEDIATELY is printed at the bottom of the bill.

```
>RUN
FROM: BUY LOW DEPARTMENT STORE
TO: JANE GILMORE
ACCOUNT # 1

YOU HAVE CHARGED $487.23 AGAINST YOUR
ACCOUNT.  THIS AMOUNT IS NOW DUE.

                        THANK YOU


FROM: BUY LOW DEPARTMENT STORE
TO: PAUL JOHNSON
ACCOUNT # 2

YOU HAVE CHARGED $874.12 AGAINST YOUR
ACCOUNT.  THIS AMOUNT IS NOW DUE.

YOUR ACCOUNT EXCEEDS YOUR CHARGE LIMIT.
PAY IMMEDIATELY!

                        THANK YOU


READY
>
```

(d) Write a program that will close the account of a customer who has paid his or her balance and is moving away. (Hint: Place all blanks in the record.)

```
>RUN
WHICH ACCOUNT IS BEING CLOSED? 2
ACCOUNT # 2 HAS BEEN CLOSED
READY
>
```

(e) Write a program that opens an account for a new customer. Have the computer search the existing records and use one that is empty. If no empty record is found, add a new one.

```
>RUN
NAME? SARA JONES
STREET ADDRESS? 75 GEORGE DYE RD.
CITY? TRENTON
STATE? NJ
ZIP CODE? 08690
THIS PERSON WILL BE ASSIGNED ACCOUNT # 2
READY
>
```

USING THE EDITOR

The TRS-80 has an editor which helps the programmer correct a program currently in memory. The programmer can best learn the use of the editor by spending time to become familiar with its different functions. A short outline of the edit commands is presented here.

EDIT

The EDIT command is used to invoke the TRS-80's built in editor. To correct the line

50 FOR Q = 1 TO 10: PRINT Q, SQR (Q) :NEXT D

the command

EDIT 50

is used. The computer will respond by printing the number of the selected line, leaving the cursor positioned one space after the line number.

Pressing the ENTER key while in EDIT mode causes the computer to print the rest of the line being edited and to record any changes made in that line. The computer then leaves the EDIT mode and returns to normal operation.

Key	Function
n Spacebar	moves cursor n spaces to the right
n ←	moves cursor n spaces to the left
L	lists line being edited
n D	deletes n characters from cursor position

`I`	puts editor in insert mode
`Shift` ↑	exit from insert mode
`X`	places cursor at end of line and allows insert
`H`	deletes all characters to the right of the cursor and allows insert
n `S` c	searches for the nth occurrence of the character (c) and places cursor at that position
n `K` c	deletes all characters up to the nth occurrence of the character (c)
n `C`	changes n characters to the right of the cursor
`E`	quits EDIT mode, saving all changes
`Q`	quits EDIT mode, canceling all changes
`A`	cancel changes and returns to EDIT mode

DISK BASIC COMMANDS

The following commands are intended for systems equipped with at least one disk unit.

CMD

The CMD command performs a number of different tasks:

CMD "D:d"   will list the directory for the disk in drive d (e.g. CMD"D:1")

CMD "Z", "ON"   duplicates all output on a printer as well as on the display screen

CMD "Z", "OFF"   cancels the effect of CMD "Z", "ON"

Program and File Names

Every program and file on a disk is identified by a unique name. The general format for a program or file name is:

<name> / <extension> . <password> : <drive#>

The name may consist of from one to eight characters (letters and numbers). The first character must be a letter.

The extension, which is optional, may be from one to three characters, starting with a letter. It is useful to standardize extensions by employing /BAS for BASIC programs and /TXT for files. This allows the user to easily distinguish between programs and files.

An optional password may be assigned to a program or file and may be from one to eight characters long, starting with a letter. The password must be specified whenever loading a program or opening a file whose name contains a password. A password prevents unauthorized users from tampering with valuable data or programs.

For example, in loading a program named JONES/BAS with the password SECRET it is necessary to type JONES/BAS.SECRET. When listing the directory of a disk, the passwords are not printed. Therefore, it is important to remember passwords.

Optionally, a drive number may be specified when using a system equipped with more than one disk unit. If a unit number is specified, the computer will perform the operation desired (such as opening a file) on the selected disk drive.

The following are valid program or file names:

> MAIL/BAS
> TALK/DAT:1
> CODES/TXT. PASSWORD
> POTATOES
> OMNI3.PAUL
> P46/A9.SIX66:0

SAVE

The SAVE command is used to store a program on a disk. Its form is:

> SAVE "\<program name\> : \<drive#\>"

For example,

> SAVE "MYPROG/BAS:1"

will save the program currently in the computer's memory on the disk in drive one, and give it the name MYPROG/BAS. Note that MYPROG/BAS:1 must be enclosed in quotation marks.

LOAD

Programs previously saved by the SAVE command may be recalled from the disk and transferred to the computer's memory by the use of the LOAD command. For example,

> LOAD "MYPROG/BAS:1"

will load MYPROG/BAS into memory from drive 1.

KILL

Unwanted programs and files stored on a disk can be removed using the KILL command. Its form is:

KILL "<program or file name>: <drive#>"

The command

KILL "MYPROG/BAS:1"

will delete MYPROG/BAS from the disk in drive one.

NAME

The NAME command is used to renumber the line numbers of a program currently in the computer's memory. Its form is:

NAME <newline>, <startline>, <increment>

Newline is the new line number of the first line of the program to be renumbered. When not specified, the computer will assume 10.

Startline is the line number of the original program where renumbering is to begin. When not specified, renumbering begins with the first line in the program and then renumbers the entire program.

Increment specifies the difference between successive renumbered program lines. If omitted, the computer assumes 10.

For example, the command:

NAME 100,,20

will renumber the entire program currently in memory, so that the first line number is 100, the second 120, the third 140, and so on. Note that startline was not specified in this example.

The NAME command will also change the line numbers used within statements so that they correspond with the new line numbers of the program.

MERGE

The MERGE command is used to combine a program in memory with one that has been previously stored on a disk. Its form is:

MERGE "<program name> : <drive#> "

For example,

MERGE "ADDENDUM/BAS:1"

will combine the program in memory with the program ADDENDUM/BAS on the disk in drive one. If the drive number is not specified, the computer will search for the program on all of the available disks, starting with drive zero. If any line numbers in the program in memory match line numbers in the program from the disk, the lines in memory will be replaced by those from the disk.

Programs are usually stored on a disk in a coded format which will not allow them to be merged with a program in memory. To be merged the program on disk must be stored in ASCII format. This is accomplished with the command:

SAVE "MYPROG/BAS:1",A

Sorting

The TRS-80 has a built in function that will alphabetize the contents of singly subscripted string variables (arrays). The general format for the command is:

CMD "O", N%, <array name> (<starting point>)

N% must be an integer variable that specifies the number of elements to be sorted and the array name is the name of the array to be sorted. Starting point specifies the element of the array where the sorting process is to begin. For example,

130 N% = 20%
140 CMD "O", N%, B$(5)

sorts the elements B$(5) to B$(24) and places the alphabetized results back in the elements B$(5) to B$(24).

PROGRAM B.1

The following program illustrates how the CMD "O" function is used to sort an array of fifteen names. The first printing lists the names unsorted, the second shows the sort of A$(4) to A$(10), and the third shows the sort of the entire fifteen names.

```
10   CLEAR 250
20   DIM A$(15)
30   FOR X = 1 TO 15
40      READ A$(X)
50   NEXT X
60   GOSUB 140
70   N% = 7
80   CMD "O", N%, A$(4)
90   GOSUB 140
100  N% = 15
110  CMD "O", N%, A$(1)
120  GOSUB 140
130  END
140  FOR Q = 1 TO 15
150     PRINT A$(Q),
160  NEXT Q
170  PRINT
180  PRINT
190  RETURN
200  DATA TOM,DICK,HARRY,LYDIA,MARY,JANE,DIANE,JEREMY,ELI
210  DATA ROBERT,LESTER,DON,CAROL,ERNIE,ERIC
READY
>RUN
```

TOM	DICK	HARRY	LYDIA
MARY	JANE	DIANE	JEREMY
ELI	ROBERT	LESTER	DON
CAROL	ERNIE	ERIC	

TOM	DICK	HARRY	DIANE
ELI	JANE	JEREMY	LYDIA
MARY	ROBERT	LESTER	DON
CAROL	ERNIE	ERIC	

CAROL	DIANE	DICK	DON
ELI	ERIC	ERNIE	HARRY
JANE	JEREMY	LESTER	LYDIA
MARY	ROBERT	TOM	

```
READY
>
```

TRSDOS OPERATING SYSTEM

Starting the System

To bring the computer up in the disk operating mode, place a copy of the TRSDOS disk in drive 0 and then turn on the computer. After a few seconds, the computer will respond by asking a series of questions.

ENTER DATE (MM/DD/YY)?

Enter the date in the form requested (e.g. 06/23/82).

ENTER TIME (HH:MM:SS)?

Enter the time in the form requested (e.g. 14:32:10). Note that the computer uses a 24 hour clock. The computer will now respond

TRSDOS READY

and print a series of periods. Type the word BASIC and then the computer will ask

HOW MANY FILES?

Enter the maximum number of files, from 1 to 15, that you expect to have opened simultaneously. If you expect to use random-access files, enter a V along with the number. For example,

HOW MANY FILES? 3V

When working in BASIC hit the ENTER key as a response to

MEMORY SIZE?

APPEND

The APPEND command is used to tack the contents of one file onto the end of another. Its form is:

APPEND <source> <destination>

For example,

APPEND FILE1/TXT FILE2/TXT

will cause the contents of the file FILE1/TXT to be added to the end of FILE2/TXT. The contents of FILE1/TXT will not be affected, but FILE2/TXT will now contain both files.

COPY

The COPY command is used to duplicate a file. Its form is:

COPY <original> <new file>

For example,

COPY PAYROLL/TXT SAFETY/TXT

will cause the computer to make an exact copy of PAYROLL/TXT and place it in a new file named SAFETY/TXT.

COPY PAYROLL/TXT:0 :1

will make an exact copy of the file PAYROLL/TXT located on drive zero and place the copy on drive one, naming it also PAYROLL/TXT.

DIR

To produce a catalogue of a disk, type

DIR:<d> <(PRT)>

which will list the directory of the disk on the specified disk drive (d). If the (PRT) option is specified, the directory will also be produced on a printer, should one be available.

RENAME

It is possible to change the name of files and programs using the RENAME command. Its form is:

RENAME <old name> TO <new name>

For example,

RENAME PAYROLL/BAS:1 TO SALARY/BAS:1

will give the program PAYROLL/BAS on drive one the new name SALARY/BAS.

DUAL

DUAL(ON) will cause all subsequent video output to be duplicated on the printer until the command DUAL(OFF) is executed.

FORMAT

New disks must be initialized, or "formatted" so that the TRS-80 can use them. After the command FORMAT is given, the computer will respond by asking a series of questions.

FORMAT WHAT DRIVE?

Enter the number of the drive containing the new disk to be formatted.

DISKETTE NAME?

Enter a name from one to eight letters and numbers, starting with a letter, that you wish to utilize as an internal label for the disk.

MASTER PASSWORD?

Enter a password made up of from one to eight letters and numbers, starting with a letter. This password is important and must be known when a disk is copied. Hence the programmer must not forget what it is.

BACKUP

The BACKUP command is used to copy an entire disk at one time. After the command BACKUP is given, the computer will ask a series of questions.

SOURCE DRIVE NUMBER?

Enter the number of the drive containing the disk to be copied.

DESTINATION DRIVE NUMBER?

Enter the number of the drive containing the disk to be copied onto.

SOURCE DISK MASTER PASSWORD?

Enter the master password of the disk to be copied.

FORMATTING OUTPUT

There are many instances when a programmer will want to have the computer's output produced in some special form. This is especially true when charts or tables are to be printed in some specific format. The PRINT USING statement is usually employed to produce formatted output.

PRINT USING

The PRINT USING statement allows an entire line of output to be formatted into zones of variable length. These zones may contain a series of numbers, strings, or a combination of both. The general form of PRINT USING is:

PRINT USING "<format>"; <variables or expressions>

The format must be a string variable or a string enclosed within quotation marks. Its purpose is to inform the computer of the format which will be employed in printing the variables or expressions. The variables or expressions must be preceded by a semicolon and separated from each other by commas.

PROGRAM D.1

This program demonstrates some simple applications of PRINT USING.

```
10 A = 25.68 : B = 3.21 : C = 2.4
20 PRINT USING "##.#    #.#      #";A, B, C
30 PRINT
40 PRINT USING "##.##     #.#      #.#"; 3.798, 2.78, 3.55
READY
>RUN
25.7    3.2     2

  3.80    2.8    3.6
READY
>
```

Notice how either variables or expressions may be used in the PRINT USING statement and also how numbers are rounded off to the desired number of decimal places.

The following table shows the valid formats that may be used in a PRINT USING statement.

Symbol	Use	Examples
#	Reserve space for one digit.	### ##
•	Indicate location of decimal point within number sign (#) field.	#.### ###.##
,	Specify location of one or more commas within a # field.	##,###.## #,###
+	Display the sign of the number being printed. The + may be placed before or after the # field.	+###.# ####.##+
−	Display a leading or trailing minus sign regardless of the sign of the number.	−###.## ###−
$$	Display a single dollar sign just prior to the leftmost digit of a # field.	$$###.## $$#,###
**	Replace any leading blanks in a # field with asterisks.	**####.## **##.##
**$	This combines ** and $$ such that a single dollar sign will be displayed just prior to the leftmost digit in a # field. Any leading spaces remaining will be filled with asterisks.	**$###.## **$#.##

↑↑↑↑	Output a number in scientific notation. Remember that ↑ prints as [.	#.### ↑↑↑↑ ###.# ↑↑↑↑
!	Output only the first character of a string.	!
%%	Output only the first two characters of a string.	%%
%<n-2 spaces>%	Output the first n characters of a string.	% % % %
<any other char>	Output any characters not in this table as though they were in a normal print statement.	ABCD Q12R

PROGRAM D.2

This program demonstrates the use of the different symbols given in the table.

```
10 PRINT USING "   ###"; 657
20 PRINT USING "   ###.###"; 63.2867
30 PRINT USING "   #,###.##"; 1287.53
40 F$ = "Over ### contributed to the goal of ##,###,###.##"
45 C = 212 : PRINT USING F$; C,23967000.92
50 PRINT USING "   +###.#        #.####+"; -42.3, 8.9172
60 PRINT USING "   ###.#+       +#.####"; -42.3, 8.9172
70 PRINT USING "We can format numbers such as +##.#"; 18.37
80 PRINT USING "   $$####.##"; 201.76
90 A = 4201.67
100 PRINT USING "Amount is: **$#,###.## of budget."; A
110 PRINT USING "Mr. Dandy gave **$####.## to charity."; 43.10
120 PRINT
READY
>RUN
   657
    63.287
  1,287.53
Over 212 contributed to the goal of 23,967,000.92
    -42.3        8.9172+
     42.3-       +8.9172
We can format numbers such as +18.4
     $201.76
Amount is: **$4,201.67 of budget.
Mr. Dandy gave ****$43.10 to charity.

READY
>
```

It is possible to place the format portion of the PRINT USING statement into a string. For example,

$$10 \ F\$ = \text{``##.\#} \qquad \#\# \qquad \% \qquad \%\text{''}$$

can be used later in a PRINT USING statement.

$$70 \ \text{PRINT USING F\$, A, B, N\$}$$

This technique is especially useful in formatting columns in a table so that they line up with their appropriate headings. The headings are typed in the line directly above the line containing the format string. By lining up the quotation marks in each of the lines, it is easy to produce the correct format. Program D.3 demonstrates this procedure.

PROGRAM D.3

```
10 PRINT "Key    Description    Cost     Qty     Total"
20 F2$ = " !   %            %  $$###.##   ###   **$#,###.##"
30 FOR L = 1 TO 6
40      READ K$, L$, C, Q
50      PRINT USING F2$; K$, L$, C, Q, C*Q
60      T = T + C*Q : Q2 = Q2 + Q
70 NEXT L
80 PRINT : J$= "### items were sold raising **$###,###.## today"
90 PRINT USING J$; Q2, T
100 DATA D, "Diskettes", 5.95, 20, K, "Cleaner", 2.29, 16
110 DATA B, "I/O Manual", 17.95, 100, R, "Ribbon", 1.99, 50
120 DATA W, "CPU Cables", 55.00, 48, Z, "Games Pkg.", 49.95, 12
READY
>RUN
Key    Description    Cost     Qty     Total
  D    Diskettes      $5.95     20    ****$119.00
  K    Cleaner        $2.29     16    ****$36.64
  B    I/O Manual     $17.95    100   **$1,795.00
  R    Ribbon         $1.99     50    *****$99.50
  W    CPU Cables     $55.00    48    **$2,640.00
  Z    Games Pkg.     $49.95    12    ****$599.40

246 items were sold raising ***$5,289.54 today
READY
>
```

D.4

CHAPTER THREE

```
1. 10 D1 = RND(101) + 49
   20 D2 = RND(101) + 49
   30 PRINT D1; "multiplied by"; D2; "is"; D1*D2
```

```
2. 10 PRINT "I'm thinking of a random number between 1 & 50."
   20 R = RND(50)
   25 FOR W = 1 TO 5 : REM W = # of wrong guesses
   30 INPUT "What is your guess"; G
   70 IF G < R THEN PRINT "Too Low!" : NEXT W : GOTO 90
   80 IF G > R THEN PRINT "Too High!" : NEXT W : GOTO 90
   85 PRINT "Correct!!!" : END
   90 PRINT "You've had 5 guesses now."
   100 PRINT "The number was"; R
```

```
3. 10 REM    R = Random number between 0 and 9
   20 REM    X = Number of random numbers resulting between 0 & 4
   30 REM    Y = Number of random numbers resulting between 5 & 9
   40 REM    L = Loop variable to generate 50 random numbers
   50 FOR L = 1 TO 50
   60 R = RND(10) - 1
   70 IF R < 5 THEN X = X + 1  ELSE Y = Y + 1
   80 NEXT L
   90 PRINT "There were"; X; "numbers between 0 and 4."
   100 PRINT "There were"; Y; "numbers between 5 and 9."
```

```
4. 10 REM    L = Loop for entering 10 numbers from keyboard
   20 REM    N = Arbitrary value entered from keyboard
   30 REM    E = Number of EVEN numbers entered
   40 REM    10-E = number of ODD numbers entered
   50 FOR L = 1 TO 10
   60 INPUT "Enter a number"; N
   70 IF (N/2) = INT(N/2) THEN  E = E + 1
   80 NEXT L
   90 PRINT E; "Even; "; 10-E; "Odd"
```

```
5.  10 CLS
    20 FOR X = 45 TO 73
    30    SET(X,18) : SET(X,19) : SET (X,30) : SET(X,31)
    40 NEXT X
    50 FOR Y = 20 TO 29
    60    SET(45,Y) : SET(46,Y) : SET(72,Y) : SET(73,Y)
    70 NEXT Y
    80 FOR X = 57 TO 61
    90    SET(X,23) : SET (X,26)
    100 NEXT X
    110 FOR Y = 24 TO 25
    120    SET(57,Y) : SET(61,Y)
    130 NEXT Y


6.  10 CLS
    20 X = 1 : Y = 24 : F = 1
    30 SET(X,Y)
    40 X = X + F
    50 RESET(X-F,Y)
    60 IF X = 127 OR X = 1 THEN F = F * -1
    70 GOTO 30
```

CHAPTER FOUR

```
1.  10 FOR X = 20 TO 24
    20    PRINT "Outer Loop:"; X
    30    FOR Y = 1 TO 3
    40       PRINT "Inner:"; Y,
    50    NEXT Y
    60    PRINT
    70 NEXT X


2.  10 FOR X = 1 TO 3
    20    INPUT L(X)
    30 NEXT X
    40 REM Print L() in reverse order now
    50 FOR X = 3 TO 1 STEP -1
    60    PRINT L(X)
    70 NEXT X


3.  10 REM Read 6 words from keyboard
    20 FOR X = 1 TO 6
    30    INPUT W$(X)
    40 NEXT X
    50 REM Pick 4 words and print them as a sentence
    60 FOR P = 1 TO 4
    70    N = RND(5)
    80    PRINT W$(N); " ";
    90 NEXT P
    100 PRINT "." : REM Period = End of sentence
```

```
4.  10 REM Read 6 words from keyboard
    20 FOR X = 1 TO 6
    30      INPUT W$(X)
    40 NEXT X
    50 REM Pick 4 words and print them as a sentence
    60 C(1) = RND(5) : REM First random number
    70 PRINT W$(C(1)); " "; : REM Always show first word
    80 FOR P = 2 TO 4
    90      C(P) = RND(5)
    100      REM Now check for duplicate random numbers
    110      FOR K = 1 TO P-1
    120          IF C(K) = C(P) THEN 90    : REM Pick another if used
    130      NEXT K
    140      PRINT W$(C(P)); " ";
    150 NEXT P
    160 PRINT "." : REM Period = End of sentence


5.  10 REM Enter the six numbers from keyboard
    20 FOR K = 1 TO 6
    30      INPUT X(K)
    40 NEXT K
    50 REM Print the six numbers in a column
    60 FOR K = 1 TO 6
    70      PRINT X(K)
    80 NEXT K
    90 REM Print the six numbers in a row
    100 PRINT
    110 FOR K = 1 TO 6
    120      PRINT X(K);
    130 NEXT K
    140 PRINT


6.  5 DIM X$(5,3)
    10 FOR I = 1 TO 5
    20      FOR J = 1 TO 3
    30          READ X$(I,J)
    40      NEXT J
    50 NEXT I
    60 REM Output X$(), making the rows become columns
    70 FOR I = 1 TO 3
    80      FOR J = 1 TO 5
    90          PRINT X$(J,I);" ";
    100     NEXT J
    110     PRINT
    120 NEXT I
    130 DATA   A,B,C,D,E,F,G,H,I,J,K,L,M,N,O
```

CHAPTER FIVE

1A.
```
10 INPUT "ARE YOU COMING OR GOING"; A$
20 IF A$="COMING"
        THEN PRINT "HELLO"
        ELSE PRINT "GOOD BYE"
30 END
```

1B.
```
1 REM SHELLSORT OF THE LIST OF CLUB MEMBERS
10 INPUT "HOW MANY NAMES IN THE LIST";N
20 FOR X=1 TO N
30     INPUT "MEMBER";M$(X)
40 NEXT X
50 S=N
60 S=INT(S/1.5) : Q=S
70 F=0
80 FOR X=1 TO N
90     Q=X+S
100    IF Q>N THEN 150
110    IF M$(X)>M$(Q)
          THEN T$ = M$(X) : M$(X) = M$(Q) : M$(Q) = T$ : F = 1
140 NEXT X
150 IF S>1 THEN 60
155 IF F=1 THEN 70
160 FOR X=1 TO N
170    PRINT M$(X)
180 NEXT X
190 END
```

2A. The problem with 2a is very easy to correct. The FOR-TO-NEXT loop in line 20 is missing the STEP command. Line 20 should read:

20 FOR X =10 TO 1 STEP -1

2B. The product in line 30 is always positive. The best way to correct this error in logic would be to eliminate line 40 and replace it with:

40 PRINT "THE PRODUCT IS POSITIVE"

CHAPTER SIX

1. X=-2

2. ```
10 INPUT N
20 X = ABS(N - FIX(N))
30 Y = INT(X * 100 + 0.5) / 100
40 PRINT "INPUT:"; N, "OUTPUT:"; Y
```

3. ```
10 DEF FNR(D) = D * 3.1415 / 180
20 DEF FND(R) = R * 180 / 3.1415
30 INPUT "DEGREES";A
40 PRINT "That is"; FNR(A); "radians."
50 PRINT
60 INPUT "RADIANS";B
70 PRINT "That is"; FND(B); "degrees."
```

CHAPTER SEVEN

1. ```
10 INPUT "NAME";N$
20 PRINT N$
30 IF N$ = "DONALD" THEN GOSUB 100
50 GOTO 10
60 REM
70 REM
100 REM   THIS IS THE CODE TO UNDERLINE
110 FOR I = 1 TO LEN(N$)
120   PRINT"-";
130 NEXT I
140 PRINT
150 RETURN
```

2. ```
10 FOR D = 1 TO 5
20    C = RND(13)
30    S = RND(4)
40    PRINT "CARD";D;"IS THE";C;"OF ";
50    ON S GOTO 60,70,80,90
60    PRINT "CLUBS" : GOTO 100
70    PRINT "DIAMONDS" : GOTO 100
80    PRINT "HEARTS" : GOTO 100
90    PRINT "SPADES"
100 NEXT D
```

CHAPTER EIGHT

```
1. 10  INPUT "A LETTER FROM THE ALPHABET PLEASE";A$
   20  PRINT "THE ASCII OF '";A$;"' IS";ASC(A$)
   30  C = ASC(A$) + 2
   40  IF C > 90 THEN C = C - 26
   50  PRINT "TWO LETTERS AFTER '";A$;"' IS '";CHR$(C);"'"
   60  GOTO 10
```

CHAPTER NINE

```
1. 10  OPEN "O",1,"MONTHS/TXT:1"
   20  FOR I = 1 TO 12
   30      READ M$
   40      PRINT #1,M$
   50  NEXT I
   60  CLOSE 1
   100 DATA JANUARY,FEBRUARY,MARCH,APRIL,MAY,JUNE,JULY
   110 DATA AUGUST,SEPTEMBER,OCTOBER,NOVEMBER,DECEMBER
```

```
2. 10  INPUT "WHAT NUMBER MONTH DO YOU WANT";N
   20  OPEN "I",1,"MONTHS/TXT:1"
   30  FOR I = 1 TO N
   40      INPUT #1,N$
   50  NEXT I
   60  CLOSE 1
   70  PRINT "MONTH";N;"IS ";N$
```

CHAPTER TEN

```
1. 1   REM    M$,M1$ = MONTH (9 CHARACTERS)
   2   REM
   3   REM
   10  OPEN "R",1,"MONTHS/TXT:1",9
   20  FIELD 1, 9 AS M$
   30  FOR M = 1 TO 12
   40      READ M1$
   50      LSET M$ = M1$
   60      PUT 1
   70  NEXT M
   90  CLOSE 1
   100 DATA JANUARY,FEBRUARY,MARCH,APRIL,MAY,JUNE
   110 DATA JULY,AUGUST,SEPTEMBER,OCTOBER,NOVEMBER,DECEMBER
```

```
2.  10 OPEN "R",1,"MONTHS/TXT:1",9
    20 FIELD 1, 9 AS N$
    30 INPUT "WHAT NUMBER MONTH";N
    40 GET 1, N
    50 PRINT "MONTH";N;"IS ";N$
    60 CLOSE 1


3.  1 REM    M$ = MONTH (9 CHARACTERS)
    2 REM    L$ = LENGTH OF FILE 'MONTHS/TXT' (2 CHARACTERS)
    3 REM
    4 REM
    10 OPEN "R",1,"MONTHS/TXT:1",9
    20 FIELD 1, 9 AS M$
    30 OPEN "R",2,"LENGTH/TXT:1",2
    40 FIELD 2, 2 AS L$
    50 LSET L$ = MKI$(LOF(1))
    60 PUT 2,1
    70 CLOSE 1,2
```

CHAPTER ONE

1.  ```
    10 PRINT "A"
    20 PRINT " B"
    30 PRINT "  C"
    40 PRINT "ABCD"
    ```

3.  ```
    >RUN
    THE VALUE OF B
     19
    ```

5.  ```
    10 READ A,B
    20 PRINT "THE SUM IS ";A+B
    30 GOTO 10
    40 DATA 12,8,9,5
    ```

7.  ```
    10 INPUT "PRICE, NUMBER OF LOAVES";P,N
    20 PRINT "TOTAL SPENT =   $";P*N/100
    ```

9.  ```
    10 INPUT X,Y
    20 PRINT "X=";X,"Y=";Y,"X*Y=";X*Y
    30 GOTO 10
    ```

11. ```
    >RUN
     300              510
      .3    .51
    ```

```
13.  >PRINT"AAA";111,222;"AAA","333";"   ";16-3*2
     AAA 111          222 AAA            333    10


15.  >RUN
     ABCDXYZ
     ABCD 7
      7 XYZ
     -4 XYZ


17.  10 PRINT 2+3+4+3+5


19.  10 READ X,Y
     20 A = 12*X+7*Y
     30 PRINT A
     40 GOTO 10
     50 DATA 3,2,7,9,12,-4


21.  10 INPUT "LENGTH, WIDTH, HEIGHT";L,W,H
     20 PRINT "VOLUME IS";L*W*H


23.  10 INPUT "HEIGHT";H
     20 INPUT "WIDTH";W
     30 INPUT "LENGTH";L
     40 INPUT "PRESENCE";P
     50 PRINT "YOUR OBJECT USES";H*W*L*P;"TESSERACTS IN FOUR SPACE"


25.  10 INPUT "HOW MANY BOOKS HAVE YOU BORROWED";B
     20 INPUT "HOW MANY DAYS LATE ARE THEY";L
     30 PRINT "YOU OWE";.10*B*L;"DOLLARS."


27.  10 INPUT "WHAT IS THE PLAYERS NAME";P$
     20 PRINT "WHAT IS ";P$;"'S";
     30 INPUT " WAGE";W
     40 T=W*.44
     50 PRINT P$;" WOULD KEEP $";W-T
     60 PRINT "HE WOULD PAY $";T;"IN TAXES."


29.  10 INPUT "WHAT IS THE BASE";B
     20 INPUT "WHAT IS THE ALTITUDE";A
     30 PRINT:PRINT"THE AREA IS";A*B*.5
```

```
31.   10  READ S1,G1,S2,G2,S3,G3,S4,G4,S5,G5
      20  S = S1+S2+S3+S4+S5
      30  G = G1+G2+G3+G4+G5
      40  T = S+G
      50  PRINT "SLOTH'S TOTAL VOTE WAS";S
      60  PRINT "HIS TOTAL PERCENTAGE WAS";100*S/T
      70  PRINT
      80  PRINT "GRAFT'S TOTAL VOTE WAS";G
      90  PRINT "HIS TOTAL PERCENTAGE WAS";100*G/T
      100 DATA 528,210,313,721,1003,822,413,1107,516,1700


33.   10  INPUT "MONTH, DAY, AND YEAR OF BIRTH";M1,D1,Y1
      20  D9 = Y1*365+M1*30+D1
      30  INPUT "TODAY'S MONTH, DAY, AND YEAR";M2,D2,Y2
      40  D8 = Y2*365+M2*30+D2
      50  S = 8*(D8-D9)
      60  PRINT "YOU HAVE SLEPT ABOUT";S;"HOURS."
```

CHAPTER TWO

```
1.    10  INPUT A,B
      20  IF A < B THEN 60
      30  IF A > B THEN 80
      40  PRINT A;"IS EQUAL TO";B
      50  GOTO 10
      60  PRINT A;"IS LESS THAN";B
      70  GOTO 10
      80  PRINT A;"IS GREATER THAN";B
      90  GOTO 10


3.    10  INPUT A$
      20  IF A$>"MIDWAY" THEN PRINT A$


5.    10  INPUT A$,B$: PRINT A$,B$: PRINT B$,A$


7.    10  INPUT A$
      20  IF A$ > "DOWN" AND A$ < "UP" THEN PRINT "A$ IS BETWEEN"


9.    10  INPUT X
      20  IF X <= 25 OR X >= 75
              THEN PRINT "NOT IN THE INTERVAL"
              ELSE PRINT "IN THE INTERVAL"
      30  GOTO 10
```

```
11.   10 FOR I = 11 TO -11 STEP -2
      20     PRINT I[3
      30 NEXT I


13.   10 FOR I = 1 TO 40
      20     PRINT "*";
      30 NEXT I : PRINT


15.   10 FOR I = 10 TO 97 STEP 3
      20     PRINT I;
      30 NEXT I


17.   10 INPUT "CREATURE";X$
      20 RESTORE
      30 FOR I = 1 TO 6
      40     READ C$,W$
      50     IF C$ = X$ THEN 90
      60 NEXT I
      70 PRINT "CREATURE ";X$;" NOT FOUND."
      80 GOTO 10
      90 PRINT "YOU CAN KILL A ";C$;" WITH A ";W$
      100 GOTO 10
      110 DATA LICH, FIRE BALL,MUMMY, FLAMING TORCH
      120 DATA WEREWOLF, SILVER BULLET,VAMPIRE, WOODEN STAKE
      130 DATA MEDUSA,SHARP SWORD,TRIFFID,FIRE HOSE


19.   Line:   <10><20><30><40><50><60><10><20><30><40>
              <50><60><10><20><30><40>


21.   10 FOR I = 1 TO 10
      20     PRINT : PRINT "---------------------"
      30     PRINT "  HAPPY HOLIDAY MOTEL"
      40     PRINT "         ROOM";I
      50     PRINT "---------------------"
      60 NEXT I


23.   10 PRINT "X","X[2","X[3"
      20 PRINT
      30 FOR I = 2 TO 10 STEP 2
      40     PRINT I,I[2,I[3
      50 NEXT I
```

```
25.   10  INPUT N
      20  FOR H = 1 TO N : REM H IS HEIGHT THE TRIANGLE IS.
      30      IF W = H THEN 70  : REM W IS WIDTH
      40      PRINT "*";
      50      W = W+1
      60      GOTO 30
      70      PRINT : W = 0 : REM RESET WIDTH FOR EACH H
      80  NEXT H


27.   10  FOR I = 1 TO 5
      20      READ N$,P : REM GET NAME , PERFORMANCE
      30      IF P >= 75 THEN 110
      40      PRINT : PRINT "DEAR ";N$;","
      50      PRINT "  I AM SO SORRY THAT I MUST FIRE YOU."
      60      PRINT "YOU HAVE BEEN SUCH A FINE EMPLOYEE"
      70      PRINT "WITH A PERFORMANCE RATING OF";P;"%"
      80      PRINT "I'M SURE YOU'LL HAVE NO TROUBLE"
      90      PRINT "FINDING ANOTHER JOB." : PRINT TAB(20);"SINCERELY,"
      100     PRINT : PRINT TAB(20);"GEORGE SHWABB":PRINT
      110 NEXT I
      120 DATA OAKLEY,69,HOWE,92,ANDERSON,96,WOLLEY,88,GOERZ,74


29.   10  INPUT "HOURS WORKED";H
      20  INPUT "HOURLY WAGE";W
      30  M = W * H
      40  IF H > 40 THEN M = M + .5*W*(H-40)
      50  PRINT "THE WAGE FOR THE WEEK IS $";M


31.   1 REM    A = AMOUNT OF MONEY LEFT
      10  A = 200     : REM INITIAL AMOUNT
      20  INPUT "HOW MUCH DOES THE ITEM COST";C
      25  IF C = 0 THEN END
      30  A = A - 1.05*C : REM 1.05 * C IS COST WITH TAX
      35  IF A < 0 THEN PRINT "YOU DON'T HAVE ENOUGH"
                   : A = A + 1.05*C : GOTO 20
      40  PRINT "YOUR TOTAL IS NOW $";A
      50  PRINT
      60  GOTO 20
```

CHAPTER THREE

```
1. 10 FOR I = 1 TO 10
   20    N = RND(0)
   30     IF N > .5 THEN PRINT N;
   40 NEXT I
```

```
3. 10 INPUT N
   20 IF N = INT(N) THEN PRINT N
   30 GOTO 10
```

```
5. 10 N = RND(4) + 1
   20 D = RND(4)
   30 Q = RND(4) - 1
   40 F = .05*N + .10*D + .25*Q : REM TOTAL AMOUNT FOUND
   50 PRINT "YOU FOUND $";F
   60 IF F > .99
         THEN PRINT "YOU CAN BUY LUNCH"
         ELSE PRINT "SORRY, YOU CAN'T BUY LUNCH"
```

```
7. 10 REM   A = AMOUNT IN BANK
   20 REM   I = WEEK NUMBER
   30 A = 11
   40 FOR I = 1 TO 4
   50    PRINT "WEEK";I;",  HOW MANY PENNIES DO YOU HAVE";
   60    INPUT N
   70    A = A + N
   80    PRINT "YOUR TOTAL IS NOW $";A/100
   90 NEXT I
```

```
9. 10 FOR I = 0 TO 1005 STEP 67
   20    PRINT@I,"*"
   30 NEXT I
```

```
11A. >RUN
       1
        2
         3
          4
                        1
                        2
                        3
                        4
```

```
11B. >RUN
     123.4          123.5
     123.45         123.46
```

13.
X	Y
1*	5*
2	0
	2
	1
	-1
3*	2*

* - THIS SHOULD BE CIRCLED.

15.
```
10 FOR I = 13 TO 147 STEP 2 : REM STEP 2 FOR ODDS ONLY
20     S = S + I
30 NEXT I
40 PRINT "THE SUM = ";S
```

17.
```
10 FOR I = 1 TO 1000
20     N = RND(9)
30    IF N/2 = INT(N/2)
          THEN E = E + 1
          ELSE O = O + 1
40 NEXT I
50 PRINT "THERE WERE";O;"ODD INTEGERS."
60 PRINT "THERE WERE";E;"EVEN INTEGERS."
```

19.
```
10 PRINT "DATE","BALANCE"
20 B = 1000 : Y = 1983
30 B = B * 1.05 : Y = Y + 1
40 PRINT "JAN 1,";Y,"$";B
50 IF B > 2000 THEN END
60 GOTO 30
```

21.
```
10 READ V
20 PI = 3.14159
30 R = (.75 * V / PI)[(1 / 3)
40 R = INT(R*100 + .5)/100
50 PRINT "RADIUS IS";R
60 GOTO 10
70 DATA 690,720,460,620
```

23.
```
10 PRINT TAB(15);"*"
20 FOR I = 1 TO 5
30     PRINT TAB(15-I);"*";TAB(15+I);"*"
40 NEXT I
50 PRINT TAB(9);"*************"
```

```
25.  10 R = 7
     20 XC = 64 : YC = 24 : REM CENTER OF "CIRCLE"
     30 FOR Y = -7 TO 7
     40    X = (R[2-Y[2)[(.5)
     50    SET (INT(XC+X+.5),(Y+YC)) : SET (INT(XC-X+.5),(Y+YC))
     60 NEXT Y


27.  10 Q = RND(8) - 1
     20 D = RND(5) - 1
     30 P = RND(10) - 1
     40 V = .25*Q + .10*D + .01*P
     50 T = Q + D + P
     60 PRINT "THERE ARE";T;"COINS, TOTALLING $";V
     70 PRINT "GUESS HOW MANY QUARTERS, DIMES, PENNIES"
     80 FOR I = 1 TO 10
     90 INPUT "GUESS";Q1,D1,P1
     100 IF Q1 = Q AND D1 = D AND P1 = P THEN PRINT "YOU GOT IT!":
         END
     110 PRINT "INCORRECT ": NEXT I
     120 PRINT "HAH, YOU DIDN'T GET IT


29.  10 Y = 10
     20 FOR X = 19 TO 33
     30    SET(X,Y)
     40 NEXT X
     50 Y = Y + 1
     60 IF Y <> 19 THEN 20
     70 END


31.  10 CLS
     20 FOR U = 0 TO 3
     30    READ N$,A,B,C,D,E,F,G
     40    R = (A + B + C + D + E + F + G) / 7 : REM SCALE TO <40
     50    FOR P = 40 TO 40 - R STEP -1
     60       SET(30 * U,P) : SET (30 * U + 1,P) : REM PLOT GRAPH
     70    NEXT P
     80    PRINT@ (960 + 15 * U),N$;
     90 NEXT U
     100 DATA GREER,18,12,9,10,16,22,14
     110 DATA MCPHERSON,12,21,19,16,28,20,22
     120 DATA RADY,18,20,14,19,11,16,23
     130 DATA WYNCOTT,23,27,18,16,21,14,24
```

CHAPTER FOUR

```
1.  10 FOR I = 1 TO 8
    20     FOR J = 1 TO 30
    30         PRINT "*";
    40     NEXT J
    50     PRINT   : REM USED TO MOVE TO NEXT LINE
    60 NEXT I
```

```
3.  10 FOR I = 1 TO 6
    20     INPUT "ENTER X(I)";X(I)
    30 NEXT I
    40 FOR I = 1 TO 5 STEP 2
    50     PRINT I,X(I)
    60 NEXT I
    70 FOR I = 2 TO 6 STEP 2
    80     PRINT I,X(I)
    90 NEXT I
```

```
5.  5 DIM A(4,12)
    10 FOR I = 1 TO 4
    20     FOR J = 1 TO 12
    30         A(I,J) = 3*I + J*J
    40     NEXT J
    50 NEXT I
    60 INPUT "N";N
    80 FOR I = 1 TO 12
    90     PRINT A(N,I);
    100 NEXT I
    110 PRINT
    120 GOTO 60
```

7A. >RUN

1	5
1	6
2	5
2	6
3	5
3	6

7B. >RUN

```
      10
      10
      10
      12
      12
      11
      14
      13
      11
```

7C. >RUN
     45   89   35


9.  ```
    10 FOR X = 40 TO 1 STEP -1
    20     FOR Y = 1 TO 10
    30         READ N
    40          IF N = X THEN PRINT N;
    50     NEXT Y
    55 RESTORE
    60 NEXT X
    70 DATA 5,27,37,16,27,8,2,40,1,9
    ```


11. ```
    10 DIM N(100)
    20 FOR X = 1 TO 100
    30     N(X) = RND(99) : REM GET A NEW RANDOM NUMBER
    35     REM   LOOP THROUGH ALL PREVIOUS NUMBER
    40     FOR Y = 0 TO X-1
    50         IF N(X) =  N(Y) THEN 90 : REM SEE IF ANY DUPLICATES
    60         NEXT Y
    70     NEXT X
    80 END
    90 PRINT "DUPLICATE AFTER";X;"NUMBERS"
    100 FOR I = 1 TO X
    110     PRINT N(I);
    120 NEXT I
    ```


13. ```
    10 FOR I = 3 TO 30
    20     FOR J = I + 1 TO 40 : REM ADD ONE SO NO DUPLICATES
    30         FOR K = J + 1 TO 50
    40             IF K*K = J*J + I*I THEN PRINT I,J,K
    50         NEXT K
    60     NEXT J
    70 NEXT I
    ```


15. ```
    10 DIM N(20)
    20 FOR I = 1 TO 20
    30     N(I) = RND(90) + 9
    40 NEXT I
    50 PRINT "ODD INTEGERS:";
    60 FOR I = 1 TO 20
    70     IF N(I)/2 <> INT(N(I)/2) THEN PRINT N(I);
    80 NEXT I
    90 PRINT:PRINT"EVEN INTEGERS:";
    100 FOR I = 1 TO 20
    110     IF N(I)/2 = INT(N(I)/2) THEN PRINT N(I);
    120 NEXT I
    ```

```
17A.  10 DIM N$(5,6)
      20 INPUT "WHAT DAY AND TIME WOULD YOU LIKE";D,T
      30 IF N$(D,T) <> "" THEN PRINT "THAT TIME IS TAKEN ":GOTO 20
      40 INPUT "WHAT IS YOUR NAME ";N$(D,T)
      50 PRINT "THANK YOU SO VERY MUCH."
      60 GOTO 20


17B.  10 DIM N$(5,6)
      15 INPUT "ARE YOU THE DOCTOR ";A$
      17 IF A$ = "YES" THEN 70
      20 INPUT "WHAT DAY AND TIME WOULD YOU LIKE";D,T
      30 IF N$(D,T) <> "" THEN PRINT "THAT TIME IS TAKEN ":GOTO 20
      40 INPUT "WHAT IS YOUR NAME ";N$(D,T)
      50 PRINT "THANK YOU SO VERY MUCH."
      60 GOTO 15
      70 INPUT "WHICH DAY";D
      80 FOR T = 1 TO 6
      90    IF N$(D,T) = "" THEN PRINT "SANKA BREAK" : GOTO 110
      100   PRINT N$(D,T)
      110 NEXT T
      120 GOTO 15


19.   10 DIM N(100)
      20 R = RND(100)
      30 FOR X = 1 TO 100
      40    INPUT "GUESS";G
      50    IF G = R THEN 150
      60    FOR Z = 1 TO X-1
      70       IF N(Z) = G THEN 130
      80    NEXT Z
      90    N(X) = G
      100   IF G > R THEN PRINT "LOWER": GOTO 120
      110   PRINT "HIGHER"
      120 NEXT X
      130 PRINT "WAKE UP! YOU GUESSED THAT NUMBER BEFORE"
      140 GOTO 40
      150 PRINT "CORRECT"
```

```
21.   1 REM     ARRAY P HOLDS POINT VALUES FOR THE BOARD
      2 REM     ARRAY B = P EXCEPT A ZERO IS ENTERED WHEN A PENNY
                HITS THE BOARD
     10 DIM P(6,6),B(6,6)
     20 REM     SET UP OUTSIDE OF BOARD FOR 1 POINT
     30 FOR I = 1 TO 6
     40     P(1,I) = 1 :P(6,I) = 1 :P(I,6) = 1 :P(I,1) = 1
     50 NEXT I
     60 REM     SET UP BOARD POSITIONS WORTH 2 POINTS
     70 FOR I = 2 TO 5
     80     P(2,I) = 2 :P(5,I) = 2 :P(I,2) = 2 :P(I,5) = 2
     90 NEXT I
    100 REM      SET UP THE THREE POINT POSITIONS
    110 P(3,3) = 3 :P(3,4) = 3 :P(4,3) = 3 :P(4,4) = 3
    120 REM     SET ARRAY B EQUAL TO ARRAY P
    130 FOR Q = 1 TO 6
    140     FOR W = 1 TO 6
    150         B(Q,W) = P(Q,W)
    160     NEXT W
    170 NEXT Q
    180 REM     NOW GET TEN RANDOM ROWS AND COLUMNS FOR PENNY TOSSES
    190 FOR T = 1 TO 10
    200     R = RND(6) : C = RND(6)
    210     B(R,C) = 0 : REM     SET HIT POSITIONS TO 0
    220     S = S + P(R,C)  : REM ADD ON POINT VALUE FOR THE HIT
    230 NEXT T
    240 REM     PRINT OUT RESULTANT BOARD
    250 FOR R = 1 TO 6
    260     FOR C = 1 TO 6
    270         IF B(R,C) = 0 THEN PRINT " X "; : GOTO 290
    280         PRINT B(R,C);
    290     NEXT C
    300     PRINT
    310 NEXT R
    320 PRINT:PRINT "SCORE IS";S


23.   1 REM     ARRAY A$ HOLDS THE LETTERS OF THE ALPHABET
      2 REM     W$ = THE WORD FORMED
     10 DIM A$(26)
     20 FOR I = 1 TO 26
     30     READ A$(I)
     40 NEXT I
     50 FOR W = 1 TO 15
     60     R = RND(7) : REM  GET RANDOM LENGTH
     70     FOR L = 1 TO R  : REM  GET WORD OF LENGTH R
     80         W$ = W$ + A$(RND(26))  : REM   ADD LETTERS ON
     90     NEXT L
    100     PRINT W$
    110     W$ = "" : REM    BLANK W$ FOR NEXT WORD
    120 NEXT W
    200 REM
    210 DATA A,B,C,D,E,F,G,H,I,J,K,L,M,N,O,P,Q,R,S,T,U,V,W,X,Y,Z
```

```
25A.   10 CLS
       15 REM    DRAW CHECKERBOARD BASE
       20 FOR X = 0 TO 127
       30    IF X/2 = INT(X/2)
                 THEN SET(X,40)
                 ELSE SET(X,39)
       40 NEXT X
       50 REM    DRAW PEGS
       60 FOR X = 1 TO 3
       70    FOR Y = 5 TO 38
       80       SET(X*30,Y)
       90    NEXT Y
       100 NEXT X
       110 REM    DRAW DISCS
       120 FOR I = 1 TO 5
       130    FOR X = 30 - 2 * I  TO  30 + 2 * I
       140       SET(X,I*7 + 1) : SET(X,I*7 + 2) : SET(X,I*7 + 3)
       150    NEXT X
       160 NEXT I


25B.   1 REM     DISK = NUMBER OF DISK BEING MOVED
       2 REM     EMPTY = THE NUMBER OF THE EMPTY SPOT IN T2
       3 REM     T1 = TOWER 1   :   T2 = TOWER 2
       4 REM     ARRAY A HOLDS THE CURRENT POSITION OF ALL DISKS
       5 REM            WITH ZERO INDICATING EMPTINESS
       10 CLS
       15 REM    DRAW CHECKERBOARD BASE
       20 FOR X = 0 TO 127
       30    IF X/2 = INT(X/2)
                 THEN SET(X,40)
                 ELSE SET(X,39)
       40 NEXT X
       50 REM    DRAW PEGS
       60 FOR X = 1 TO 3
       70    FOR Y = 5 TO 38
       80       SET(X*30,Y)
       90    NEXT Y
       100 NEXT X
       110 REM    DRAW DISCS
       120 FOR I = 1 TO 5
       125    A(I,1) = I : A(I,2) = 0 : A(I,3) = 0
       130    FOR X = 30 - 2 * I  TO  30 + 2 * I
       140       SET(X,I*7 + 1) : SET(X,I*7 + 2) : SET(X,I*7 + 3)
       150    NEXT X
       160 NEXT I
       180 REM
       190 REM
```

```
200 REM   MOVEMENT
210 PRINT@ 896, : PRINT@ 896,"FROM TOWER TO TOWER";
220 INPUT T1,T2
230 DISK = 0
240 REM    START AT TOP OF T1 AND SEARCH FOR A DISK
250 FOR X = 1 TO 5
260 REM     SEE IF WE HAVE FOUND A DISK YET
270    IF DISK > 0 OR A(X,T1) = 0 THEN 340
280 REM     IF ONE IS FOUND SET DISK AND CLEAR OLD SPOT
290    DISK = A(X,T1) : A(X,T1) = 0
300    FOR D = 30*T1 - 2*X  TO 30*T1 + 2*X
310       RESET(D,X*7 + 1): RESET(D,X*7 + 2): RESET(D,X*7 +3)
320    NEXT D
330    SET(T1*30,X*7+1): SET(T1*30,X*7+2): SET(T1*30,X*7+3)
340 NEXT X
350 IF DISK = 0 THEN PRINT@ 896,"NO DISK THERE!            " :
    FOR J = 1 TO 300 : NEXT J : GOTO 210
360 EMPTY = 0
370 REM     START AT BOTTOM AND SEARCH FOR AN EMPTY SPOT
380 FOR X = 5 TO 1 STEP -1
390    IF EMPTY = 0 AND A(X,T2) = 0 THEN EMPTY = X
400 NEXT X
410 IF EMPTY = 5 OR A(EMPTY+1,T2) >= DISK THEN 430
420 PRINT@896,"YOU CAN'T DO THAT        ": T2 = T1 :   GOTO 360
430 REM    PLOT DISK AT A(EMPTY,T2)
440 FOR DRAW = 30*T2 - 2*DISK TO 30*T2 + 2*DISK
450    Y = EMPTY*7 +1
460    SET(DRAW,Y) : SET(DRAW,Y+1) : SET(DRAW,Y+2)
470 NEXT DRAW
480 A(EMPTY,T2) = DISK
490 IF A(1,2) = 1 OR A(1,3) = 1 THEN 510
500 GOTO 210
510 PRINT@ 960,"GOOD SHOW OL' CHAP"


27.  10 M=500
     20 FOR X=1 TO 21
     30     FOR Q=1 TO 4
     40             M=M+M*.06/4
     50     NEXT Q
     60     PRINT "AT THE END OF YEAR";X;"THERE IS $";M
     70     M=M+60
     80 NEXT X
```

CHAPTER FIVE

1. a) This program will generate an "Out of DATA in 10" error. Line 10 attempts to read a fourth data element from line 40. A possible correction might read;

   40 DATA 2,3,4,5

   where the value 5 becomes the fourth data element.

   b) This program will endlessly print .5 because no new data is read in. Correct line 40 as follows:

   40 GOTO 10

   c) Lines 20 and and 30 each contain syntax errors. The function "*/" referenced at line 20 is illegal. The statement may be corrected to read:

   20 PRINT A*B+C

   to indicate multiplication, or:

   20 PRINT A/B+C

   to indicate division of A by B. Line 30 may be corrected by placing quotation marks around "D/F=" to read:

   30 PRINT "D/F=";D/F

   In addition, the variables D and F should be defined, or else a division by zero will result in line 30.

   d) The conditional clause at line 20 is incomplete. The user has not specified what variable should be 10. The obvious variable is F, so that line 20 reads:

   20 IF F>5 OR F<10 THEN 40

   A comma or a semicolon must be inserted between the variables F and G at line 40 so that the computer understands that they are two separate elements:

   40 PRINT F,G

e) The FOR-TO-NEXT loops are improperly nested:

```
10   FOR X=1 TO 8
20     FOR Y=1 TO 3
30       X=X+Y
40     NEXT X
50   NEXT Y
60   PRINT X
70   END
```

Line 40 and 50 may be corrected as follows:

```
40   NEXT Y
50   NEXT X
```

Also, changing the value of variables used in FOR-TO-NEXT loops is not recommended practice such as at line 30.

f) This program will continuously print the sum of 3, 6, and 9 since new data is not being read at line 10. Correct line 40 as follows:

```
40 GOTO 10
```

3. >RUN
   —6   6
   READY
   >

5. a) The computer will return the error "Syntax Error in 20". Since it appears that the variable "X" is intended to contain formula weight, line 20 may be corrected to read:

```
20 INPUT "FORMULA WEIGHT";X
```

b) When this program attempts to branch to line 50 at line 35, it will not find line 50, and the error message "Undefined line number in 35" will be printed. Change line 35 to:

```
35 IF Y=X THEN A=A+1 : GOTO 55
```

c) Note that both lines 10 and 20 do not contain the same number of closing parentheses as opening parentheses, thereby causing an "Illegal function call in 10". The computer reports the first error encountered so the error in line 20 goes undiscovered. The first opening parenthesis is not necessary in either of these lines.

d) Upon encountering line 30, the computer will print the error message "Syntax Error in 30". The line in question should read:

30 IF X>200 THEN 10

e) When the computer runs this program, it will print "Type mismatch in 20" and terminate the run. The problem arises from trying to add a floating point variable to a string variable. Variables can be of several types. They can be integers (which means they have no decimal places), floating point or real (which means they have decimal places), or string variables. Assuming the intent of this program was to sum all the numbers between 1 and 26, the best way to correct this program is to change all occurrences of "A$" to "A".

20   A=A+X
40   PRINT A

f) The error enountered in this example is "Out of string space in 20". "A$" in line 20 uses all of the string space allotted to it (when undefined the computer assumes 50). To correct this program it is necessary to allot more space at the beginning of the program. This is done with the CLEAR command:

5 CLEAR 80

7. The computer stores all decimal numbers in binary form. Because of this, small "rounding errors" are introduced into stored numbers. When these errors are compounded as in the large summation at line 30 (100 and 1000 times), it leads to very visible miscalculations as seen when this program is run. In this case the error was small.

CHAPTER SIX

```
1.  10 INPUT N
    20 IF N < 0 THEN PRINT "NO NEGATIVE NUMBERS ALLOWED" : GOTO 10
    30 PRINT "N =";N," SQUARE ROOTS = + OR -";SQR(N) : GOTO 10
```

```
3A.    PRINT 3[2[3
          729
       READY
3B.    >PRINT 5-4[2
          -11
       READY
3C.    >PRINT 3*(5+16)
           63
       READY
3D.    >PRINT 5+3*6/2
          14
       READY
3E.    >PRINT 640/10/2*5
          160
       READY
3F.    >PRINT 5+3*4-1
          16
       READY
3G.    >PRINT 2[3[2
          64
       READY
3H.    >PRINT 2[(3[2)
          512.001
       READY
3 I.   >PRINT 64/4*.5+((1+5)*2[3)*1/(2*4)
          14


5.     10 INPUT N
       20 PRINT SGN(N)*N
       READY
       >RUN
       ? -14
         14


7.     10 PRINT "RADIANS","DEGREES"
       20 FOR A = 0 TO 3 STEP .25
       30     PRINT A,A*180/3.141592653
       40 NEXT A


9.     10 INPUT N
       20 N = N * 3.1415926535/180
       30 C = COS(N)
       40 S = SIN(N)
       50 T = TAN(N)
       60 IF C > S AND C > T
               THEN PRINT "COSINE =";C
               ELSE IF S > T
                       THEN PRINT "SINE =";S
                       ELSE PRINT "TANGENT =";T
```

```
11.   10 DEF FNF(X) = 9*X[3 - 7*X[2 + 4*X - 1
      20 INPUT "A,B";A,B
      30 PRINT FNF(B) - FNF(A)


13.   10 PRINT " X";TAB(9);"LN(X)";TAB(24);"EXP(X)"
      20 PRINT
      30 FOR X = 1 TO 15
      40    PRINT X;TAB(7);LOG(X);TAB(22);EXP(X)
      50 NEXT X


15.   >RUN
        5               -4              3               4


17.   >RUN
      FNF(-4 ) IS NEGATIVE
      FNF(-2 ) IS NEGATIVE
      FNF( 0 ) IS NEGATIVE
      FNF( 2 ) IS ZERO
      FNF( 4 ) IS POSITIVE
      FNF( 6 ) IS POSITIVE


19.   >RUN
      -3
      -2
      -1
       0
       1
       2
       3
       4


21.   10 INPUT "R AND THETA (IN DEGREES) :";R,T
      20 T = T * 3.141592653/180
      30 X = R * COS(T)
      40 Y = R * SIN(T)
      50 PRINT "(X,Y) = (";X;",";Y;")"


23.   10 FOR X = 1 TO 100
      20    Y = ABS(SIN(X)*1000)
      30    R = INT(Y)/16 - INT(INT(Y)/16)
      40    PRINT R
      50 NEXT X
```

```
25.   10 FOR N = 0 TO 6.2 STEP .2
      20    U = SIN(N)
      30    PRINT TAB(20 * U + 22);"SHAZAM!"
      40 NEXT N


27.   10 PI = 3.1415926535
      20 INPUT "N";N
      30 CLS
      40 REM    DRAW AXES
      50 XO = 64 : YO = 24   : REM   CENTER
      60 FOR X = 0 TO 127
      70    SET(X,YO)
      80 NEXT X
      90 FOR Y = 0 TO 47
      100     SET(XO,Y)
      110 NEXT Y
      120 REM
      130 REM    DO PLOT
      140 FOR X1 = 0 TO 127
      150    X = (X1 - XO) / 16 : REM SHRINK X
      160    Y = SIN(N * PI * X) * 10 : REM * 10 TO SCALE Y
      170    Y1 = INT(YO - Y + .5)  : REM ROUND TO NEAREST INTEGER
      180    IF (Y1 >= 0) AND (Y1 < 48) THEN SET(X1,Y1)
      190 NEXT X1
```

CHAPTER SEVEN

```
1.    10 GOSUB 400
      20 FOR J=1 TO 40
      30    PRINT "*";
      40 NEXT J
      50 GOSUB 400
      60 FOR J=1 TO 3
      70    PRINT "!",
      80 NEXT J
      90 GOSUB 400
      100 FOR J=1 TO 20
      110    PRINT "AB";
      120 NEXT J
      130 END
      400 PRINT
      410 I=I+1
      420 PRINT "PART";I
      430 RETURN
```

```
3.   10 INPUT "ONE,TWO,THREE,FOUR";X
     20 IF X<>1 AND X<>2 AND X<>3 AND X<>4 THEN 10
     30 ON X GOTO 40,60,80,100
     40 PRINT "DON'T LET YOUR COMPUTER TURN TO TRASH!"
     50 END
     60 PRINT "DON'T LET BUGS GET IN YOUR TRASH."
     70 END
     80 PRINT "STUDY HARD AND YOU WON'T NEED A TRUSS."
     90 END
     100 PRINT "NEVER PLAY WITH TRASH."
     110 END


5A.   RUN
      <10><20><30><70><40><10><20><30><50><40><10><20><30><60><40><10>
      <20><90><100>
      READY


5B.  >RUN
      N= 3              Z= 1              P= 4
      READY
      >


7.   10 READ A,B,C
     20 GOSUB 200
     30 IF L=1 THEN 70
     40 R=A*B/2
     50 PRINT "AREA=";R,"PERIMETER=";A+B+C
     60 GOTO 10
     70 PRINT "NOT A RIGHT TRIANGLE"
     80 GOTO 10
     200 L=0
     210 IF A+B<=C THEN 250
     220 IF A+C<=B THEN 250
     230 IF B+C<=A THEN 250
     240 IF INT(A[2+B[2)=INT(C[2) THEN 260
     250 L=1
     260 RETURN
     270 DATA 3,4,5,0,1,1,2,2,2,12,5,13
     280 END
```

```
9.  10 INPUT "WITHDRAWAL(1),DEPOSIT(2), OR CALCULATE INTEREST(3)";D
    15 IF D <> 1 AND D<>2 AND D<>3 THEN 10
    20 ON D GOSUB 120,150,180
    30 PRINT "YOUR BALANCE STANDS AT";B;"DOLLARS."
    40 GOTO 10
    115 REM    WITHDRAWAL LOOP
    120 INPUT "HOW MUCH WOULD YOU LIKE TO WITHDRAW";A
    130 IF A >= 0 AND B - A > 0 THEN B = B - A : RETURN
    140 GOTO 120
    145 REM    DEPOSIT LOOP
    150 INPUT "HOW MUCH WOULD YOU LIKE TO DEPOSIT";A
    160 IF A >= 0 THEN B = B + A : RETURN
    170 GOTO 150
    180 INPUT "HOW MANY MONTHS SINCE LAST CALCULATION";M
    190 Q = M / 3
    200 IF Q < 1 THEN PRINT "TOO SOON" : RETURN
    210 FOR C = 1 TO Q
    220    B = B + .0575 / 4 * B
    230 NEXT C
    240 RETURN


11. 10 ON ERROR GOTO 70
    20 FOR X=-5 TO 5
    30      J=10/X
    40       PRINT J
    50 NEXT X
    60 GOTO 90
    70 IF ERR/2+1=11 THEN PRINT "DIVISION BY ZERO"
    80 RESUME 50
    90 END
```

CHAPTER EIGHT

```
1.  10 INPUT "NAME";N$
    20 FOR I = 1 TO LEN(N$)
    30    PRINT ASC(MID$(N$,I,1));
    40 NEXT I


3.  10 READ X%
    20 PRINT CHR$(X%);
    30 GOTO 10
    40 DATA 65,83,67,73,73,32,68,73
    50 DATA 68,32,84,72,73,83,33
    60 END
```

```
5.  1 REM     A$ = ORIGINAL STRING
    2 REM     L$,M$,R$ = LEFT, MID, RIGHT STRINGS OF ORIGINAL
    3 REM
    4 REM
    10 A$="THREE!@#$%STRING@#$%FUNCTIONS"
    20 L$=LEFT$(A$,5) : REM    SETS L$ EQUAL TO "THREE"
    30 M$=MID$(A$,11,6) : REM   SETS M$ EQUAL TO "STRING"
    40 R$=RIGHT$(A$,9) : REM    SETS R$ EQUAL TO "FUNCTIONS"
    50 PRINT L$;" ";M$;" ";R$
    60 END


7.  1 REM     A$ = ORIGINAL STRING
    2 REM     P = POSITION IN STRING
    3 REM     N = ASCII OF A CHARACTER
    4 REM
    5 REM
    10 INPUT "YOUR STRING";A$
    20 FOR P=LEN(A$) TO 1 STEP -1
    30     N=ASC(RIGHT$(A$,P))
    40     PRINT N;
    50 NEXT P
    60 END


9.  1 REM     A$ = A STRING FROM DATA
    2 REM     L% = LENGTH OF A STRING
    3 REM     B$ = A CHARACTER IN A STRING
    4 REM
    5 REM
    10 READ A$
    20 L%=LEN(A$)
    30 FOR X%=1 TO L%
    40     B$=MID$(A$,X%,1) : REM  PULLS OUT ONE CHARACTER FROM A$
    50     IF ASC(B$)=69 THEN 70
    60     PRINT B$;
    70 NEXT X%
    80 PRINT
    90 GOTO 10
    100 DATA QUEEN, LENGTH, REMEMBER
```

11.

Binary	Decimal
1011	11
10100	20
1111	15
1110	14
1010011	83
110011	51
1011100	92
1101111	111
11000000	192
10000111	135

13.
```
1 REM    A$ = THE FIRST 12 LETTERS OF THE ALPHABET
2 REM    L% = THE LENGTH OF THE STRING TO BE PRINTED
3 REM
4 REM
10 FOR C%=ASC("A") TO ASC("L")
20      A$=A$+CHR$(C%)
30 NEXT C%
40 FOR L%=1 TO 12
50      PRINT LEFT$(A$,L%)
60 NEXT L%
70 END
```

15.
```
READY
>RUN
 87
 72
 55
 54
READY
>
```

17.
```
10 FOR X%=1 TO 15
20      C%=RND(26)+64
30      PRINT CHR$(C%);
40 NEXT X%
50 END
```

```
19.  5 CLEAR 500
    10 FOR X = 1 TO 100
    20     A$ = A$ + CHR$(RND(95)+31)
    30 NEXT X
    40 FOR Y = 1 TO 100
    50     C = ASC(MID$(A$,Y,1))
    60     IF (C>64 AND C<91) OR (C>96 AND C<123)
              THEN L = L + 1
              ELSE IF (C>47 AND C<58)
                      THEN N = N + 1
                      ELSE M = M + 1
    70 NEXT Y
    80 PRINT "THERE ARE";L;"LETTERS,";N;"NUMBERS, AND"
    90 PRINT M;"MISCELLANEOUS CHARACTERS."


21A. 10 CLEAR 500  : REM  CLEARS SPACE FOR A$
    20 INPUT "MESSAGE TO ENCODE ";M$
    30 FOR I%=1 TO LEN(M$)
    40     C%=ASC(MID$(M$,I%,1))
    50     IF C%<65 OR C%>90 THEN 90
    60     C%=C%+2
    70     IF C%>90 THEN C%=C%-26
    80     A$=A$+CHR$(C%)
    90 NEXT I%
    100 PRINT "ENCODED MESSAGE: ";A$
    110 END


21B. 10 CLEAR 500
    20 INPUT "MESSAGE TO DECODE? ";M$
    30 FOR I%=1 TO LEN(M$)
    40     C%=ASC(MID$(M$,I%,1))
    50     IF C%<65 OR C%>90 THEN 80
    60     C%=C%-2
    70     IF C%<65 THEN C%=C%+26
    80     A$=A$+CHR$(C%)
    90 NEXT I%
    100 PRINT "MESSAGE: ";A$
    110 END
```

```
23.   1 REM    S%() = STORES SENTENCES (UP TO 30)
      2 REM    N%() = STORES NUMBEF OF OCCURRENCES OF EACH TARGET
      3 REM    R% = RECORDS NUMBER UF OCCURRENCES IN A SENTENCE
      4 REM
      5 REM
      10 DIM S$(30),N%(9)
      20 CLEAR 1000
      30 REM    BEGIN INPUT LOOP
      40 C%=C%+1
      50 LINE INPUT "SENTENCE?";S$(C%)
      60 IF LEN(S$(C%))=0 THEN 90
      70 S$(C%)=CHR$(32)+S$(C%)+CHR$(32)
      80 GOTO 40
      90 REM    BEGIN PROGRAM
      100 FOR L%=1 TO C%-1
      110     RESTORE
      120     FOR W%=1 TO 9
      130             READ T$
      140             GOSUB 220
      150             N%(W%)=N%(W%)+R%
      160     NEXT W%
      170 NEXT L%
      180 PRINT "ARTICLES:";N%(1)+N%(2)+N%(3)
      190 PRINT "ADVERBS:";N%(4)
      200 PRINT "PUNCTUATION MARKS:";N%(5)+N%(6)+N%(7)+N%(8)+N%(9)
      210 GOTO 300
      220 REM    BEGIN GOSUB LOOP
      230 R%=0
      240 FOR P%=1 TO LEN(S$(L%))
      250     IF MID$(S$(L%),P%,LEN(T$))=T$ THEN R%=R%+1
      260 REM    LINE 240 FINDS OCCURRENCES OF THE TARGET STRING
      270 NEXT P%
      280 RETURN
      290 DATA " A ", " AN ", " THE ", "LY ", ".", "!", "?", ";",","
      300 END


25.   1 REM    W$() = STORES WORDS
      2 REM
      3 REM
      10 REM    BEGIN INPUT LOOP
      20 CLEAR 100
      30 DIM W$(11)
      40 C%=C%+1
      50 PRINT "WHAT IS YOUR";C%;
      60 INPUT "WORD";W$(C%)
      70 IF C%<=10 AND LEN(W$(C%))>0 THEN 40
      80 REM    BEGIN PROGRAM LOOP
      90 FOR L%=1 TO C%-1
      100     PRINT CHR$(ASC(W$(L%)));
      110 NEXT L%
      120 END
```

```
27.  1 REM    N$ = YOUR NUMBER
     2 REM
     3 REM
     10 INPUT "WHAT IS YOUR BINARY NUMBER";N$
     20 D%=0
     30  FOR I%=1 TO LEN(N$)
     40     IF ASC(MID$(N$,I%,1))=49 THEN D%=D%+2[(LEN(N$)-I%)
     50 NEXT I%
     60 PRINT "IT'S DECIMAL EQUIVALENT IS";D%
     70 GOTO 10
     80 END
```

CHAPTER NINE

```
1A.  10 DIM R(50)
     20 FOR X = 1 TO 50
     30    R(X) = RND(21) - 1
     40 NEXT X
     50 OPEN "O",1,"RANUM:1"
     90 REM
     100 REM    NOW WRITE TO THE FILE
     110 FOR I = 1 TO 50
     120    PRINT #1,R(I)
     130 NEXT I
     140 CLOSE 1
```

```
1B.  1 REM    R = THE NUMBER READ FROM THE FILE
     2 REM    S = THE SUM OF ALL R'S
     10 OPEN "I",2,"RANUM:1"
     20 FOR I = 1 TO 50
     30    INPUT #2,R
     40    S = S + R
     50 NEXT I
     60 CLOSE 2
     70 PRINT "THE SUM IS";S
```

```
3A.  10 OPEN "O",1,"SEQ:1"
     20 FOR I = 1001 TO 1128
     30    PRINT #1,I
     40 NEXT I
     50 CLOSE 1
```

```
3B.  10 OPEN "I",1,"SEQ:1"
     20 INPUT "WHICH PLACE IN THE SEQUENCE";P
     30 FOR I = 1 TO P
     40    INPUT #1,N
     50 NEXT I
     60 PRINT "THAT IS";N


5A.  1 REM    N$ = ARRAY TO HOLD THE NAMES
     2 REM    F$ = ARRAY TO HOLD THE NAME OF THE FRATERNITY
     3 REM    A = ARRAY TO HOLD THE AGES
     10 CLEAR 200: DIM N$(30),F$(30),A(30)
     20 FOR X = 1 TO 30
     30    INPUT "NAME ";N$(X)
     40    INPUT "FRATERNITY ";F$(X)
     50    INPUT "AGE";A(X)
     60 NEXT X
     70 REM
     100 REM NOW WRITE TO THE FILE
     110 OPEN "O",1,"FRAT:1"
     120 FOR I = 1 TO 30
     130    PRINT #1,N$(I);",";F$(I);",";A(I)
     140 NEXT I
     150 CLOSE 1


5B.  1 REM    N$ = NAME
     2 REM    F$ = FRATERNITY
     3 REM    A  = AGE
     10 OPEN "I",1,"FRAT:1"
     20 OPEN "O",2,"SIGMA:1"
     30 FOR X = 1 TO 30
     40    INPUT #1,N$,F$,A
     50    IF F$ = "SIGMA CHI" THEN PRINT #2,N$;",";A
     60 NEXT X
     70 CLOSE 1,2
```

```
5C.  1 REM    N$ = ARRAY TO HOLD NAMES
     2 REM    P  = ARRAY TO HOLD A 1 IF A STUDENT HAS BEEN SEATED
     10 DIM N$(30),P(30)
     20 OPEN "I",1,"FRAT:1"
     30 FOR I = 1 TO 30
     40    INPUT #1,N$(I),F$,A
     50 NEXT I
     60 CLOSE 1
     70 REM
     100 REM NOW GET RANDOM SEATING
     110 FOR X = 1 TO 5
     120    FOR Y = 1 TO 5
     130       R = RND(30)
     140       IF P(R) = 1 THEN 130 : REM SEE IF STUDENT IS SEATED
     150       PRINT N$(R);"   ";
     160    NEXT Y
     165 PRINT
     170 NEXT X


7A.  1 REM    H = ARRAY TO HOLD TIME IN HOURS
     2 REM    F = ARRAY TO HOLD TEMP IN FAHRENHEIT DEGREES
     10 OPEN "O",1,"NIT:1"
     20 PRINT "ENTER NIT'S DATA"
     30 FOR A = 1 TO 6
     40    INPUT "TIME";H(A)
     50    INPUT "TEMPERATURE";F(A)
     60 NEXT A : PRINT
     70 REM    NOW PRINT TO THE FILE
     80 FOR B = 1 TO 6
     90    PRINT #1,H(B);",";F(B)
     100 NEXT B
     110 CLOSE 1
     200 REM    THIS IS WIT
     210 OPEN "O",1,"WIT:1"
     220 PRINT "ENTER WIT'S DATA"
     230 FOR A = 1 TO 6
     240    INPUT "TIME";H(A)
     250    INPUT "TEMPERATURE";F(A)
     260 NEXT A : PRINT
     270 REM    NOW PRINT TO THE FILE
     280 FOR B = 1 TO 6
     290    PRINT #1,H(B);",";F(B)
     300 NEXT B
     310 CLOSE 1
```

```
7B.  1 REM     T = ARRAY WHICH HOLDS TMP IN POSITION TIME*10
     2 REM     H = TIME IN HOURS
     3 REM     F = TMP IN FAHRENHEIT DEGREES
     10 DIM T(100)
     20 OPEN "I",1,"NIT:1"
     30 OPEN "I",2,"WIT:1"
     40 OPEN "O",3,"MERGE:1"
     50 FOR L = 1 TO 6
     60     INPUT #1,H,F : GOSUB 90 : REM    PUT DATA IN ARRAY T
     70     INPUT #2,H,F : GOSUB 90
     80 NEXT L : GOTO 200
     90 REM    IF T(H*10) IS EMPTY THEN PUT THE TEMP IN
     100 REM       ELSE AVERAGE THE VALUES
     110 IF T(H*10) = 0
            THEN T(H*10) = F
            ELSE T(H*10) = (T(H*10)+F)/2
     120 RETURN
     130 REM
     200 REM    NOW PRINT TO THE FILE MERGE
     210 FOR Z = 0 TO 100
     220    IF T(Z) <> 0 THEN PRINT #3, Z/10;",";T(Z)
     230 NEXT Z
     240 CLOSE 1,2,3


7C.  10 OPEN "I",1,"MERGE:1"
     20 IF EOF(1) THEN CLOSE 1 : END
     30     INPUT #1,H,F
     40     PRINT H,F
     50 GOTO 20


9A.  10 DIM S$(10,5)
     15 ON ERROR GOTO 200
     20 OPEN "I",1,"SHOW:1"
     30 FOR I = 1 TO 51
     40     INPUT #1,X,Y,S$(X,Y)
     50     IF EOF(1) THEN 80
     60 NEXT I
     70 CLOSE 1 : PRINT "I AM SORRY, WE HAVE A PACKED HOUSE." : END
     80 CLOSE 1 : INPUT "YOUR NAME";F$
     90 INPUT "WHAT SEAT WOULD YOU LIKE (ROW, COLUMN)";X1,Y1
     100 IF S$(X1,Y1) <> "" THEN PRINT "THAT SEAT IS TAKEN" : GOTO 90
     120 PRINT "DRAMA CLUB SHOW" : PRINT F$;" HAS"
     130 PRINT "RESERVED ROW";X1 : PRINT "SEAT";Y1;"FOR"
     140 PRINT "JULY 4, 1983" : PRINT
     150 OPEN "E",1,"B:SHOW.TXT" : REM APPEND THE LIST W/NEW PERSON
     160 PRINT #1,X1;",";Y1;",";F$
     170 CLOSE 1 : END
     200 REM    IF ERROR OCCURRED THERE MUST BE NO FILE SO MAKE ONE
     210 CLOSE 1 : OPEN "O",1,"SHOW:1"
     220 PRINT #1,"0,0,B"
     230 CLOSE 1 : RESUME
```

```
9B.  1 REM    X = ROW OF PERSON SEAT AS INPUT FROM THE FILE SHOW
     2 REM    Y = COLUMN OF PERSONS SEAT AS INPUT FROM THE FILE SHOW
     3 REM    S$ = ARRAY TO HOLD THE PERSONS NAME AT ROW X, COLUMN Y
     10 CLEAR 500
     20 DIM S$(10,5)
     30 OPEN "I",1,"SHOW:1"
     40 FOR I = 1 TO 50
     50     IF EOF(1) THEN 80
     60     INPUT #1,X,Y,S$(X,Y)
     70 NEXT I
     80 CLOSE 1
     100 PRINT "EMPTY SEATS FOR JULY 4TH DRAMA SHOW.":PRINT
     110 FOR R = 1 TO 10
     120     FOR S = 1 TO 5
     130         IF S$(R,S) <> "" THEN 150
     140         PRINT "ROW";R;"SEAT";S
     150     NEXT S
     160 NEXT R


9C.  10 CLEAR 500 : DIM S$(10,5)
     20 OPEN "I",1,"SHOW:1"
     30 FOR I = 1 TO 51
     40     IF EOF(1) THEN 70
     50     INPUT #1,X,Y,S$(X,Y)
     60 NEXT I
     70 PRINT "ROWS DOWN, SEATS ACROSS":PRINT
     75 FOR R = 1 TO 10
     80     FOR S = 1 TO 5
     85         IF S$(R,S) = "" THEN S$(R,S) = "EMPTY"
     90         PRINT TAB(14 * (S-1));S$(R,S);
     100     NEXT S
     105 PRINT
     110 NEXT R
     120 CLOSE 1
```

CHAPTER TEN

```
1A.   1 REM    L$,L1$ = LETTER (1 CHARACTER)
      2 REM
      3 REM
      10 CLEAR 75
      20 OPEN "R",1,"ALPHABET/TXT:1",1
      30 FIELD 1, 1 AS L$
      40 FOR L = 1 TO 26
      50    READ L1$
      60    LSET L$ = L1$
      70    PUT 1
      80 NEXT L
      90 CLOSE 1
      100 DATA A,B,C,D,E,F,G,H,I,J,K,L,M,N,O,P,Q,R,S,T,U,V,W,X,Y,Z


1B.   1 REM    L$,L1$ = LETTER (1 CHARACTER)
      2 REM
      3 REM
      10 CLEAR 75
      20 OPEN "R",1,"ALPHABET/TXT:1",1
      30 FIELD 1, 1 AS L$
      40 FOR L = 1 TO 5
      50    GET 1, RND(26)
      60    PRINT L$;
      70 NEXT L
      80 CLOSE 1


3A.   1 REM    S$,S1$ = SAYING (128 CHARACTERS)
      2 REM    N = NUMBER OF SAYINGS
      3 REM
      4 REM
      10  CLEAR 500
      20  OPEN "R",1,"SAYINGS/TXT:1",128
      30  FIELD 1, 128 AS S$
      40  INPUT "HOW MANY SAYINGS";N
      50  FOR S = 1 TO N
      60     LINE INPUT S1$ : LSET S$ = S1$
      70     PUT 1
      80     PRINT
      90  NEXT S
      100 CLOSE 1
```

```
3B.  1 REM    S$ = SAYING (128 CHARACTERS)
     2 REM    S = NUMBER OF SAYING
     3 REM
     4 REM
     10 CLEAR 500
     20 OPEN "R",1,"SAYINGS/TXT:1",128
     30 FIELD 1, 128 AS S$
     40 INPUT "WHICH SAYING";S
     50 IF S > LOF(1) THEN PRINT "THERE AREN'T THAT MANY" : GOTO 40
     60 GET 1, S
     70 PRINT S$
     80 CLOSE 1


5A.  1 REM    F,F$ = FULL-SIZED CARS (2 CHARACTERS)
     2 REM    M,M$ = MID-SIZED CARS (2 CHARACTERS)
     3 REM    C,C$ = COMPACT CARS (2 CHARACTERS)
     4 REM    M1,M1$ = MONT
     5 REM
     6 REM
     10  OPEN "R",1,"CARSALES/TXT:1",6
     20  FIELD 1, 2 AS F$, 2 AS M$, 2 AS C$
     30  FOR M1 = 1 TO 12
     40     READ M1$
     50     PRINT M1$;" SALES"
     60     INPUT "FULL-SIZED";F : LSET F$ = MKI$(F)
     70     INPUT "MID-SIZED";M : LSET M$ = MKI$(M)
     80     INPUT "COMPACT";C : LSET C$ = MKI$(C)
     90     PUT 1
     100    PRINT
     110 NEXT M1
     120 CLOSE 1
     130 DATA JANUARY,FEBRUARY,MARCH,APRIL,MAY,JUNE
     140 DATA JULY,AUGUST,SEPTEMBER,OCTOBER,NOVEMBER,DECEMBER
```

```
5B.   1 REM    F$ = FULL-SIZED (2 CHARACTERS)
      2 REM    M$ = MID-SIZED (2 CHARACTERS)
      3 REM    C$ = COMPACT (2 CHARACTERS)
      4 REM    M1 = MONTH
     10   OPEN "R",1,"CARSALES/TXT:1",6
     20   FIELD 1, 2 AS F$, 2 AS M$, 2 AS C$
     30   PRINT "ENTER A NEGATIVE NUMBER TO STOP"
     40   INPUT "WHICH MONTH (1-12)";M1
     50   IF M1 < 0 THEN 160
     60   CLS
     70   GET 1, M1
     80   PRINT @320, "FULL-SIZED:"
     90   PRINT @448, " MID-SIZED:"
    100 PRINT @576, "   COMPACT:"
    110 FOR F = 1 TO CVI(F$) : SET(24 + F,15) : NEXT F
    120 FOR M = 1 TO CVI(M$) : SET(24 + M,21) : NEXT M
    130 FOR C = 1 TO CVI(C$) : SET(24 + C,27) : NEXT C
    140 PRINT @768, "";
    150 GOTO 40
    160 CLOSE 1


7A.   1 REM    N$ = NAME (12 CHARACTERS)
      2 REM    A1$ = ADDRESS (15 CHARACTERS)
      3 REM    S1$ = STATE   (2 CHARACTERS)
      4 REM    S2$ = SALARY (4 CHARACTERS)
      5 REM    S3$ = SAVINGS (4 CHARACTERS)
      6 REM    A2$ = AGE (2 CHARACTERS)
      7 REM    S4$ = SEX (1 CHARACTER)
      8 REM    C$ = MAKE OF CAR (8 CHARACTERS)
      9 REM    Y$ = YEAR OF CAR (2 CHARACTERS)
     10 REM
     11 REM
     20 CLEAR 500
     30 OPEN "R",1,"NAME/TXT:1",29
     40 FIELD 1, 12 AS N$, 15 AS A1$, 2 AS S1$
     50 OPEN "R",2,"SALARY/TXT:1",8
     60 FIELD 2, 4 AS S2$, 4 AS S3$
     70 OPEN "R",3,"AGESEX/TXT:1",3
     80 FIELD 3, 2 AS A2$, 1 AS S4$
     90 OPEN "R",4,"AUTO/TXT:1",10
    100 FIELD 4, 8 AS C$, 2 AS Y$
    110 FOR ID = 1 TO 10
    120    GET 4, ID
    130    IF C$ <> "FORD    "   THEN 200
    140    GET 3, ID
    150    IF S4$ = "F" OR CVI(A2$) <= 30 THEN 200
    160    GET 2, ID
    170    IF CVS(S2$) <= 20000 THEN 200
    180    GET 1, ID
    190    PRINT N$, A1$, S1$
    200 NEXT ID
    210 CLOSE 1,2,3,4
```

```
7B.  1 REM    N$ = NAME (12 CHARACTERS)
     2 REM    A1$ = ADDRESS (15 CHARACTERS)
     3 REM    S1$ = STATE (2 CHARACTERS)
     4 REM    S2$ = SALARY (4 CHARACTERS)
     5 REM    S3$ = SAVINGS (4 CHARACTERS)
     6 REM    C$ = MAKE OF CAR (8 CHARACTERS)
     7 REM    Y$ = YEAR OF CAR (2 CHARACTERS)
     8 REM
     9 REM
    10  CLEAR 500
    20  OPEN "R",1,"NAME/TXT:1",29
    30  FIELD 1, 12 AS N$, 15 AS A1$, 2 AS S1$
    40  OPEN "R",2,"SALARY/TXT:1",8
    50  FIELD 1, 4 AS S2$, 4 AS S3$
    60  OPEN "R",3,"AUTO/TXT:1",10
    70  FIELD 3, 8 AS C$, 2 AS Y$
    80  FOR ID = 1 TO 10
    90     GET 2, ID
    100    IF CVS(S2$) <= 15000 OR CVS(S3$) >= 2000 THEN 150
    110    GET 3, ID
    120    IF C$ <> "CHEVY" AND C$ <> "FORD" AND C$ <> "VW"
                     THEN 150
    130    GET 1, ID
    140     PRINT N$
    150 NEXT ID
    160 CLOSE 1,2,3


7C.  1 REM    N$ = NAME (12 CHARACTERS)
     2 REM    A1$ = ADDRESS (15 CHARACTERS)
     3 REM    S1$ = STATE (2 CHARACTERS)
     4 REM    A2$ = AGE (2 CHARACTERS)
     5 REM    S4$ = SEX (1 CHARACTER)
     6 REM    C$ = MAKE OF CAR (8 CHARACTERS)
     7 REM    Y$ = YEAR OF CAR (2 CHARACTERS)
     8 REM
     9 REM
    10  CLEAR 500
    20  OPEN "R",1,"NAME/TXT:1",29
    30  FIELD 1, 12 AS N$, 15 AS A1$, 2 AS S1$
    40  OPEN "R",2,"AGESEX/TXT:1",3
    50  FIELD 2, 2 AS A2$, 1 AS S4$
    60  OPEN "R",3,"AUTO/TXT:1",10
    70  FIELD 3, 8 AS C$, 2 AS Y$
    80  FOR ID = 1 TO 10
    90     GET 2, ID
    100    IF S4$ = "F" OR CVI(A2$) >= 35 THEN 160
    110    GET 3, ID
    120    IF C$ <> "FORD" THEN 160
    130    GET 1, ID
    140    IF S1$ <> "NJ" THEN 160
    150     PRINT N$, A1$
    160 NEXT ID
    170 CLOSE 1,2,3
```

```
9A.  1 REM     N$,N1$ = NAME (20 CHARACTERS)
     2 REM     A$,A1$ = STREET ADDRESS (25 CHARACTERS)
     3 REM     C$,C1$ = CITY (15 CHARACTERS)
     4 REM     S$,S1$ = STATE (2 CHARACTERS)
     5 REM     Z$,Z1$ = ZIP CODE (5 CHARACTERS)
     6 REM     B,B$ = BALANCE (4 CHARACTERS)
     7 REM     A = ACCOUNT NUMBER
     8 REM
     9 REM
     10  CLEAR 500
     20  OPEN "R",1,"CHARGE/TXT:1",71
     30  FIELD 1, 20 AS N$, 25 AS A$, 15 AS C$, 2 AS S$,
             5 AS Z$, 4 AS B$
     40  FOR A = 1 TO 10
     50     PRINT "THIS WILL BE ACCOUNT #";A
     60     INPUT "NAME";N1$ : LSET N$ = N1$
     70     INPUT "STREET ADDRESS";A1$ : LSET A$ = A1$
     80     INPUT "CITY";C1$ : LSET C$ = C1$
     90     INPUT "STATE";S1$ : LSET S$ = S1$
     100    INPUT "ZIP CODE";Z1$ : LSET Z$ = Z1$
     110    LSET B$ = MKS$(O)
     120    PUT 1
     130    PRINT
     140 NEXT A
     150 CLOSE 1


9B.  1 REM     N$,N1$ = NAME (20 CHARACTERS)
     2 REM     A$,A1$ = STREET ADDRESS (25 CHARACTERS)
     3 REM     C$,C1$ = CITY (15 CHARACTERS)
     4 REM     S$,S1$ = STATE (2 CHARACTERS)
     5 REM     Z$,Z1$ = ZIP CODE (5 CHARACTERS)
     6 REM     B,B$ = BALANCE (4 CHARACTERS)
     7 REM     A = ACCOUNT NUMBER
     8 REM     T$ = TRANSACTION FLAG
     9 REM     A1 = TRANSACTION AMOUNT
     10 REM
     11 REM
     20  CLEAR 500
     30  OPEN "R",1,"CHARGE/TXT:1",71
     40  FIELD 1, 20 AS N$, 25 AS A$, 15 AS C$, 2 AS S$,
             5 AS Z$, 4 AS B$
     50  PRINT "ENTER A NEGATIVE NUMBER TO STOP THE PROGRAM"
     60  INPUT "ACCOUNT #";A
     70     IF A < O THEN 180
     80     INPUT "CHARGE (C) OR PAYMENT (P)";T$
     90     INPUT "AMOUNT";A1
     100    GET 1, A
     110    B = CVS(B$)
     120    IF T$ = "C" THEN B = B + A1 ELSE B = B - A1
     130    LSET B$ = MKS$(B)
     140    PUT 1, A
     150    PRINT "TRANSACTION RECORDED"
     160    PRINT
     170 GOTO 60
     180 CLOSE 1
```

```
9C.  1 REM     N$ = NAME (20 CHARACTERS)
     2 REM     A$ = ADDRESS (25 CHARACTERS)
     3 REM     C$ = CITY (15 CHARACTERS)
     4 REM     S$ = STATE (2 CHARACTERS)
     5 REM     Z$ = ZIP CODE (5 CHARACTERS)
     6 REM     B$ = BALANCE (4 CHARACTERS)
     7 REM
     8 REM
    10  CLEAR 500
    20  OPEN "R",1,"CHARGE/TXT:1",71
    30  FIELD 1, 20 AS N$, 25 AS A$, 15 AS C$, 2 AS S$,
           5 AS Z$, 4 AS B$
    40  IF EOF(1) THEN 230
    50      GET 1
    60      IF N$ = STRING$(20," ") THEN 50
    70      PRINT "FROM: BUY LOW DEPARTMENT STORE"
    80      PRINT "TO: ";N$
    90      PRINT "ACCOUNT #";LOC(1)
   100      PRINT
   110      PRINT "YOU HAVE CHARGED $";CVS(B$);"AGAINST YOUR"
   120      PRINT "ACCOUNT.   THIS AMOUNT IS NOW DUE."
   130      IF CVS(B$) > 800 THEN GOTO 190
   140      PRINT
   150      PRINT "                          THANK YOU"
   160      PRINT : PRINT
   170 GOTO 40
   180 END
   190 PRINT
   200 PRINT "YOUR ACCOUNT EXCEEDS YOUR CHARGE LIMIT."
   210 PRINT "PAY IMMEDIATELY!"
   220 GOTO 140
   230 CLOSE 1
```

```
9D.  1 REM      N$ = NAME (20 CHARACTERS)
     2 REM      A$ = ADDRESS (25 CHARACTERS)
     3 REM      C$ = CITY (15 CHARACTERS)
     4 REM      S$ = STATE (2 CHARACTERS)
     5 REM      Z$ = ZIP CODE (5 CHARACTERS)
     6 REM      B$ = BALANCE (4 CHARACTERS)
     7 REM      A = ACCOUNT NUMBER
     8 REM
     9 REM
    10  CLEAR 500
    20  OPEN "R",1,"CHARGE/TXT:1",71
    30  FIELD 1, 20 AS N$, 25 AS A$, 15 AS C$, 2 AS S$,
           5 AS Z$, 4 AS B$
    40  INPUT "WHICH ACCOUNT IS BEING CLOSED";A
    50  LSET N$ = STRING$(20," ")
    60  LSET A$ = STRING$(25," ")
    70  LSET C$ = STRING$(15," ")
    80  LSET S$ = STRING$(2," ")
    90  LSET Z$ = STRING$(5," ")
    100 LSET B$ = MKS$(0)
    110 PUT 1, A
    120 PRINT "ACCOUNT #";A;"HAS BEEN CLOSED"
    130 CLOSE 1


9E.  2 REM      A$,A1$ = STREET ADDRESS (25 CHARACTERS)
     3 REM      C$,C1$ = CITY (15 CHARACTERS)
     4 REM      S$,S1$ = STATE (2 CHARACTERS)
     5 REM      Z$,Z1$ = ZIP CODE (5 CHARACTERS)
     6 REM      B$ = BALANCE (4 CHARACTERS)
     7 REM      A = ACCOUNT NUMBER
     8 REM
     9 REM
    10  CLEAR 500
    20  OPEN "R",1,"CHARGE/TXT:1",71
    30  FIELD 1, 20 AS N$, 25 AS A$, 15 AS C$, 2 AS S$,
           5 AS Z$, 4 AS B$
    40  FOR A = 1 TO LOF(1)
    50     GET 1, A
    60     IF N$ = STRING$(20," ") THEN 90
    70  NEXT A
    80  A = LOF(1) + 1
    90  INPUT "NAME";N1$ : LSET N$ = N1$
    100 INPUT "STREET ADDRESS";A1$ : LSET A$ = A1$
    110 INPUT "CITY";C1$ : LSET C$ = C1$
    120 INPUT "STATE";S1$ : LSET S$ = S1$
    130 INPUT "ZIP CODE";Z1$ : LSET Z$ = Z1$
    140 LSET B$ = MKS$(0)
    150 PRINT "THIS PERSON WILL BE ASSIGNED ACCOUNT #";A
    160 PUT 1, A
    170 CLOSE 1
```

INDEX